MAPPING TRAUMA AND ITS WAKE

ROUTLEDGE PSYCHOSOCIAL STRESS SERIES
Charles R. Figley, Ph.D., Series Editor

MAPPING TRAUMA AND ITS WAKE

Autobiographic Essays by Pioneer Trauma Scholars

Edited by Charles R. Figley

Routledge
Taylor & Francis Group
New York   London

Published in 2006 by
Routledge
Taylor & Francis Group
270 Madison Avenue
New York, NY 10016

Published in Great Britain by
Routledge
Taylor & Francis Group
2 Park Square
Milton Park, Abingdon
Oxon OX14 4RN

Printed in the United States of America on acid-free paper
10 9 8 7 6 5 4 3 2 1

International Standard Book Number-10: 0-415-95140-2 (Hardcover)
International Standard Book Number-13: 978-0-415-95140-1 (Hardcover)
Library of Congress Card Number 2005011318

Library of Congress Cataloging-in-Publication Data

Mapping trauma and its wake : autobiographic essays by pioneer trauma scholars / Charles R. Figley, editor ; with chapters by the leading pioneers in the study and treatment of trauma, Ann Wolbert Burgess ... [et al.].
    p. ; cm. -- (Routledge psychosocial stress series ; 31)
    Includes bibliographical references and index.
    ISBN 0-415-95140-2 (hardback : alk. paper)
    1. Post-traumatic stress disorder--Research. 2. Psychic trauma--Research. 3. Psychiatrists--Biography. 4. Psychologists--Biography. [DNLM: 1. Stress Disorders, Post-Traumatic--Personal Narratives. 2. Research Personnel--Personal Narratives. WZ 112 M297 2005] I. Figley, Charles R., 1944- II. Series.

RC552.P67M358 2005
616.85'21'0922--dc22
                                     2005011318

Taylor & Francis Group
is the Academic Division of Informa plc.

Visit the Taylor & Francis Web site at
http://www.taylorandfrancis.com

and the Routledge Web site at
http://www.routledge-ny.com

To Joseph Wolpe, MD, the pioneer of trauma treatment theory

Contents

Series Note

The Routledge Psychosocial Stress Book Series is delighted to welcome this book about and by the pioneers of trauma to the oldest trauma book series. The series is the first to focus on traumatic stress, the first book having been published in 1978. It is therefore only fitting that a book about and by trauma scholar pioneers be published in this pioneering series.

The series strives to attract and publish books introducing new areas of inquiry or understanding that immediately or eventually help prevent, cope with, or eliminate unwanted human stress and promote the resultant benefits. The list of books in the series is available at the front of this book.

Several pioneers with chapters in this book have contributed to the series. Most recently, among these, has been John Wilson's book *The Post-traumatic Self*. Others who have published either books or chapters in the series include Ann Wolbert Burgess, Yael Danieli, Charles R. Figley, Matthew J. Friedman, Mardi Horowitz, Robert Jay Lifton, Frank Ochberg, Beverley Raphael, Bessel van der Kolk, and Lars Weisaeth.

Consistent with the aim of the series of contributing to understanding trauma and its consequences, *Mapping Trauma and Its Wake: Autobiographic Essays by Pioneer Trauma Scholars* advances the field. This collection of personal, autobiographical essays was written by trauma scholars recognized for their significant contributions to the field by the International Society for Traumatic Stress Studies and the Academy of Traumatology. Each scholar was asked to address four fundamental questions but remained otherwise free in structuring his or her chapter. The purpose of the collection is to recognize the similarities and differences among these scholars, punctuate the significance and interrelatedness of their contributions, and inspire current and future trauma scholars to strive to make equally important lifetime contributions to understanding and helping the traumatized. This is a special project of the Academy of Traumatology with support from the Green Cross Foundation.

Charles R. Figley, Ph.D., Editor
Routledge Psychosocial Stress Book Series

Acknowledgments

Among the many people who were instrumental in some way in bringing this book to fruition are the following: Dr. Patricia L. Johnson (*Traumatology* assistant editor), Dr. Ellisa Benedek (University of Michigan), Allison Stieber (assistant to Dr. Robert Jay Lifton), Michaela Nevin (Dr. Ursano's personal assistant), Pamela K. Leadbitter-Shaver and Mary K. Estes (assistant to and daughters of Lawrence Kolb), Margarite Salinas (administrative assistant to Mardi J. Horowitz), Scott Lindstrom (assistant to Dr. Lenore Terr), Kathy Letizio (assistant to John Wilson), Dr. Bruce Thyer (Florida State University School of Social Work), the International Society for Traumatic Stress Studies, and the Academy of Traumatology staff. I offer a special note of thanks to colleagues who reviewed the submissions and provided tactful and supportive editorial suggestions. They include Frank Ochberg, Matthew Friedman, Lars Weisaeth, Spencer Eth, Dan Weiss, Robert Michels, Craig Van Dyke, Robert Ursano, Carol Fullerton, Rick Kolb (for assistance with the photos of Lawrence Kolb, his father), Annette Berenger (personal assistant to Prof. Beverley Raphael), Lynn Ochberg (for assisting Frank, as always), Molly Hall, Professor Harry Kreisler (UC-Berkeley Institute of International Studies, for providing a portion of the first draft of Dr. Lifton's chapter), Ann Norwood, Judy Herman, Sandy McFarlane, Rachel Yehuda, Anne Burgess, Francine Shapiro, John Fairbank, Onno van der Hart, and Roger Pitman. Also, I am grateful to my family, who tolerated my going on and on about this project; they include Kathy Regan Figley, Laura Figley, Geni Figley, Jessica Chynoweth, Mike Chynoweth, Sandy Elliott, Mike Elliott, and Amy Elliott. Dana Bliss, Brook Cosby, and George Zimmar of Routledge worked hard to keep this project on target and on time during the endless e-mail exchanges. I appreciate their professionalism and patience.

Contributors

MAPPING TRAUMA AND ITS WAKE:
AUTOBIOGRAPHIC ESSAYS BY PIONEER TRAUMA SCHOLARS

Edited by
Charles R. Figley

With chapters by the leading pioneers in the study and treatment of trauma:

Ann Wolbert Burgess, RN, DSciN
Yael Danieli, Ph.D.
Charles R. Figley, Ph.D.
Matthew J. Friedman, M.D., Ph.D.
Judith Lewis Herman, M.D.
Mardi Horowitz, M.D.
Lawrence C. Kolb, M.D.
Henry Krystal, M.D.
Robert Jay Lifton, M.D.
Frank Ochberg, M.D.
Beverley Raphael, M.D.
Zahava Solomon, Ph.D.
Lenore Terr, M.D.
Robert J. Ursano, M.D.
Bessel van der Kolk, M.D.
Lars Weisaeth, M.D.
John P. Wilson, Ph.D.

Introduction

CHARLES R. FIGLEY

The idea for this book emerged from my reading of a biography of Albert Einstein (Folsing, 1997), which noted that the only autobiography written by Einstein was in the form of a chapter in a book edited by Paul Arthur Schilpp (1949) as part of his *Library of Living Philosophers* (LLP). The plan of the LLP was to approach a leading philosopher and request an "intellectual autobiography," or authorized biography, of his or her publications. In the resulting book, this autobiographical work would be followed by a series of expository chapters and critical essays written by noted exponents and opponents of the philosopher's perspective. The LLP autobiographies often illuminated how these ideas grew into significant philosophical movements. Of special interest is how they reflected their originators' own special and personal experiences.

This approach to understanding the person behind the perspective would, it seemed to me, be relevant to any field of study, including traumatology. And it seemed to me that just as Einstein was motivated to write his only autobiography by this approach, the same method might entice the pioneers of traumatology to do likewise. This, the resulting book, offers evidence that the enticement worked.

The history of modern traumatology comprises only a few decades. Although traumatology was originally a narrow specialty of surgery, its scope has become wide, with a focus on the individual's psychosocial, emotional, and psychobiological reactions to traumatic events as well as the roles of medical injury and mitigation.

The explosion of this information has outpaced our ability to comprehend its history. Who better to tell that history than the history makers? The Society for Traumatic Stress Studies was established in 1985, a mere 5 years after the diagnosis of posttraumatic stress disorder (PTSD) was first presented. Over the years the (now international) society has served as the leading organization dedicated to the creation and dissemination of new knowledge in traumatology. Starting in 1988, the society established the Pioneer Award to represent both the lifetime achievements of the recipients and their pivotal role as pioneers in the field. In 1995, as a reflection of the growing significance of the field, the Pioneer Award was renamed the Lifetime Achievement Award, which remains the top award given by this learned society. Therefore, what better way to select those whose work represents the core and history of the field than to choose these award-winning scholars?

This is the first of several volumes of autobiographies written by traumatologists. Several winners of the society's award, including Edna Foa and Robert Pynoos, were unable to contribute to this book but have promised to do so in the next one. They are founding members of the Academy of Traumatology, and internationally, recognized pioneers are included in this book in addition to those recognized by U.S. society. Others will contribute to future volumes.

ABOUT THE TITLE

The primary title of this book, *Mapping Trauma and Its Wake*, represents two important concepts. First, pioneers of a new field, like the explorers of a new land, contribute primarily because they were the first to tell about their experience and to link what is known with what is unknown. The "maps they drew" were the initial reports of the traumatized, such as Robert Lifton's discussions of Vietnam veterans and the bombings of Japan; Danieli's accounts of the survivors of the Nazi camps and the effects on their children; and Terr's reports of the traumatized children of Chowchilla. Attention is given also to the trauma of war (Weiseth, Ursano), sexual assault (Burgess), and prolonged abuse (Herman). The mapping of trauma and its wake has also included pioneering laboratory research such as that of Lawrence Kolb, and its biomedical applications, such as those discussed by Friedman. The maps of theory (e.g., van der Kolk), constructs (e.g., Figley), context (e.g., Ochberg), and assessment (e.g., Horowitz, Wilson) were needed, too, and these were provided by most of the pioneers, along with innovative strategies of research (e.g., Solomon), treatment (e.g., Krystal), and the unique features of grief and loss (e.g., Raphael).

The other meaning of the primary title is associated with the 1985 book *Trauma and Its Wake: The Research and Treatment of Post-Traumatic Stress Disorder* (Figley, 1985). This was an historic volume that was also published in book series on psychosocial stress because it was the forerunner of the *Journal of Traumatic Stress* (JTS). The third volume of *Trauma and Its Wake*[1] was not published. Rather, its chapters appeared in the first volume of JTS in 1988.

The subtitle *Autobiographic Essays by Pioneer Trauma Scholars* reflects my decision to let those most responsible for drawing the maps of trauma and its wake relate the field's history through their own personal and professional experiences. Just as Schilpp (1949) believed that autobiographical essays by leading scholars would help tell the history of the modern philosophy of science, the editor and publisher of the present volume were confident that its pioneers would do the same for traumatology.

ABOUT THE PIONEERS

The pioneers who were selected for this volume represent some but not all of the scholars who built the field. Those less known or who became known for their work more recently are noted throughout this volume and will have an opportunity to express their views in future ones.

The pioneers who contributed to this book make up a remarkable group. Their names are listed on the "Contributors" page. Yet their names and work are well known even to the more casual consumers of scholarly literature in the field. Their ages range from the late 50s to 93—a remarkable span. Most are psychiatrists, but psychology, social work, and nursing are represented as well. Though most are Americans, their countries of origin include Israel, the Netherlands, and Norway. Most have traveled and lectured throughout the world. Thus, the contributors to this historic book and the beginnings of the field are international and multidisciplinary, spanning age, gender, areas of expertise, and specialty.

ABOUT THE CHAPTERS

The organization of this book is simple. The chapters are arranged by author, alphabetically. Authors were free to decide the way they would tell their story as long as, along the way, they answered four questions. Some organized their chapters with the questions (e.g., Horowitz). Others answered the questions at the end, in a separate section (e.g., Lifton). Most, however, answered the questions in the general context of their chapters.

Chapter 1, "Putting Trauma on the Radar Screen," was written by Ann Burgess. Dr. Burgess is the van Ameringen Professor of Psychiatric Mental Health Nursing and has received many awards, including the society's 1993 Pioneer Award and the Episteme Award from the Sigma Theta Tau international Honor Society of Nursing. She has played a significant role in changing beliefs, attitudes, and practices involving the victims of crime, particularly the crime of sexual assault. Much of her chapter tells the story, which starts in 1972, of her groundbreaking research on the circumstances and consequences of rape. She credits her contributions to the science and sociology of rape trauma to her friend and colleague

Lynda Lytle Holmstrom. These two, known affectionately as the "rape ladies," put rape on the radar screens of science and mental health practice.

Chapter 2, "It Was Always There," was written by Dr. Yael Danieli, a psychologist and the founder and director of the Group Project for Holocaust Survivors and Their Children in New York City. She is the 1995 winner of the society's Lifetime Achievement Award, its third president, and a cofounder. She starts her chapter with a brief discussion of her childhood, on a Tel Aviv kibbutz under British mandate prior to Israel's birth in 1948. Much of her chapter focuses on her many experiences and achievements on behalf of world peace and the United Nations, and with special attention to the social psychology of survivorship and secondary trauma among the children of Holocaust survivors. Part of her chapter is devoted to her efforts, through the society and on behalf of the society, at the United Nations.

Chapter 3, "From Veterans of War to Veterans of Terrorism: My Maps of Trauma," was written by Dr. Charles R. Figley, who is currently a professor at the Florida State University School of Social Work and director of the Traumatology Institute. He has won numerous awards, including the society's last Pioneer Award (1994) and the National Organization for Victim Assistance Shaffer Research Award; he was chosen Family Psychologist of the Year by the American Psychological Association in 1996, became a Penn State University Alumni Fellow in 2004, and was recently awarded a Fulbright Senior Research Fellowship. His chapter, as the title implies, begins with a discussion of his studies of war veterans and ends with a description of his current research on the survivors of terrorism. He combines notes on his personal life with reflections on his career, starting with his service in the Marine Corps and in the Vietnam War through his involvement at the start of both Society for Traumatic Stress Studies and the *Journal of Traumatic Stress* in 1985 as well as the founding of the Green Cross and the Academy of Traumatology.

Chapter 4, "Making It Up as I Went Along," was written by Matthew J. Friedman, currently a professor of psychiatry at Dartmouth and cofounder and director of the acclaimed National Center for PTSD in White River Junction, Vermont. He has won numerous awards, including the society's Lifetime Achievement Award. Professor Friedman admits, at the start of his essay, to having had no clear career passion. Although he had experienced anti-Semitism at first hand and was deeply affected by the Holocaust, it took the traumatic death by suicide of his only sibling, his younger brother Dick, to make him become a trauma pioneer. Soon thereafter, Dr. Friedman took a staff psychiatrist position at the Veterans Administration Medical Center in White River Junction, Vermont (where, he says, the locale was far more the initial attraction than working with veterans); there, his work ignited a fire that had already been kindled.

Chapter 5, "My Life and Work," was written by Judith Lewis Herman. Dr. Herman, in addition to being a professor of clinical psychiatry at Harvard University Medical School, is also director of training at Cambridge Hospital's Victims of Violence Program, in the department of psychiatry. Her long and distinguished career emerged from her passion for dissent, initially introduced by her parents, which continued at Harvard. The women's liberation movement primed her sensitivity to sexism and, after finishing her medical internship, led her to join a women's consciousness-raising[2] group in 1970. This opened her eyes to the derogation of women in everyday life; also, as a doctor, she was able to be far more sensitive to and connected with female patients. As a result and inevitably, she discovered that the incidence of incest was far greater than had been reported. This led her to team up with Lisa Hirschman, who had just finished her training in psychology. Together, they found the courage to challenge the current psychiatric establishment and publish their first paper in *Signs* (a women's studies journal) in 1976. This work was based on 20 cases of incest just from the surrounding community. The rest, and her career, was then history.

Chapter 6, "A Life in but Not Under Stress," was written by Mardi Horowitz, professor of psychiatry at University of California at San Francisco. He, perhaps more than any other person, conceived of posttraumatic stress disorder. Dr. Horowitz adopts a rather straightforward structure in describing his long and illustrious career. For example, in response to the question about how he became interested in the field, he notes that it was associated with stressful events in his life before he was 10 years old: being sent away from home to school at age 5, surviving a hemorrhaging tonsillectomy, witnessing the mauling of two children by a dog, and being violently attacked by two older boys. Later on, he also nearly drowned as a patrolman for the Fish and Wildlife Service. Horowitz notes that more meaningful than the experiences themselves was his "mindfulness about it all. I learned to observe the workings of my own consciousness, especially in review of my error in judgment." This mindfulness provided an important context as he completed his education and entered psychiatry. In the course of his military service, he became interested in studying the imagery of trauma, and a development grant from the National Institute of Mental Health enabled him to pursue research in this area. He began to realize that "intrusive thoughts in the form of images were frequently derived from perceptions during a traumatic event. The postcombat and postaccident cases in military settings gave concordant observations. They also frequently involved fantasy elaborations and distortions of actual perceptions." These initial speculations grew into his theory of traumatic stress and his important contributions to the field.

Chapter 7, "Fully Primed," by Lawrence C. Kolb, covers a greater span of time than any of the other chapters. His photo from 1947, which is included, illustrates this. Professor Kolb, now retired and living on the Georgia coast, won the society's first Pioneer Award. In the 1960s, he was not only chair of the department of psychiatry at Columbia University Medical School but also, consecutively, president of the American Psychological Association and of the American Board of Psychiatry and Neurology. He became the first "Distinguished Physician in Psychiatry" in the U.S. Department of Veterans Affairs. Among Kolb's numerous achievements was the discovery, from observations in his laboratory, that there is an abnormal physiologic disturbance in the brains of those with chronic PTSD. Indeed, it was Kolb's laboratory, along with the work of other pioneers who contributed to this book, that provided most of the data to justify the diagnosis of PTSD. The recognition of this abnormality ushered in the neurology of traumatology, which went far beyond psychiatry and mental health. As a result, the medical management of patients with PTSD and other diagnoses linked to war-related psychological trauma has improved significantly. Nearly every major development within the Veterans Administration leading to the more appropriate diagnosis, treatment, and management of PTSD, including the emergence of the National Center for PTSD, retains the fingerprints of Larry Kolb. For this and many other reasons he has won numerous awards, including the society's 1991 Pioneer Award.

Chapter 8, "Psychoanalytic Approaches to Trauma: A Forty-Year Retrospective," was written by Henry Krystal. Dr. Krystal, Michigan State University Professor Emeritus of Psychiatry, explains in the opening of his chapter that his family once resided in Sosnowiec, Poland; a deadly childhood condition and 3-month hospitalization was his first trauma, which he survived thanks to his mother's devoted care. This experience, he explains, led to a number of important insights. He notes that "primary" childhood narcissism—the feeling that one is loved and lovable, resulting from the "programming" of the child in a state of secure attachment to the mother—was the most important single asset promoting the survival of Holocaust victims. His journey to the United States and his medical and analytic training in Michigan provided important tools for what was to become an extraordinary and distinguished career. His scholarly contributions to the psychoanalysis of trauma and, in particular, the horror of the Holocaust and its survivors are recognized internationally. As a result, he has won many awards, including the society's Pioneer Award in 1992 and the International Psychoanalytic Association's Hayman Prize for his paper on resilience in 1999.

Chapter 9, "Some Reflections" was written by Robert Jay Lifton, currently Harvard University Visiting Professor of Psychiatry. Dr. Lifton is among the best-known and highly celebrated of the trauma pioneers featured in this book and was the first winner of the Pioneer Award in 1985. Lifton notes that his interest in trauma began with his early years in Japan, while serving in the military. This resulted in the first of many books that focused on the nature and consequences of trauma. He notes that he has, since childhood, been fascinated by imagery (especially in sports), history, and social justice. This explains to some degree his many contributions to the elucidation of trauma in so many different contexts. His earliest work, on thought reform, or "brainwashing," led to his study of Hiroshima and marked the beginning of his approach to psychology and history. He notes at the end of his chapter that Hiroshima " . . . was a major turning point because it combined everything I had become concerned with: a large and historical event, and advocacy in confronting and combating nuclear weapons." Yet perhaps his greatest contributions are associated with his work on Nazi doctors—two books and two personal immersions. Certainly his concepts will live on: psychic numbing, doubling, and the symbolization of immortality.

Chapter 10, "There Is Reason in Action," was written by Frank Ochberg. Dr. Ochberg, Michigan State University Clinical Professor of Psychiatry and Adjunct Professor of Criminal Justice, is chairman emeritus of the Dart Center for Journalism and Trauma. He is also the former associate director of the National Institute of Mental Health, former director of the Michigan Department of Mental Health, and the 2003 winner of the society's Lifetime Achievement Award. His chapter is a highly personal recollection of his distinguished and colorful career, which began 1968, when he was 28 years old and halfway through a psychiatry residency at Stanford. With encouragement from his wife, Lynn, and the guidance of faculty, he helped to establish the Stanford Committee on Violence and Aggression. Dr. Ochberg and his Stanford colleagues wrote his first book, *Violence and the Struggle for Existence*. He was then accepted into an elite group, the Mental Health Career Development Program, and by 1973 had moved up the ranks to become director of the Services Division of the NIMH. Once in this position, he was asked to serve on the U.S. Attorney General's National Task Force on Terrorism and Disorder. It was the beginning of a long-term relationship between, as he puts it, "cops and shrinks." This led to a 1976 assignment to the work-study program at The Maudsley, London's premier psychiatric teaching hospital. It was during this period that he made one of his more famous discoveries, which became known as the Stockholm syndrome, defined as an unexpected bond that forms between captor and captive. Although he did not name this syndrome, he defined it. As associate director for Crisis Management of NIMH he undertook a year-long study of the U.S. Secret Service. Among his other efforts, he served as the only male member of the Committee on Women of the American Psychiatric Association (APA), which is credited with having kept Hysterical Personality Disorder out of the Diagnostic and Statistical Manual (DSM). He and his colleagues also paid close attention to the concerns of victimized women, among other things picketing APA meetings until the APA trustees agreed to boycott states that refused to ratify the Equal Rights Amendment.

Another chapter in Dr. Ochberg's distinguished career comprised his service as Director of the Michigan Department of Mental Health. Though the position did not last long, it opened the door to establishing the first residential treatment facility for trauma victims in America, called the Dimondale Stress Reduction Center. The Dart Foundation was so impressed with his efforts that they helped him to cocreate the Michigan Victim Alliance, the Dart Center for Journalism and Trauma, the Critical Incident Analysis Group, the National Center for Critical Incident Analysis, and Gift from Within. Dr. Ochberg notes that his most significant achievements in the trauma field may lie in the seeding and nourishing of these networks.

Chapter 11, "Life, Trauma and Loss," was written by Beverley Raphael, the third winner (1987) of the Lifetime Achievement Award. Dr. Raphael is director of the Centre for Mental Health for New South Wales and emeritus professor in psychiatry from the University of Queensland. Professor Raphael is a fellow of the Australian Academy of Social Sciences. She organized her chapter by the four primary questions. The events that shaped her life included, first, surviving World War II as a child in Australia. She started out as a general practitioner with no particular interest in trauma until she became interested in the many war veterans she treated; the labels "inadequate personality" or "anxiety neurosis" led her to "learn something of their ways of dealing with what had happened in the war, as well as the strong cultural prescription of the time." This eventually led to her training in psychiatry in 1964, with a special interest in Caplan's model of "preventive intervention," or crisis intervention, that she quickly extended to other life crises, including hysterectomy, first pregnancy, and later in studies of response to accidental injury and natural disasters (starting with Cyclone Tracey of Christmas Eve, 1974).

Dr. Raphael's significant achievements include her research on bereavement as a stressor—and its psychological, social, and mental health concomitants—with the aim of developing appropriate mental health responses. In her work she has differentiated the phenomena of bereavement reactions and traumatic stress reactions and developed evidence-based guidelines for responses to disaster and terrorism. She notes in the latter part of her chapter that there is much to do in the field and is especially interested in improving the research and understanding of resilience in populations affected by disasters and terrorism. She also notes that it is important to further develop interventional strategies for those bereaved and traumatized by exposure to disaster or terrorism and has pointed out another half dozen areas that are ripe for research.

Chapter 12, "Choices Made, Promises Kept," was written by Zahava Solomon, who is a distinguished professor of social work and former dean of the Bob Shapel School of Social Work at the University of Tel Aviv, Israel. She is the 1997 winner of the Robert S. Laufer Memorial Award for Outstanding Scientific Achievement. This award is given to an individual or group responsible for an outstanding contribution to research in the PTSD field. She is full professor and director of the Adler Research Center at Tel Aviv University. Like some of the other authors, she has organized her chapter around the four standard questions. As to the emergence of her interest in trauma, she notes that all Israelis are influenced by the struggle to establish and protect the Jewish state. Israel, therefore, has become a virtual laboratory of stress. Dr. Raphael emphasizes the important role played by the Israeli army "in our collective and individual existence, as well as…the high toll that the ongoing strife can take—on fighters, their families, and other civilians." As a daughter and niece of Holocaust survivors, she was constantly reminded of its long-lasting horrors. As she notes, "trauma study is not merely an academic but [a] deeply personal matter." She describes surviving the Sinai campaign of 1956 as a child and being in the 11th grade during the Six-Day War, which erupted in June 1967. Only 3 kilometers separated her family's home from the Arab forces. She vividly remember her mother—who had spent her adolescence in the Auschwitz death camp and lived through the Israeli War of Independence as well as the Sinai campaign—whispering quietly to herself, "Till when? How many more wars do I have to go through in my lifetime?" Then came the Yom Kippur War in October 1973. It was now Zahava's turn as wife and mother to worry. She saw in her husband, on his return from the Syrian front, what she would later describe as combat stress reactions.

The turning point of her career came with the 1982 Lebanon War, shortly after her return from the United States with a doctorate in psychiatric epidemiology. As a member of the research branch of the Israeli Defense Force Mental Health Department, she was instrumental in transforming the department into the first major research facility focusing on combat stress. She set up a casualty file to record the number and characteristics of all casualties, examined the clinical features for common patterns, and looked at data on predisposition and types of treatment interventions. By the time the first Gulf War broke out in 1991, she was a mature scholar, well recognized in her field. Her expertise would be needed, because civilians were the targets. These circumstances offered Professor Solomon another opportunity to study the psychological reactions of people under stress. The El-Aqsa intifada, which continues at this writing (though there are hopeful signs of peace), has caused hundreds of deaths and injuries to Israelis from all walks of life and demographic categories.

Professor Solomon counts among her greatest achievements her quantitative research on the stress of combat as it affected not only soldiers as well as prisoners of war and their families but also civilians exposed to violence. Her studies have resulted in the publication of six books and 50 book chapters, more than a dozen monographs, and more than 200 articles in scientific journals in several languages. She has brought early and significant attention to secondary trauma, starting with combat stress but also including many other traumatic circumstances. Furthermore, she has noted vulnerability and resilience factors, including personality traits and social and cultural factors; societal attitudes to traumatized individuals; and issues of counter transference.

Dr. Solomon ends her chapter with a plea for more attention to several areas of research. First she notes the need to understand the special nature of vulnerability and resilience. Professor Solomon also emphasizes the importance of assessing acute stress as a risk factor for PTSD. She believes that it is imperative to devise effective evidence-based interventions for the treatment of PTSD that specifically focus on blocking or arresting the crystallization of acute stress reactions into chronic PTSD, inhibiting development of the disorder before it occurs, and interrupting or slowing its progression. She also urges more attention to understanding the prolonged and repeated trauma that so frequently occurs in Israel, Northern Ireland, the inner cities, and war zones. She also urges far more attention to understanding traumatized children and victims of secondary traumatization. Finally, she urges more cross-disciplinary research focusing on the issues outlined above.

Chapter 13, "Memoirs of a Childhood Trauma Hunter," was written by Lenore Terr. Dr. Terr is a clinical professor of psychiatry at the Langley Porter Psychiatric Institute at the University of California, San Francisco. The first among her many awards was the NIMH's Career Teacher award. She is also a winner of the Blanche Ittleson Award for her research on childhood trauma. Terr begins her chapter with a description of her first psychiatric patient in 1962, months after Terr gave birth, and her confrontation with child abuse. This led to her documenting similar cases in each department of her hospital. And, she reports, she "was hooked." Dr. Terr noted that in the early sixties, psychological trauma was fragmented into such areas as "battle fatigue," "rape," "incest," "accident," "torture," "civilian casualties of war," and "battered child syndrome." So she chose the last until she almost single-handedly established the field of child trauma. A large section of her chapter is devoted to her classic investigation of the Chowchilla kidnapping, which started on July 15, 1976, when 26 summer-school children from the California town of Chowchilla disappeared, along with their school bus and driver. Fortunately, the children and driver were able to escape after being imprisoned in an underground pit. Their captors were found; they confessed and served long jail sentences. Her years of investigation led to numerous publications and the identification of some lasting concepts using the core symptoms and signs found at Chowchilla: mental mechanisms, such as omen formation, future foreshortening, perceptual distortion, fears of the mundane, specific trauma-related fears, posttraumatic play, reenactment, characteristics of traumatic memory, how traumatic childhood dreams are expressed and changed over time, and posttraumatic thought patterns. These found their way into the APA's description of PTSD in children. The next section of her chapter focuses on the range of childhood trauma that could be considered normal; she notes that small traumatic events may affect taste, preferences, and interests as well as fears. The rest of the chapter is a review of her various projects, many of which have resulted in books—a pattern similar to that of Robert Lifton's career. Dr. Terr ends her chapter with a series of questions for current and future child traumatologists.

Chapter 14, "Autobiographical Essay," by Robert J. Ursano, is organized around the four primary questions. Dr. Ursano is professor and chairman of the Department of Psychiatry, Uniformed Services University of the Health Sciences, E. Edward Hebert School of Medicine in Bethesda, Maryland, and director of the Center for the Study of Traumatic Stress. Winner of the society's Lifetime Achievement Award in 1999, he became, in that same year, editor in chief of the venerable journal *Psychiatry*. Professor Ursano began his career with his work at the U.S. Air Force School of Aerospace Medicine, which included his first studies of trauma in the late 1970s; these focused on repatriated prisoners of the Vietnam War. This work led to changes in the Uniform Code of Military Conduct and to disability payments for the repatriated prisoners. He also discusses his later association with the Gander, Newfoundland, air disaster, the largest peacetime loss the Army had ever suffered. Since that time, in the past 20 years, he has had contact with nearly every major disaster our nation has faced, through consultation, education, or research. These events have included plane crashes in New York City and around the nation; earthquakes in California and Armenia (then part of the USSR); hurricanes in Florida and typhoons in Hawaii; the Khobar Towers bombing; *USS Cole* attack; embassy bombings in Kenya; wars in Iraq; peacekeeping in Somalia; and extensive involvement following the 9/11 terrorist attack, the anthrax attacks, and sniper attacks in Washington, DC. Dr. Ursano has held many leadership positions, including the first chair of the American Psychiatric Association's Committee on Psychiatric Aspects of Disaster and also chair of the first task force of the APA to develop the treatment guidelines for PTSD and ASD. He ends his chapter by suggesting that PTSD may be the first preventable psychiatric disorder and notes that the establishment of an extreme-stress brain bank will facilitate this goal and our neurobiological understanding of this and other "event related" disorders.

Chapter 15, "The Body Keeps the Score," is a brief autobiography by Bessel van der Kolk. The title comes from a well-known phrase that appears in several of his papers and represents the essence of his important contributions to traumatology. He is currently professor of psychiatry at Boston University Medical School and Clinical Director of the Trauma Center at HRI Hospital in Brookline, Massachusetts. Like other pioneers, he has been both president of the society and winner of the society's Lifetime Achievement Award. His interest in traumatology began with one of his first patients, a Vietnam War combat veteran who wanted to be free from his painful symptoms, later known as PTSD. Professor van der Kolk's work integrates developmental, biological, psychodynamic, and interpersonal aspects of the impact of trauma and its treatment. Because of his multidisciplinary approach and personal curiosity he has, perhaps more than any other modern traumatologists, helped to stimulate creativity among practitioners. This has led to important innovations in the assessment, treatment, and prevention of unwanted consequences from traumatic events.

Chapter 16, "Becoming a Psychotraumatologist," was written by Lars Weisaeth. Like other chapter authors in this volume, Professor Weisaeth was profoundly affected by World War II. He notes early in his chapter that he was born during the Nazi occupation of his homeland of Norway; "virtually all my memories from those [early] years are war-related, the vast majority of them involving some kind of danger." He credits these "minor or moderately stressful experiences" with his specialization within the field. Equally important, it appears, was his military service prior to medical school. This provided access to the culture of the military at home and abroad that enabled him to work later as a military psychiatrist and with war veterans. He credits his experiences in teaching and practicing at the University of Oslo's department of psychiatry as part of the medical faculty and work with Professor Arne Sund, M.D. as the deciding factors of his specialization in psychotraumatology stating in 1975. The rest of the chapter is a useful review of the history of the study of trauma in Norway with special emphasis on and credit to Leo Eitinger, whom Professor Weisaeth credits as "the father of Norwegian psychiatry related to stress, the military, and disaster." Starting with his 1976 paper at the Nordic Psychiatric Conference in Finland on "the traumatic anxiety syndrome," Professor Weisaeth was poised for a defining event in his professional life. This event was the September 15, 1976 Sandefjord petrochemical plant explosion. His research led to a series of publications including a two-volume monograph. The rest of the chapter discusses his work among peacekeepers with PTSD, the 1980 Oil-Rig Disaster: PTSS-10 in the North Sea, and various other studies and activities. These activities included his international collaborations. The final section of the chapter includes his discussion of his current position at the National Centre for Violence and Traumatic Stress Studies. He ends the chapter with an optimistic view that the field is the "most promising for prevention in psychiatry." But what is lacking, he asserts, is convincing and compelling evidence of the value of our treatment efforts.

The final chapter is entitled "From Crisis Intervention to Bosnia: The Trauma Maps of John P. Wilson." Dr. John Wilson is currently a professor of psychology at Cleveland State University. Though trained as a development and personality psychologist, Dr. Wilson became interested in traumatized war veterans very early in his career and, by 1978, had completed one of the first comprehensive studies of Vietnam War veterans for the Disabled Americans Veterans. Cofounder of the society and its second president, Professor Wilson is a recent Fulbright Fellow and Distinguished Visiting Professor of Psychology at the University of Croatia Medical School, where he drew upon his 9 books, 20 monographs and many dozens of journal articles, including such topics as the trauma of war, countertransference and the assessment and treatment of PTSD. These achievements are well represented in his chapter. He traces the beginning of his career to his initial encounter with a Vietnam vet who was a student in one of his classes and was instrumental in acquiring the grant from the Disabled American Veterans that made Dr. Wilson's Forgotten Warrior Project possible. Having described his many achievements and challenges, Dr. Wilson ends, as his title suggests, with the story of his work in Bosnia.

ABOUT JOSEPH WOLPE

As editor, the dedication of this book is my choice. In the past, I have dedicated my books to family members. I dedicate this book to Joseph Wolpe because I see him as one of the first pioneer traumatologists (Figley, 2002). Although we were not friends or even acquaintances, I flew from Tallahassee to Los Angeles to attend his funeral and meet his wife, Anna, and his children. I had that much respect for Dr. Wolpe and his work. He first became interested in trauma as a young South African psychiatrist in the 1940s, when he was responsible for treating combat veterans returning from the battlefields of Europe and North Africa in World War II. He immediately recognized that traditional theories of psychiatry would not do and appreciated the emerging social learning theory and its originators. With more of an interest in research than practice, he began to replicate the studies of Pavlov and others.

More than sixty years ago, in his paper "Reciprocal Inhibition as the Main Basis of Psychotherapeutic Effects," Wolpe (1954) asserted that the successful treatment of anxiety disorders was due to what he called "reciprocal inhibition." Wolpe suggested that reciprocal inhibition, first applied outside psychology, was the active ingredient in desensitization (i.e., complete or partial suppression of anxiety responses). Wolpe's theory suggested that stress reactions or fear can be eliminated when the sufferer is exposed to both the source of the fear and anything that was "physiologically antagonistic" to fear reactions. This implied a technique that would condition a new response to the originally feared stimulus. Originally, in animal studies, food was the physiologic antagonist, used first by Pavlov with dogs and then by Wolpe with cats. Food and associated cues counteracted the fear conditioning. With his technique of systematic desensitization, Wolpe substituted food-related cues with evocation of the relaxation reflex to counteract conditioned fear in human beings. The rest is history; but, with some exceptions (Heriot & Pritchard, 2002; Wolpe & Plaud, 1995; Poppen, 1995), Wolpe's treatment and experimental methods were adopted and improved upon by behaviorists over the next 60 years, with little credit to him or the reciprocal inhibition theory. This is why Joseph Wolpe was the first inductee to the Academy of Traumatology and winner of the first Golden Award.

Let us hope that this book helps us to remember the important contributions that have already been made, to build on them and go beyond them. As Chaim Shatan, another pioneer, has noted:

> I propose that [we] . . . go beyond the treatment of new trauma populations: the long-range cure of war-related trauma requires prevention of traumatic stress. We traumatologists can continue to provide first aid as "stretcher bearers of the social order," sophisticated, compassionate, with growing scientific knowledge, but picking up the wounded rather than preventing them from being wounded. Or we can try to eliminate the sources of PTSD in the social order, to dismantle the army-and-enemy system, a human invention, an institutionalized manhunt . . . . Otherwise, PTSD—an outgrowth of war and persecution—will remain with us unchanged, under whatever name, from shell shock to K.Z. syndrome, from DSM-III to DSM-X (Shatan, 1992, p. 20; cited in Bloom, 2000).

Far from being the final statement on the pioneers of trauma, this book, we hope, will provide steppingstones to preventing the unwanted and promoting the wanted consequences of trauma. At the very least, we hope that this book will offer some degree of understanding and appreciation of the living pioneers' explanations in mapping trauma and its wake and how they differentiated the steppingstones of trauma work from stumbling blocks in the field of traumatology.

REFERENCES

Bloom, S. L. (2000). Our hearts and our hopes are turned to peace: origins of the International Society for Traumatic Stress Studies. In A. Y. Shalev, R. Yehuda, & A. C. McFarlane (Eds.), *International handbook of human response to trauma* pp. 27–50. New York: Kluwer Academic/Plenum Publishers.

Figley, C. R. (2002). Theory-driven and research-informed brief treatments. In C. R. Figley (Ed.), *Brief Treatments for the traumatized* (pp. 3–28). Westport, CT: Greenwood Press.

Folsing, A. (1997). *Albert Einstein: A biography*. New York: Penguin Books.

Roberts, S., Weaver, A.J., Flannelly, K. J., & Figley, C. R. (2003). Compassion fatigue among chaplains and other clergy after September 11th. *Journal of Nervous and Mental Disease, 191*,11, 756–758.

Poppen, R. (1995). *Joseph Wolpe*. London: Sage.

Reyna, L. (1998). Joseph Wolpe—pioneer: A personal remembrance. *Journal of Behavior Therapy and Experimental Psychiatry, 29*, 187–188.

Schilpp, P. A. (1949). *Albert Einstein: Philosopher-scientist*. Evanston, IL: Living Philosophers, Inc.

Shatan, C. (1992, June). Enemies, armies, and PTSD: Divided consciousness and war—our next assignment. Paper presented at the First World Conference of the ISTSS, Amsterdam, Netherlands.

Sherrington, C. S. (1906). *The integrative action of the nervous system.* New Haven, CT: Yale University Press.

Wendt, G. R. (1936). An interpretation of inhibition of conditioned reflexes as competition between reaction systems. *Psychological Review, 43,* 258–281.

Wolpe, J. (1954). Reciprocal inhibition as the main basis of psychotherapeutic effects. *American Medical Association Archives of Neurology and Psychiatry, 72,* 204–226.

Wolpe, J. (1958). *Psychotherapy by reciprocal inhibition.* Stanford, CA: Stanford University Press.

Wolpe, J. (1993). Commentary: The cognitivist oversell and comments on symposium contributions. *Journal of Behavior Therapy and Experimental Psychiatry, 24,* 141–147.

Wolpe, J., & Plaud, J. J. (1995). Pavlov's contribution to behavior therapy: The obvious and the not so obvious. *American Psychologist, 52,* 966–972.

ENDNOTES

1. Volume 2 was published in 1986 (Figley, 1986).
2. The term "consciousness raising" was invented by her friend and Harvard classmate Kathie Sarachild, of the New York Red Stockings.

1

Putting Trauma on the Radar Screen

ANN WOLBERT BURGESS

My work on rape trauma started as a research project. Credit for any of my contributions to the science and sociology of rape trauma must include my colleague, Lynda Lytle Holmstrom. Without her, I never would have started the study. Both of us were newly hired at Boston College. Holmstrom had just finished a research project on two-career families and was searching for a topic that was relevant to women's lives and to the relationship between men and women. She had heard many reports by women at consciousness-raising groups in the late 1960s about physical assaults that had been made on them by men. And yet, it seemed that despite the common occurrence of assault against women and its strong impact on the people involved, researchers seldom picked up on this behavior as a research topic. Thinking about this disparity led Holmstrom to the idea, initially only vaguely formulated, of studying rape and especially rape victims. Her next step was to meet with me (Burgess), with whom she had done some interdisciplinary teaching at Boston College, to discuss how one might go about such a study. As I listened, I did a memory search on what I knew about rape and its victims. I came up with a blank. Having been educated in Boston, I had learned mainly the psychoanalytic theories, so nothing Holmstrom was

17

saying about rape matched what I was taught—which piqued my curiosity. It led me to tell her that if she wanted to add a clinical or counseling component to the study, I would be interested in collaborating with her. We then discussed how an interdisciplinary approach might be an especially fruitful way to deal with the problem, and how the academic expertise of a sociologist and the clinical expertise of a psychiatric nurse complemented each other. We became a team (Holmstrom & Burgess, 1978).

In venturing forward in the spring of 1972, the first thing we discovered was that rape victims were hard to find. Our initial inquiries were not successful. First, we tried locating victims through the courts, only to be confronted with innumerable delays and also to learn that only a very small percentage of cases made it through the system.

We then asked some criminologists for advice and made some contacts in the criminal justice system. Although people were polite to us, they were not very helpful in terms of locating victims. Third, we tried contacting the police. That proved totally impossible, as our calls were never returned. So we then turned to the medical hierarchy of a large municipal hospital—Boston City Hospital—where a large percentage of victims were taken. A colleague in the department of psychiatry referred us to medical personnel on the emergency services; again, people were polite but also thought of many reasons why we could not begin our study. After trying these four entry points into the system, we were still not getting very far. No one had refused us, but neither was anyone helping us or moving very fast.

Impatient with delays, we tried a fifth approach: the nursing hierarchy at Boston City Hospital. And they moved with utmost speed. Anne G. Hargreaves, Executive Director of Nursing Services and Nursing Education, told us that the emergency department saw many rape victims and, to her knowledge, no psychological services were being provided. Hargreaves put us in touch with the assistant director of nursing for emergency services, who met with us. She then arranged for us to meet at once with the three shifts of staff nurses, the people who would be most in contact with us as we worked. She introduced us as interested in doing "some clinical work." The research aspect was noted but not emphasized. We exchanged ideas. The staff nurses expressed polite interest, made some inquiries, explained what they had done with rape victims in the past, and told us some of the obstacles they thought we might face—for example, that the police were often in a hurry and might rush us. But most important, they agreed to telephone us each time a rape victim was admitted. Two days later, a rape victim was brought to the hospital and the nurses called us promptly at 1:40 a.m. And they, as well as the administrative staff, continued to call us for an entire year. Their tremendous and conscientious help was essential to the success of the project.

Access to the hospital was the first step. We also needed the cooperation of the individual victims. The nurse or physician on duty typically told the victims about us. Their explanations varied, depending on their perceptions of us. Some emphasized that we did counseling, others said we were doing a study. Because victims were often in great distress when we met them, we provided a handout repeating the information that the Victim Counseling Program had two aims: (1) to provide counseling through an initial visit at the hospital and by telephone for follow-up and (2) to study the problems the victim experienced as a result of being assaulted. This same information was also posted on the wall of the examination room. All victims met with us and agreed to telephone follow-up calls.

A part of our study was also to observe what happened at court. We would accompany the victim and occasionally would be asked about why we wanted to stay. We answered that we were from the hospital, provided counseling services to rape victims, and studied rape victims' problems. Upon hearing that explanation, the judges ruled that we had a direct interest in the case and could stay.

At Boston City Hospital, over a 1-year period, we interviewed all persons (n = 146) admitted through the emergency department with a complaint of rape, provided crisis counseling, and accompanied them through the court process. We called the victim's trauma response "rape trauma syndrome" and published the resulting paper in the *American Journal of Psychiatry* in 1974. The study was twofold, having a clinical focus on victim response to rape and an institutional focus. The study made clear that rape does not end with the assailant's departure; rather, the profound suffering of the victim can be diminished or heightened by the response of those who staff the police stations, hospitals, and courthouses. Ironically, the institutions that society has designated to help victims may in fact cause further damage (Holmstrom & Burgess, 1978).

How We Were Perceived

The staff nicknamed us the "rape ladies." For the most part they went out of their way to help us, so we assumed that our presence had some legitimacy in their eyes. Perhaps the thing that established us most was our willingness to be on 24-hour call to the hospital. The staff subjected us to good-natured teasing about whether we had the stamina to last a year.

The physicians who examined the victims accepted our presence on the emergency ward. We were careful to explain to the physicians our credentials and what we were doing, but still they often misperceived us. One physician thought we were from the hospital's Social Services and sometimes entered that on the patient's medical record. Another assumed we were nuns because we taught at Boston College; he told us, laughing, of this misperception one night after suddenly realizing that one of us was very pregnant. And still another thought we did this kind of work "to earn a little extra money on the side."

Victims saw us as part of the hospital system. Despite our careful explanation, our exact training and position were not always understood. Victims called us, or asked us if we were, social workers, "workers," psychiatrists, "shrinks," doctors, counselors, or religious women. Several inquired if we were rape victims ourselves.

The Experience of Interdisciplinary Research

Could a sociologist and a psychiatric nurse work together? In the beginning, we did not know. We had very different backgrounds. Holmstrom brought to the project training in sociology and anthropology, research experience analyzing the careers of professional couples, an interest in the sociology of the professions and medical sociology, knowledge of feminist literature, and experience in the women's movement. I, in contrast, brought training in nursing and psychiatric care, previous work with a wide range of emotional problems, and experience in many hospitals, private practice, and the training of other clinicians. Through mutual education we each expanded our range of skills and conceptual framework. And through countless discussions, we came to make analytic sense out of our data. The resulting conceptualizations were very much a joint product.

DUAL MOTIVATION FOR THE STUDY: THE WOMEN'S MOVEMENT

Lynda Holmstrom was influenced to initiate a study of rape victims because of her understanding of the women's movement, and I was influenced because of my nursing education and experience. Both are key to understanding our purpose in studying rape victims. As background, the women's rights movement had enjoyed a number of births, phases, and rebirths since the beginning of the 19th century. Initially, the movement concerned itself with legal recognition of women to secure their rights to vote, to own and control property, and to participate in public affairs. The movement in the 20th century focused on educational opportunities, equal employment, and the impact of sexism on women's lives. For a growing number of women, this freedom meant more than a choice of nontraditional roles, jobs, and lifestyles; for many it meant confronting restrictions on women's personal lives. Analysis of these restrictions began to emerge from the dialogue of "consciousness raising" (CR) groups, a new organizing tool of the women's movement whereby women discussed their experiences and problems of being female in a modern society. Frequently viewed by men as hotbeds of radical feminism, the reality was simply that attending such a discussion group was the most assertive action many of the women of that day were capable of taking. But it was within the supportive environment of the CR groups that women found the courage to share private experiences never before shared, such as incest and rape (Largen, 1985).

These disclosures of former victims had a profound effect on their listeners. The revelations represented an unprecedented breakthrough of the silence that had surrounded the topic of rape for centuries. The act of rape has been an inherent part of women's lives throughout recorded history—a theme of literature, poetry, theater, art, and war; it is an act that a pre-1970 society tended to view more through the mocking eyes of *Playboy* magazine. At best, it was a subject considered too delicate to raise, as noted by Largen (1985); at worst, it was a subject that generated derision, blame, or distrust of the victim.

In the early 1970s, when police departments and rape crisis centers first began to address the crime of rape, little was known about rape victims or sex offenders. The issue of rape was just beginning to be raised by feminist groups, and the 1971 New York Speak-Out on Rape had been held. Contemporary feminists who raised the issue early were Susan Griffin, in her now classic article on rape as the "all-American" crime; and Germaine Greer, in her essay on "grand rapes" (legalistically defined) and "petty rapes" (everyday sexual ripoffs). Susan Brownmiller wrote the history of rape and urged people to deny its future. The general public was not particularly concerned about rape victims; very few academic publications or special services existed; funding agencies did not see the topic as important; and health policy was almost nonexistent.

The antirape movement began to attract women from all walks of life and political persuasions. Various strategies began to emerge, one of them being the self-help program now widely known as the "rape crisis center." One of the first such centers was founded in Berkeley, California, in early 1972, known as Bay Area Women Against Rape (BAWAR). Within months of the opening of the Berkeley center, similar centers were established in Ann Arbor, Michigan; Washington D.C.; and Philadelphia. Lynda Holmstrom and I founded a hospital-based rape counseling service at Boston City Hospital, and in Minneapolis, Linda Ledray, RN, PhD, founded a similar service. Centers soon were replicated and services flourished. Although volunteer ranks tended to be composed of a large number of university students and instructors, they also included homemakers and working women. The volunteer makeup usually reflected every age, race, socioeconomic class, sexual preference, and level of political consciousness. Volunteers were, however, exclusively women. Among the women, the most common denominators were a commitment to aiding victims and to bringing about social change (Largen, 1985). As Susan Brownmiller noted, the amazing aspect of the proliferation of the grass-roots women's groups was that such an approach to the problem of rape had never been suggested by men: That women should organize to combat rape was an invention of the women's movement.

In retrospect, the history of the rape crisis centers in the United States has been one of enormous struggle. The struggle was to overcome indifference, apathy, changing social trends, and lack of stable resources, yet it was willingly engaged in from the belief in the rightness of the cause—a cause that, despite the struggles, had its share of successes. Feminists identified a social need and a way of responding to it. Centers, begun without role models, became role models themselves for other crime victims, specifically for battered women and their children. Though never having reached the ultimate goal of eradicating rape through social change, they nonetheless were the instigators of social change essential to the rights of women (Largen, 1985).

CONTRIBUTIONS AND ACHIEVEMENTS

Rape, until the 1970s, thrived on prudery, misunderstanding, and silence. It was not until the 1980s that academic and scientific publications on the subject multiplied. A review of articles on the psychological effects of rape and interventions for rape victims in the posttraumatic period located 78 references between 1965 and 1976, with 36 on the effects of rape and 42 on intervention. Two of the papers were coauthored by Burgess and Holmstrom in 1973 and 1974.

But studying the lot of the victim was only half of the equation in rape. To fully appreciate the impact of rape on a victim, it was necessary to understand the assailant.

Holmstrom and I had met A. Nicholas Groth at a tiny (about 15 people attended) conference on rape in 1973, where we informally talked about rape victims coming into an emergency ward. Groth (one of the featured speakers) impressed us for several reasons. First, he talked of his interviews with rapists at the Massachusetts Treatment Center, where he was a clinical psychologist. Some of what he said matched what we had heard from victims, but other parts, of course, did not. Second, after the conference he (as he had promised) sent us material; and third, he was interested in collaborating with us on a paper on motivational intent of issues related to power, anger, and sexuality rather than primarily sex, citing the amount of sexual dysfunction during rape. Child sexual abuse victims told us (and we wrote) of the pressure, sex, and secrecy used in the act, and the child molesters told of how they pressured children for sex using attention and material goods as the exchange (Burgess, 2002).

Funding opportunities for further research to expand on these findings became available to Burgess as the problem of child sexual abuse and child pornography became more visible. Serial murderers and the role of physical abuse, child sexual abuse, and lack of supportive and/or blaming parents provided key variables to understanding a possible transition from victim to victimizer (Ressler, Burgess, & Douglas, 1988). Another key colleague was research psychologist Robert Prentky, who was director of research at the Massachusetts Treatment Center and had extensive data and understanding of serial sex offenders. Our first paper together focused on prevention and analyzed victim response by rapist type (Prentky & Burgess, 2000). The collaboration has continued on issues such as the presumptive role of fantasy in serial sexual homicide, the cost-benefit analysis of the rehabilitation of child molesters, child molesters who abduct, and the new research opportunities on the developmental antecedents of sexual violence, including the most extreme form of sexual violence: serial homicide.

Financial help for funding research and services came from Congress in the 1970s. In response to a growing crime rate and concern over the problem of rape, Sen. Charles Mathias of Maryland had introduced a bill in September 1973 to establish the National Center for the Prevention and Control of Rape (NCPCR). The purpose of the bill was to provide a focal point within the National Institutes of Health from which a comprehensive national effort could be undertaken to do research, develop programs, and provide information leading to aid for victims and their families, to rehabilitation for offenders, and, ultimately, to the curtailment of rape crimes. The bill was passed by overwhelming vote in the 93rd Congress, vetoed by President Ford, and successfully reintroduced. The NCPCR was established through Public Law 94-63 in July 1975 and Burgess was the chair for the first advisory committee to the new center. However, by the late 1980s, momentum for the study of rape had significantly diminished and the NCPCR was closed. It was not until 1994 that funding again became available when Congress passed the Violence Against Women Act (VAWA) as part of the Violent Crime Control and Law Enforcement Act, and an Office on Violence Against Women in the U.S. Department of Justice was established. With funding, many other vulnerable target populations for sexual assault—children, adolescents, the developmentally delayed, and patients with physical and/or mental impairments—have been the subject of varying degrees of clinical and empirical scrutiny. Like the elderly, when any of these populations reside in an institutional setting, the risk for abuse increases simply as a function of their dependence on staff for safety, protection, and care.

Indeed, the decade of the 1990s catapulted sexual assault from relative obscurity to high profile in the legal and public health arenas (Prentky & Burgess, 2000). Despite the considerable attention given to the diversity and ubiquity of sexual assault, it is all the more noteworthy that one of the most vulnerable groups of victims, the residents of nursing homes (estimated to be 1.5 million persons in 1997), remain in obscurity. It is interesting that the NCPCR funded the first research on elderly victims of sexual assault in October 1975, but by 2000 there was still less than scant literature on the topic. Although the reasons for our failure to tackle forthrightly the problem of sexual abuse of the elderly and nursing home residents are unclear, we can certainly posit two explanations: (1) the incomprehensibility, and hence rejection, of claims of sexual assault on nursing home residents and, perhaps most important, (2) ageism—or generalized negative attitudes, if not outright hostility, toward older and cognitively impaired people (Burgess, 2002). With that as background, a pilot study of 20 sexually abused nursing home residents identified barriers to effective health care interventions. First, delayed reporting of the sexual abuse resulted in failure to obtain timely medical evidentiary examinations, delayed treatment for injuries and infection, and an absence of medical or psychological follow-up care. Second, there was difficulty in performing evidentiary rape examinations due to leg contractures and cognition/memory problems. Indeed, in a number of the victims, the fetal position and muscular rigidity made examination impossible. Third, there was evidence of wide variations in the evidentiary examination for sexual assault, such as the lack of colposcopic photographs. And fourth, the offenders (who were arrested) were either employees of the nursing homes or residents and, without prompt victim identification, were suspected to have abused more than one victim (Burgess, 2002).

PEOPLE WHO INFLUENCED AND SIGNIFICANTLY ASSISTED MY RESEARCH

I have already identified Lynda Lytle Holmstrom as the most influential colleague contributing to my work with trauma victims and have mentioned other colleagues who have collaborated with their own research and mine. But here are a few more influential people.

Anne G. Hargreaves was my professor in psychiatric nursing as an undergraduate at Boston University. She continued to be my mentor and in 1972 was Executive Director of Nursing Services and Nursing Education for the Department of Health and Hospitals, City of Boston. She opened a door to the rape study by giving permission for my colleague Lynda Holmstrom and me to begin our research with rape victims who were being admitted to Boston City Hospital's emergency department. We had approached all nursing directors of large emergency departments in the Boston area and all except Anne Hargreaves said we would need the approval of medicine. Hargreaves told us that providing crisis intervention for rape victims was the domain of nursing and we needed no further approval. In 1974, she wrote the foreword to our first book on rape and said, "Rape is a total public policy issue. . . . This book should be especially helpful to those involved in the immediate crisis situation, the hospital staff and the police, who are most often the first on the scene. . . . Readers of this book, hopefully, may find a change in their attitudes toward the victims of rape."

Anne Hargreaves is legendary for her no-nonsense approach to health care. She was a consummate Renaissance woman who fought long hard battles for nursing. She has significantly influenced many students in her long career in nursing.

The Power of Publication

The study that began in the emergency department at Boston City Hospital in 1972 sought to document the "career" of the rape victim through the institutional systems of law enforcement, the hospital, and the court. And while clinical research of this type was not funded in those days (Lynda Holmstrom and I wrote unsuccessful grant proposals to three agencies), the important act that opened the door to begin to educate nursing and law enforcement specifically about rape was the publication of our very first article in the 1973 *American Journal of Nursing*, titled "The Rape Victim in the Emergency Ward." That article described rape as having a traumatic aftermath and supported the idea of nursing intervention being effective as a first step in reducing the consequences of this violent act.

The fact that rape occurs and is an act of conquest is documented in the Bible as well as in war annals. It is endemic to humankind and was undoubtedly practiced by cavemen. But in 1972, when Lynda Holmstrom and I launched our research, there were very few clinically based articles that dealt with the incidence of rape or the impact of rape on the victim and/or family. And there was little information on the offender. While the violent acts and the suffering they caused had been noted since the origins of humanity, few considered these events from a health standpoint.

My choice of the *American Journal of Nursing* (AJN) for the first descriptive article on the rape victim was instrumental for my collaboration with research and training with the special agents of the Behavioral Science Unit at the FBI Academy in Quantico, Virginia. And the FBI sought me out because of a nurse whom I did not even know at the time.

As background, in 1973, the FBI Training Division had been assigned to instruct in the area of rape and sexual assault victimology. None of the agents were so trained. Roy Hazelwood, Supervisory Special Agent assigned to Quantico, was conducting a training on homicide investigation with the Los Angeles Police Department (LAPD). He mentioned his new assignment to the class. Rita Knecht, a detective with the LAPD who was also a registered nurse working part-time in the emergency department on weekends, told Hazelwood of the AJN article on rape victims. Knecht suggested that Hazelwood contact me, which he did. With that, I began training FBI special agents at Quantico on rape victims and offenders.

The association with the FBI agents—especially Bob Ressler, John Douglas, Roy Hazelwood, and Ken Lanning—led to several research projects on serial offenders and profiling, now called "criminal investigative analysis." I later sought out Rita Knecht at a training academy session specifically to thank her for the major role she had played in my career.

Sometimes being invited to speak at a conference opens a door to other researchers studying similar issues. One such conference was the 1979 Purdue University conference, to which I was invited as a speaker by Charles Figley. As I listened to Figley's account of his work on combat stress, it became clear to me that similar dynamics were involved in prolonged trauma situations such as sexual abuse suffered by children and women. Discussions around these issues led to a valued friendship as well as an opportunity to be part of Figley's conference on Iranian hostages.

Another important influence on my work is my colleague and friend Carol R. Hartman, RN, DNSc., an expert nurse-therapist who significantly influenced me specifically in the area of conceptualizing the practice of trauma therapy. Hartman was a classmate of mine during my doctoral study at Boston University School of Nursing. Together we studied under June Mellow, who directed the program to prepare nurses as nurse-psychotherapists. Two factors prompted me to seek out Hartman as a collaborator. In my clinical practice with rape victims, I was finding that a significant percentage were "moving on" with their lives but were still suffering from the rape trauma. I needed someone to help analyze the problem. Second, the interviews with serial sex offenders were coming in from the FBI agents and I needed some help in analyzing the motivational intent. Our work together was critical in efforts to develop theories of the neurobiology of trauma. Before we learned of the influence of neuroscience and trauma, we believed certain changes occurred in the victims that were not readily amenable to extinction. As best we tried, there were just some behaviors that did not respond to existing treatment methods. Something had changed profoundly in these victims' whole neurologic systems. The only model we knew of at that time that led to such changes was imprinting. Our work with victims led to our description of a trauma model—that is, the neurobiology of trauma. As research came along to back up the observations, in the 1990s, the changes were to be observed through brain imaging. The implications of that model were to look at intervention in a more eclectic manner. We realized we had to tailor interventions to the specific responses of individuals to their trauma. This is where the use of hypnotherapy, support systems, safety, and ego support became primary beyond merely uncovering the trauma. In fact, releasing memories of the event could be damaging if the victim were not strong enough psychologically to deal with them. These findings led to some principles involved in setting up therapy. The work on the problems of memory has been debated. Nevertheless, these are early clinical observations and must be understood in that context. Critical to this phase of study was our work with very young, preverbal children.

Another phase of study was our work with sexual killers. The work of Brittain and MacCulloch and colleagues (cited in Ressler, Burgess, & Douglas, 1988) served as a foundation for our hypothesis that the motivation for sexual murder is based on fantasy. We began to look at the impact of fantasy on personality and reviewed with the FBI agents all of their interviews with killers and the role of fantasy in the lives of people who could not make a connection with other people. These killers' empathy was used for narcissistic gain rather than to connect with others. Fantasy was their dominant emotional experience and its acting out became an important part in the escalation and triggering of a violent response. Out of that work came the model for profiling serial offenders (Ressler, Burgess, & Douglas 1988).

EVENTS IN MY LIFE LEADING TO MY INTEREST IN TRAUMA

I came to the trauma field as a result of having been invited to collaborate on a research project with Lynda Holmstrom rather than because there were any specific events that sparked my interest. However, I stayed in the field and made it a focus of research and practice. As I pondered how to answer "why," I realized that my experiences as a nursing student and as a nurse prepared me for work with trauma victims.

I had been music major in high school and had dreams of becoming a concert pianist. My only sibling, a brother, was very talented, playing jazz piano in a band. I thought I might follow in his footsteps. But my mother's Swiss background led her to urge me to have steady work (such as that of a teacher or nurse), and my father's physician brothers also encouraged me to enter the health field. Medicine did not interest me, but nursing seemed a second best to music. Even in college I was able to choreograph a production to raise money for a student nursing fund.

I was admitted to Boston University, a 4-year school that would grant me a BS degree and make me eligible to take my RN exam. However, my early experience of hospital nursing opened my eyes to the kind of oppression women experienced in the workplace. I saw that nurses were taught to give up their seats to doctors and to eat in separate dining rooms. If a patient problem developed, the nurse was looked to first. There was a complete devaluation of nurses' work. Nurses were not even allowed to describe blood as blood; we had to call it red fluid. Doctors dominated the work setting; nurses were seen as the "handmaidens."

Fortunately, there was a developing group of nursing leaders who staked their reputations on asserting themselves. Nursing leaders who kept pushing nursing forward—Anne Hargreaves, Marie Farrell, June Mellow, Rose Godbout and Anne Kibrick—taught me.

While I was struggling with nursing, Lynda Holmstrom was looking at the broader issue of women's rights; as we began to examine what happened with rape victims, these two issues dovetailed. We found that the victims were being blamed for the rapes, jokes were made about them, there was little available in services for victims and no follow-up, and funding agencies were not interested in the topic. As I became more involved with victim counseling, the injustices I saw gave energy to our continuous fight for victims.

HOPE FOR CURRENT AND FUTURE SCHOLARS TO BUILD ON MY WORK

More than thirty years ago, I had never heard of forensic nursing and never dreamed that it would play such an important role in my nursing career. Fast forward to the 21st century. Forensic nursing is now on nursing's radar screen. Forensics is a part of all nursing.

HOW FAR HAVE WE COME?

The first wave of change in the rape trauma field came with advances in the investigation and prosecution of rape cases. In the investigation of rape, which interfaced in the 1970s with the emergency department, the improved scientific collection of evidence has improved the forensic part of the process. This, in turn, has improved the prosecution of cases, because evidence greatly assisted at trial. But more important, the issue of blaming the victim lessened as the perception of the victim improved by being able to explain victim trauma and behavior. Concurrently, women's groups worked with legislators, which led to judicial rulings about the limits of cross-examination of the victim, such as rape shield laws. These were important changes, because attitudes had to be corrected, and part of what helped was the careful documentation of symptom manifestation and its presentation over time. There developed a clinical observational basis upon which a variety of behaviors became more understandable in terms of the impact of trauma on the psychological and neurologic functioning of the victim. These insights were expanded to apply not only to the adult rape victim but also to child victims and special populations such as physically or cognitively handicapped and the elderly. All of this, of course, led to the development of the study of rape within the justice department, which provided funds for extensive research and training of judicial staff. This became truly a multidisciplinary activity, so that law enforcement and the judiciary became part of the team not only to deliver the message but also to train and add pertinent questions to the ongoing investigation of the trauma victim's response to rape. A body of knowledge on the behavior of perpetrators developed, which became a significant contribution in the investigation of serial rapists and sexual abusers (Douglas et al., 1992).

The basic study of rape trauma and the follow-up work of victims, both children and adults, over time contributed to the development of a variety of approaches to treatment (Crowell & Burgess, 1996). This has paralleled efforts by others to figure out ways to abate the behavior of perpetrators. Understanding the symptom manifestations of sexually reactive children has led to interventions to prevent reenactment behaviors. The study of offenders has helped to elucidate their psychodynamics in targeting victims. Perpetrators target victims for several reasons, among which are the victims' vulnerability and/or accessibility, or they may be targeted for more personal reasons, such as specific characteristics. This has led us to look at the perpetrator behavior of stalking. That is, studying the behavior of the stalker (usually male) who interjects himself into the victim's life by writing, phoning, following, and so on. The targeted persons become aware and anxious, sometimes not knowing who the pursuer is. But there is a second type of surveillance, learned through interviews with offenders, where the victim and her habits are studied for characteristics but the offender is clandestine and does not interject himself until the attack. This understanding is important for rape prevention and education (Douglas et al., 1992).

FUTURE WORK IN THE TRAUMA FIELD

There is much to be done in the research arena. A commonly reported clinical and theoretical explanation for the origin of sexually aggressive behavior, particularly behavior with an early onset, is "recapitulation"—the notion that a person will repeat history or do what was done to him (or her). Over time, this hypothesis went from being a "silver bullet," to a tarnished bullet, to a complex bullet. Although the cycle of violence is neither inevitable nor inexorable, there is ample speculation and some empirical evidence that sexual violence may, at the very least, increase the risk for subsequent sexual violence. Increasing the risk implies the interplay of other factors that may aggravate or mitigate risk (see Prentky & Burgess, 2000).

Although research in this area clearly is needed, sufficient work has been done to suggest reasonable speculations. Prentky and Burgess have hypothesized, for instance, that protracted sexual abuse that is intrusive and/or violent is importantly related to the development of sexually deviant and aggressive fantasies and may well increase the risk of sexually aggressive behavior, especially when there is caregiver instability. Thus, morbidity factors include age of onset of sexual abuse, relationship to offender, duration of abuse, and invasiveness and/or violence of abuse (Prentky & Burgess, 2000).

In work with juvenile sex offenders, it became apparent that after the juveniles detailed their crimes in an interview, they would have an emotional reaction and memory of their own abuse. Staff soon realized they had the victim of a childhood trauma to treat, not just an offender. Whatever attitude staff had initially toward the juveniles, they began to understand the juvenile's abuse, distress, and vulnerability. This knowledge was the start of new intervention and treatment planning.

The future of rape trauma work is tenuous. First, adequate research and scholarship is always disrupted by groups that organize to fight on many levels: legal, print, media, or bogus publications. The future of scholarship depends on the scholars' intestinal fortitude to fight. In reality, the funding of trauma research has been very limited. Social policy and legislation designed to manage sexual violence is often in disarray, and the academic community has failed to embrace sexual violence as a topic of scholarly inquiry.

Nursing is and will continue to be a major player in the trauma field. The antirape movement was part of the momentum that helped catapult nursing to the status of a major provider of health care services to victims of abuse. It opened doors for nurses to develop interdependent relationships with other health care providers, initiate courses and programs of research in victimology and traumatology, influence legislation and health care policy, provide expert testimony in criminal and civil legal cases, and define the new specialty of forensic nursing. However, sexual violence still affects hundreds of thousands of women's and children's lives each year, and health care professionals could be even more influential in case finding and treatment of trauma as well as in designing research protocols for the interventions aimed at preventing abuse and decreasing the number of victims. The foothold of skilled investigator nurses in emergency departments and their preparation for collecting and presenting evidence as well as testifying in judicial proceedings is a major contribution.

Trauma is now on the radar screen for all disciplines. The pioneers have provided the foundation for the next generation, and they need to keep motivating young clinicians and scholars to forge ahead.

Ann Wolbert Burgess, 1970

REFERENCES

Burgess, A. W. (2002). *Violence through a forensic lens*. King of Prussia, PA: Nursing Spectrum.

Crowell, N., & Burgess, A. W. (Eds.) (1996). *Understanding violence against women*. Washington, D.C.: National Academy of Science Press.

Douglas, J. E., Burgess, A. W., Burgess, A. G., & Ressler, R. K. (1992). *Crime classification manual*. San Francisco: Jossey-Bass Publishers.

Holmstrom, L. L., & Burgess, A. W. (1983). *The victim of rape*. New Brunswick, NJ: Transaction Books. (Originally published in 1978 in New York by John Wiley & Sons.)

Largen, M. A. (1985). The anti-rape movement: Past and present. In A. W. Burgess (Ed.), *Rape and sexual assault* (pp. 1–13). New York: Garland Press.

Largen, M. A. (1988). Rape-law reform: An analysis. In A. W. Burgess (Ed.), *Rape and sexual assault II* (pp. 271–292). New York: Garland Press.

Prentky, R. A., & Burgess, A. W. (2000). *Forensic management of sexual offenders*. New York: Kluwer Academic/Plenum Publishers.

Ressler, R. K., Burgess, A. W., & Douglas, J. E. (1988). *Sexual homicide: Patterns and motivation*. New York: Free Press.

2

It Was Always There

YAEL DANIELI

Several interacting arcs of events and people trace the development of my interest in trauma. The first is my growing up on a Kibbutz, then in Tel Aviv, under British mandate prior to Israel's birth in 1948, then through the building of Israel and the ensuing wars. I remember clearly the sense of extended family and community in the Kibbutz in particular and in the country in general; the total idealism and willing sacrifice, commitment and determination, and joy in building our own state. But the British mandate meant, for example, that we could not have lights on at night for fear of attacks and that, in a country where the sun often does not set until after 8:00 p.m., the curfew did not allow us to be outdoors between 6:00 p.m. and 6:00 a.m. I still carry the legacy of these curfews, the sense of oppression and resentment, the small ways in which we children rebelled against the British mandate, our attempts to mask anxiety and fear, and our ever-strengthened commitment that was to become, in time, almost characterologic. I also remember being awakened on a New Year's Eve by British soldiers singing *Auld Lang Syne*. My mother told me that they were lonely and missed their wives, children, and parents, which helped to humanize "the enemy."

During the same period, news of the Holocaust was seeping in. Almost everyone around me had come to Palestine from Europe as a pioneer, leaving family members behind. Disbelief and attempted denial gave way to shock, palpable concern, dread, and anticipatory grief. Some survivors who tried to reach the shores of Israel were reinterned by the

British in concentration camps in Cyprus. Others who reached Israel were sent immediately to fight her War of Independence and were killed. Most were welcomed to share in building this new, free land for the Jewish people, where such a slaughter would "never happen again." Intended as a powerfully positive message, "never again" also concealed disdain and contempt (and related guilt) for the victims and the survivors (Danieli, 1982a); this existed at least until the Eichmann trial in 1962. Ever since my childhood, the survivors were my teachers of trauma and its aftermath.

Complexity was present at all times: The themes of rebirth, renewal, resilience, and hope; danger, vulnerability, and sadness—but never without humor and joy, sometimes to the detriment of necessary mourning. But "Yom Hashoah," the national annual day of collective observance and commemoration rituals, united all citizens in shared grief and sorrow. This complexity foretold the understanding, also in my framework (see below), that vulnerability and resilience exist simultaneously rather than being mutually exclusive, as some in the field have held.

Then came the "aliah" (immigration) of refugees from the Arab countries. We were recruited, as teenagers, to help them integrate into the culture. For example, my classmates and I taught refugee women how to use a sewing machine. Israel's wisdom in involving the children in the upbringing of the country and appreciating its multiculturalism cannot be overstated.

Many of these memories are not in themselves traumatic or traumatogenic, but they did shape my thinking, consciously and unconsciously, about posttrauma (re)building of societies that I was to become involved in later in South Africa, Bosnia, and Rwanda, among others.

The more direct intellectual arc began when I chose the phenomenology of hope as the initial topic of my doctoral dissertation at New York University. (Ironically, it was my Christian doctoral advisor, Robert R. Holt, who reminded me that hope was the Israeli anthem.) For this study, I conducted in-depth interviews with people whose hope had been challenged in situations ranging from the seemingly trivial (missing a bus) to the extreme (concentration camps, terminal illness, war imprisonment).

I remember colleagues uniformly discouraging me from interviewing Holocaust survivors: "They don't talk to anybody." This proved to be as far from my experience as possible. Typically, I would come to a survivor's home (to study people in their own environment) after work. They would seat me in the kitchen, and they would talk nonstop, sometimes until the next morning. They had been waiting for someone who would listen.

Every survivor without exception said that no one would listen to or believe their Holocaust experiences. This pervasive postwar societal reaction led them to conclude that no one who had not gone through the same experience could understand; thus they opted for silence. Their children recounted similar experiences. It was even more striking and shattering to me as an idealistic graduate student of clinical psychology to hear them say that psychotherapists, too, would not listen, thereby participating in what I consequently termed the "conspiracy of silence."

My pained outrage at the survivors' resulting sense of isolation and betrayal has been channeled into all aspects of my professional work since: research, clinical, theoretical, teaching/training, organizational, and advocacy.

As a researcher, I focused on studying the phenomenon of the conspiracy of silence, its origins, meanings, and aftermath. That resulted in two main bodies of literature. The first was entitled *Therapists' Difficulties in Treating Survivors of the Nazi Holocaust and Their Children* (Danieli, 1982), or countertransference (for lack of a better word then), which became the new topic of my doctoral dissertation (Danieli, 1982a). I was motivated first by the realization that whereas society has a moral obligation to share its members' pain, psychotherapists and researchers have, in addition, a professional contractual obligation. When we fail to listen, explore, understand, and help, we too inflict the "trauma after the trauma" (Rappaport, 1968), or "the second injury" to victims (Symonds, 1980) by maintaining the conspiracy of silence. I also believed that studying experienced, well-analyzed, introspective professionals would provide insights into the conspiracy of silence of the larger society and that of bystanders.

In order of frequency, some of the major categories of countertransference phenomena systematically examined in my study were as follows:

1. Various modes of defense against listening to Holocaust experiences and against therapists' inability to contain their intense emotional reactions (e.g., numbing, denial, avoidance, distancing, clinging to professional role, reduction to method and/or theory)
2. Affective reactions such as bystander's guilt; rage, with its variety of objects; dread and horror; shame and related emotions (e.g., disgust and loathing); grief and mourning; "me too"; sense of bond; privileged voyeurism
3. Specific relational context issues, such as those involving the relationship between parent and child or victim and liberator; also viewing the survivor as hero and attention and attitudes toward Jewish identity

These themes are reported, described, illustrated, and discussed in detail in a series of articles (Danieli, 1980, 1984, 1988a, 1994). The findings include a comparison between psychotherapists who were survivors or children of survivors and those who were not. Many of the reactions were found to be in response to patients' Holocaust stories rather than to their behavior. The unusual uniformity of psychotherapists' reactions suggested that they were responding to the Holocaust, the one fact that all the otherwise different patients had in common. I therefore suggested that it is appropriate to name them countertransference reactions to the Holocaust (the trauma events), rather than to the patients themselves and noted their similarity "to alexithymia, anhedonia, and their concomitants and components, which, according to Krystal, characterize survivors" (Danieli, 1981, p. 201). Extending the term to reflect the fact that therapists' difficulties in treating other victim/survivor populations may similarly have their roots in the nature of the victimization, I suggested the term *event countertransference*.

During the same early period, in an initial session, S.L., a frail, agitated young man, intermittently interrupted his incoherent rambling with the refrain-like phrase "my mother gave me gray milk"; this not only became a leitmotif of his therapy but also formed an indelible metaphor portending the development of my thinking and understanding of the what and how of transmission of the effects of the Holocaust in particular and of trauma in general. His "very old" father was "from Auschwitz," the sole survivor of a family that had included a wife and two sons who perished "in the ovens." S.L. was named after his murdered half-brothers. His father met S.L.'s 17-year younger and "beautiful" mother upon arriving in the United States. S.L. believed that, although American-born, his mother must have absorbed ashes from his father and passed them to him through her milk. For years, as myriad survivors and their children attempted to break the conspiracy of silence with me, I relived with them that alarming sense of acute pain, flooding helplessness, and outrage, particularly acute in conceiving this pain as "Hitler's posthumous victory."

The other body of literature was on the dialectical relationship between the aftermath of the Holocaust and the post-Holocaust conspiracy of silence as it affected survivors (and their children) throughout their lives, particularly in times of even normal transitions that they nonetheless tended to experience as a return of or further trauma. This kind of analysis requires a lifelong and multigenerational perspective and an in-depth exploration of processes such as mourning, separation, survivor's and bystander's guilt, rage, and shame. I am grateful to Helen Block-Lewis, Judith Herman's mother, for encouraging me to do such explorations with survivor's guilt, and to Henry Krystal for dialogues on the survivors' aging process.

As a clinician I reached out to other psychotherapists to develop the first program since World War II to provide psychological help for Holocaust survivors and their children. We established the Group Project for Holocaust Survivors and their Children (GPHSC) to counteract their profound sense of isolation and alienation and compensate for their neglect by the mental health professions. Formally begun in 1975 by volunteer psychotherapists in the New York City area, led by Lisette Lamon-Fink and myself, GPHSC recognized the vital importance of mutual and self-help and has capitalized on group and community modalities from its inception. Survivors could at last talk about their memories and experiences, explore their feelings with one another, comprehend the long-term consequences in their lives of the Holocaust and the conspiracy of silence that followed it, and share their current concerns (Danieli, 1982a). Group and community therapeutic modalities also affirm the central role of "we-ness" and the need for a collective search for meaningful response (Danieli, 1985c) and help rebuild a sense of extended family and community, which were lost during the Holocaust. In addition, they have helped psychotherapists compensate for and modulate their own difficulties in treating survivors and children of survivors. Whereas a therapist alone may feel unable to provide a "holding environment" (Winnicott, 1965) for his or her patient's feelings, the group as a unit is able to. The group functions as an ideal absorptive entity for abreaction and catharsis of emotions, especially negative ones that are otherwise experienced as uncontainable.

The Project's goals, which are preventive as well as reparative, are predicated on two major assumptions: (1) that integration of Holocaust experiences into the totality of the survivors' and their children's lives, and awareness of the meaning of post-Holocaust *adaptational styles* (see below), will be liberating from the trauma and facilitate mental health and self-actualization for both, and (2) that awareness of transmitted intergenerational processes will inhibit transmission of pathology to succeeding generations.

In the context of *teaching/training*, it is important to emphasize that *event countertransference* reactions may inhibit professionals even from studying, certainly from correctly diagnosing and treating, the effects of trauma. Recognizing the grave need for training, the GPHSC has provided short- and long-term countertransference and training seminars and individual supervision to professionals since 1975. Regarding event countertransferences as dimensions of a professional's inner, or intrapsychic, conspiracy of silence about the trauma allows us to explore and confront these reactions to the trauma events prior to and independent of the therapeutic encounter with the victim/survivor patient. To work through event countertransference, I gradually developed an exercise process (Danieli, 1994) that has proven helpful in numerous workshops, training institutes, "debriefing" of "front liners," short- and long-term seminars, and in consultative short- and long-term supervisory relationships around the world. Ameliorating these reactions in bystanders may lessen the societal conspiracy of silence as well.

The giants in the field of the psychiatric effects of the Holocaust on its survivors, the originators of some of the central concepts of our thinking to this day, the survivor's syndrome, survivor's guilt, and psychic numbing among others—including Henry Krystal, William Niederland, Leo Eitinger,

Edie de Wind, and Robert Jay Lifton—most influenced and generously taught me when no other means of training existed. When I entered the field, indeed, the only diagnostic term used was the "survivor's syndrome," and it was applied rather indiscriminately to all cases of survivors, even extending to the expectation that children of survivors would manifest a single transmitted "child-of-survivor syndrome" (e.g., Phillips, 1978). What I saw were heterogeneous, lifelong, and intergenerational familial styles of adaptation. Choosing the family rather than the individual as the unit of analysis, I delineated a typology of four posttraumatic adaptational styles: the victim families, the fighter families, the numb families, and families of "those who made it." The heterogeneity of these families' responses to their Holocaust and post-Holocaust experiences, beyond notions of the survivor's syndrome and of posttraumatic stress disorder (PTSD), emphasizes the need to guard against expecting all victims/survivors to behave in a uniform fashion and to match appropriate therapeutic interventions to particular forms of reaction.

The multigenerational work culminated in the publication in 1998 of the *International Handbook of Multigenerational Legacies of Trauma*, for which I commissioned a worldwide network of researchers, clinicians, and scholars from 32 populations around the world, many for the first time, to contribute. Topics included the Nazi Holocaust, World War II, genocide, the Vietnam war, intergenerational effects revealed after the fall of the Soviet Union, the experiences of indigenous peoples and citizens after the fall of repressive regimes, as well as the effects of crime and urban violence, infectious and life-threatening diseases, and the emerging biology of intergenerational trauma.

This book established the universal existence of intergenerational transmission of trauma and its effects and validated concerns shared by many experts. In the past, multigenerational transmission had been treated as a secondary phenomenon, perhaps because it is not as obviously dramatic as the horrific images of traumatized people. Recoiling when viewing such images, particularly of victimized children today, the mind does not take in that children not yet born could inherit a legacy and memories not of their own but that will shape their lives nevertheless. That the same images may shape the lives of generations to come, sometimes unconsciously, often by design, is even harder to comprehend and accept.

Given a lifetime PTSD rate of 7.8% in the U.S. general population (Kessler, et al., 1995), it is clearly a relatively common condition. Even if only a minority of such sufferers are or will be involved in parenting, the number of children upon whom intergenerational effects will have an impact is enormous. In other groups and societies, where the rates of trauma exposure are much higher, an even greater proportion of the population is affected, with consequent intergenerational implications.

Applying the lessons from my work with survivors and children of survivors of the Nazi Holocaust, I have expanded to victims/survivors of other genocides and human-made massive trauma. I served as consultant to South Africa's Truth and Reconciliation Commission and to the Rwandan government, among others, on reparations for victims, which grew to working with Rwanda's victims. I have also led a long-term project in the former Yugoslavia that I had named "Promoting a Dialogue" and the local participants named, much more appropriately, "Democracy Cannot Be Built with the Hands of Broken Souls."

IBUKA, the Rwandan umbrella organization for victims of the genocide, asked me in 1999 to help bring Holocaust survivors there to "teach [us] how to live after death." This request led to the historic first meeting of all Holocaust and genocide groups in Kigali, Rwanda, in November 2001, where we created the International Network of Survivors and Friends of Survivors of Holocaust and Genocide. Closing the meeting, I suggested that one of the lessons I had learned was to drop the "n" in "Never again." The headlines of today's newspapers tell us why.

As a theorist, I struggled to delineate the nature and encompass the extent of the destruction of catastrophic massive trauma and to account for its different contextual dimensions and levels as well as the diversity of it and in the response to it. I concluded that only a multidimensional, multidisciplinary integrative framework would be adequate. I therefore termed it *Trauma and the Continuity of Self: A Multidimensional, Multidisciplinary, Integrative (TCMI) Framework* and used it to guide mutual collaborative work with numerous experts in all related disciplines. A summary of the TCMI framework can be found in Danieli (1998, 2003, 2005).

Organizationally, I have been privileged to take part in the forefront of two pioneer organizations representing differing yet related perspectives on victims: Victimology was born out of criminology to balance the rights of the victims with those of the accused or offender and led to the birth in 1979 of the World Society of Victimology. The modern history of traumatology, with its focus on the psychosocial, emotional, and psychobiological reactions to traumatic events, is a 1980s offshoot of mental health, in particular the Scientific Committee on the Mental Health Needs of Victims of the World Federation for Mental Health, and led to the birth of the (very quickly International) Society for Traumatic Stress Studies (ISTSS) in 1985, a mere 5 years after the diagnosis of PTSD.

As one of the founders of the ISTSS and its third (1988–1989) president, I have found this society to be an integral part of my life for the last 20 years. To have the society represent as many victim populations and concerns, become the heretofore absent voice of teaching/training on the effects of trauma, and universalize its vision as much as possible were three of my missions. Having established the Chaim Danieli Young Professional Award for excellence in service and research, in memory of my father, to encourage them in furthering their work, I commissioned, as president, more than 200 members of the society to contribute to the initial (1989) Report of the Presidential Task Force on Curriculum, Education, and Training (see Danieli & Krystal, 1989). This report contained model curricula in psychiatry, psychology, social work, nursing, creative arts therapy, clergy, and media; organizations, institutions, and public health; paraprofessionals and other professionals; and undergraduate education. The report was adopted by the United Nations (E/AC.57/1990/NGO.3). I also established the ISTSS's consultative status with the UN, initiated the concept of world meetings, and served as the international chair of its first world meeting in Amsterdam, the Netherlands, in June 1992.

I view informed advocacy as teaching extended to the world (my work has been translated into at least 12 languages). Sometimes, however, I think of an effective lobbyist as a combination of a missionary and a pest.

In terms of advocacy, my efforts to bring what I had learned and was continuously learning to the international community in a more formal way began when, in the early 1980s, Eugene Brody, then secretary-general of the World Federation for Mental Health (WFMH), asked me to represent the federation at the United Nations. My international self was definitely tempted. However, being Israeli, I doubted that I could have much impact at the UN. I told him that I would give it 6 months and, if proved effective, I would continue. My first involvement in the world of nongovernmental organizations (NGOs) at the UN led to serving as vice-chair of the Executive Committee on Non-Governmental Organizations associated with the UN Department of Public Information and Chair of its publications committee.

Since that time, I have worked at and with the United Nations—with varying degrees of satisfaction and frustration—through informed advocacy to bring mental health and trauma concerns to the UN, and the UN to the fields of mental health and trauma.

As a founding member and later chair of the WFMH Scientific Committee on the Mental Health Needs of Victims, initially under the guiding wing of Irene Melup of the then UN Crime Prevention and Criminal Justice Branch, and with the continuous friendship of Roger Clark of Rutgers University School of Law, I have participated in developing, drafting, promoting, adapting, and implementing all UN instruments relating to victims. Most notably, these have been the UN Declaration of Basic Principles of Justice for Victims of Crime and Abuse of Power (40th UN General Assembly Resolution 34, 1985) and all subsequent resolutions related to it; Basic Principles and Guidelines on the Right to a Remedy and Reparation for Victims of Gross Violations of International Human Rights Law and Serious Violations of International Humanitarian Law; and the establishment of and the victims' role in the International Criminal Court, which is its most unique feature and most important contribution to international law. My lawyer friends say that I have drafted more laws than most lawyers.

I have served as consultant to the UN Crime Prevention and Criminal Justice Branch, on the board of its International Scientific and Professional Advisory Council, and as vice-chair of the Executive Committee of the NGO Alliance on Crime Prevention and Criminal Justice. I have also served as a consultant to UNICEF, the Office of the UN High Commissioner for Human Rights, and various governmental and media organizations, including the Associated Press and CNN, on trauma and victim/survivors' rights and care.

A major goal of all of these efforts has been to assert the commitment of the international community to victims; to combat impunity and adopt provisions under law for justice and redress, acknowledging the victims' suffering, and securing restitution, compensation, rehabilitation, satisfaction and guarantees of nonrepetition for them.

Indeed, delineating the necessary components for healing in the wake of massive trauma that emerged from interviews with survivors of the Nazi Holocaust, Japanese and Armenian Americans, victims from Argentina and Chile, and professionals working with them, both in and outside their countries in my study for for the UN Commission of Human Rights expert group drafting the resolution, helped develop the Basic Principles and Guidelines on the Right to a Remedy and Reparation for Victims of Gross Violations of International Human Rights Law and Serious Violations of International Humanitarian Law (Resolution E/CV.4/2005/L.48).

I have also edited, for and on behalf of the United Nations, three books. The first, *International Responses to Traumatic Stress* (Danieli, Rodley, & Weisaeth, 1996) grew out of the realization of the appalling global scope of trauma and victimization and the necessity of international endeavors on behalf of the victims. For the first time, UN and NGO contributions were treated equally, emphasizing the essential partnership between them. The second, the UN book on the 50th anniversary of the Universal Declaration of Human Rights, examined human rights from the victims' standpoint; and the third, *Sharing the Front Line and the Back Hills...* (Danieli, 2002), addressed the price paid by protectors and providers—peacekeepers, humanitarian aid and justice workers, and the media—in the midst of crisis and the responsibilities of their organizations to train and support them before, during, and after their missions. (As tragic ironies sometimes do, that book came out on September 13, 2001, and proved directly relevant to many of the caregivers in my home city, New York.) Both the advocacy process of creating these books and the books themselves have significantly affected the UN's language, programs, and policies and those of many other organizations around the world.

Since September 11, 2001, in collaboration with more than 260 colleagues around the world and throughout the United States, I have focused on two new books related to terrorism. The first, in keeping with my international perspective, is *The Trauma of Terrorism: Sharing Knowledge and Shared Care, An International Handbook.* The second, *On the Ground After September 11: Mental Health Responses and Practical Knowledge Gained,* for me, is a love gift to New York, which has always excited me with its richness, diversity, and culture. I have loved living here and being a New Yorker. On September 11, for the first time, I felt toward New York as I have felt my whole life toward Israel and later toward the countless victims around the world I have tried to help: protective, caring, and committed.

All my books were intended to be used in practical ways, to relieve and prevent suffering and for informed advocacy, as well as to contribute to traumatic stress studies. Authors were recruited from around the world and from many different disciplines, reflecting, in part, various stages of anguish in confronting their subjects as well as different ways of knowing and means of access. Many belong to the populations they write about, which makes more difficult their struggle to create enough distance for writing yet adds authenticity to the words to which they give voice. Starting with my human rights book, I began including among the chapters "voices" of actual victim/survivors and their protectors and providers, which not only renders the material far more accessible but also acknowledges that they are the experts on their experiences and are partners in our mutual journey of discovery.

I am grateful to the more than 500 authors who contributed to my books alone and to my numerous supervisees who enriched my understanding. They augment what I have learned from my most important teachers: my patients.

One of my mother's greatest gifts to me was to make history totally alive. The love of history and the commitment to learn from it instilled by both my parents have been a major force in my life. I often wonder whether this led, at least in part, to my interest in the multigenerational legacies of trauma, which integrates the psychological and historical perspectives. They also inspired a consuming curiosity about the world and a sense of being a citizen of it.

Within the field of traumatic stress, I have found it satisfying that many of my concepts, including those of the conspiracy of silence and the multigenerational transmission of trauma, have become part of the language, and that many concepts from the mental health field in general and from the field of trauma in particular have become an integral part of the language at the UN. But much more work needs to be done, especially in terms of international collaboration.

I belong to the generation that preceded PTSD. After it was adopted, most everyone seems to have become addicted to the diagnosis. Increasingly, colleagues have been discovering that PTSD did not encompass many of the survivors' essential experiences. In attempting to correct the situation, including the possible inappropriateness of PTSD for nonwestern cultures (Engdahl, 2005), the field seems to be returning to the fuller picture that had been provided by the survivor's syndrome. I would like future trauma scholars to develop further, in research as well as in clinical and theoretical work, both my concept of posttrauma adaptational styles and the heterogeneous typology I have elaborated.

Colleagues like Brian Engdahl, Bill Schlenger, and John Fairbank have been my generous scientific advisors, with whom I spent numerous hours seeking to bridge the gap between the clinical and the research perspectives. It is essential that the field continue in this direction, particularly in fully recognizing the time dimension and the long-term and multigenerational perspectives and implications in its studies. But it still pains me that what we have learned from the aftermath of the Holocaust is not naturally referred to or included in the thinking and in many writings in the field. I hope that this will be remedied.

Most importantly, our task must be to do our utmost to teach policy makers, be it locally, nationally, and/or internationally, and impress upon them that the consequences of decisions they frequently make with short-term considerations in mind can not only be lifelong but also multigenerational and are in stark contrast to their rhetoric of making the world a safer and better place for our generation and for generations to come. The issue is not only how and how many resources they choose to commit to victims' care but also the untold multidimensional costs—economic, psychosocial, educational, and political, to name but a few—over time and down through generations that will be incurred if they fail to provide for them.

Everything I have learned began with victims/survivors of the Nazi Holocaust and continued with victims/survivors of genocide and other massive traumata all over the world, such as South Africans, Cambodians, Bosnians, Rwandans, and indigenous people. To have been both a witness and a participant in the search for truth about humanity's unremitting shame and harm has left me feeling privileged. Our work calls on us to confront, with our patients and within ourselves, extraordinary human experiences. This confrontation is profoundly humbling in that at all times these experiences challenge our view of the world and test the limits of our humanity (Danieli, 1994b, p. 371). But taking the painful risk of bearing witness does not mean that the world will listen, learn, change, and become a better place.

I would like to dedicate this chapter, as I did the Lifetime Achievement Award, and the fifth meeting of the society when I was its president, to all victims/survivors everywhere, whose simple human dignity, moral courage, and profound generosity enable us—the professionals—to reach beyond the veil of rage and tears to touch the truth, without which no one can be free.

Yael Danieli, 1974

REFERENCES

Danieli, Y. (1982a). Therapists' difficulties in treating survivors of the Nazi Holocaust and their children. *Dissertation Abstracts International*, 42(12-B, Pt 1), 4927. (UMI No. 949–904.)

Danieli, Y. (1982b). *Group project for Holocaust survivors and their children.* Prepared for the National Institute of Mental Health, Mental Health Services Branch. Contract #092424762. Washington, DC: NIMH.

Danieli, Y. (1982c). Families of survivors of the Nazi Holocaust: Some short- and long-term effects. In C. D. Spielberger, I. G. Sarason, & N. Milgram (Eds.), *Stress and anxiety* (Vol. 8) (pp. 405–421). New York: McGraw-Hill/Hemisphere.

Danieli, Y. (1984a). Psychotherapists' participation in the conspiracy of silence about the Holocaust. *Psychoanalytic Psychology*, 1(1), 23–42.

Danieli, Y. (1985a). Separation and loss in families of survivors of the Nazi Holocaust. Academy Forum, 29(2), 7–10.

Danieli, Y. (1985b). The treatment and prevention of long-term effects and intergenerational transmission of victimization: A lesson from Holocaust survivors and their children. In C. R. Figley (Ed.), *Trauma and its wake* (pp. 295–313). New York: Brunner/Mazel.

Danieli, Y. (1988a). Confronting the unimaginable: Psychotherapists' reactions to victims of the Nazi Holocaust. In J. P. Wilson, Z. Harel, & B. Kahana (Eds.), *Human adaptation to extreme stress* (pp. 219–238). New York: Plenum.

Danieli, Y. (1988b). Treating survivors and children of survivors of the Nazi Holocaust. In F. M. Ochberg (Ed.), *Post-traumatic therapy and victims of violence* (pp. 278–294). New York: Brunner/Mazel.

Danieli, Y. (1988c). The use of mutual support approaches in the treatment of victims. In E. Chigier (Ed.), *Grief and bereavement in contemporary society:* Vol. 3. *Support Systems* (pp. 116–123). London: Freund Publishing House.

Danieli, Y. (1989a). Mourning in survivors and children of survivors of the Nazi Holocaust: The role of group and community modalities. In D. R. Dietrich, & P. C. Shabad (Eds.), *The problem of loss and mourning: Psychoanalytic perspectives* (pp. 427–460). Madison, WI: International Universities Press.

Danieli, Y., & Krystal, J. H. (1989b). *The initial report of the presidential task force on curriculum, education and training of the Society for Traumatic Stress Studies.* Chicago: The Society for Traumatic Stress Studies.

Danieli, Y. (1992). Preliminary reflections from a psychological perspective. In T. C. van Boven, C. Flinterman, F. Grunfeld, & I. Westendorp (Eds.), The right to restitution, compensation and rehabilitation for victims of gross violations of human rights and fundamental freedoms. *Netherlands Institute of Human Rights [Studie- en Informatiecentrum Mensenrechten]*, Special issue No.(196–213).

Danieli, Y. (1993). The diagnostic and therapeutic use of the multi-generational family tree in working with survivors and children of survivors of the Nazi Holocaust. In J. P. Wilson & B. Raphael (Eds.), *International handbook of traumatic stress syndromes* (pp. 889–898). New York: Plenum Publishing. [Stress and Coping Series, Donald Meichenbaum, Series Editor].

Danieli, Y. (1994a). Countertransference, trauma and training. In J. P. Wilson and J. Lindy (Eds.), *Countertransference in the treatment of post-traumatic stress disorder* (pp. 368–388). New York: Guilford Press.

Danieli, Y. (1994b). As survivors age: Part I. *National Center for Post Traumatic Stress Disorder Clinical Quarterly, 4*(1), 1–7.

Danieli, Y. (1994c). As survivors age: Part II. *National Center for Post Traumatic Stress Disorder Clinical Quarterly, 4*(2), 20–24.

Danieli, Y. (1994d). Trauma to the family: Intergenerational sources of vulnerability and resilience. In J. T. Reese & E. Scrivner (Eds.), *The law enforcement families: Issues and answers* (pp. 163–175). Washington, D.C.: U.S. Department of Justice Federal Bureau of Investigation.

Danieli, Y. (1994e). *Resilience and hope. Children worldwide* (pp. 47–49). Geneva: International Catholic Child Bureau.

Danieli, Y., Rodley, N. S., & Weisaeth, L. (Eds.) (1996a). *International responses to traumatic stress: humanitarian, human rights, justice, peace and development contributions, collaborative actions and future initiatives.* Amityville, NY: Baywood Publishing. [Published for and on behalf of the United Nations.]

Danieli, Y. (1996b). Who takes care of the caretakers? The emotional life of those working with children in situations of violence. In R. J. Appel & B. Simon (Eds.), *Minefields in their hearts: The mental health of children in war and communal violence* (pp. 189–205). New Haven, CT: Yale University Press.

Danieli, Y. (Ed.) (1998). *International handbook of multigenerational legacies of trauma.* New York: Kluwer Academic/ Plenum Publishing Corporation.

Danieli, Y. (1999a). Intergenerational legacies of trauma in police families. In J. M. Violanti & D. Paton (Eds.), *Police trauma: Psychological aftermath of civilian combat.* Springfield, IL: Charles C Thomas.

Danieli, Y., Stamatopoulou, E., & Dias, C. J. (Eds.) (1999b). *The Universal Declaration of Human Rights: fifty years and beyond.* Amityville, NY: Baywood Publishing. [Published for and on behalf of the United Nations.]

Danieli, Y. (Ed.) (2002). *Sharing the front line and the back hills: international protectors and providers, peacekeepers, humanitarian aid workers and the media in the midst of crisis.* Amityville, N Y: Baywood Publishing.

Danieli, Y., Engdahl, B., & Schlenger, W. E. (2003). The psychological aftermath of terrorism. In F. M. Moghaddam & A. J. Marsella (Eds.), *Understanding terrorism: Psychological roots, consequences, and interventions* (pp. 223–246). Washington, D.C.: American Psychological Association.

Danieli, Y., Brom, D., & Sills, J. B. (Eds.) (2005a). *The trauma of terrorism: sharing knowledge and shared care, an international handbook.* Binghamton, NY: Haworth Press.

Danieli, Y., & Dingman, R. (Eds.) (2005b). *On the ground after September 11: mental health responses and practical knowledge gained.* Binghamton, NY: Haworth Press.

Engdahl, B., Kastrup, M., Jaranson, J., & Danieli, Y. (1999b). The impact of traumatic human rights violations on victims and the mental health profession's response. In Y. Danieli, E. Stamatopoulou, & C. J. Dias (Eds.), *The Universal Declaration of Human Rights: Fifty years and beyond* (pp. 337–335). Amityville, NY: Baywood Publishing. [Published for and on behalf of the United Nations.]

Sirkin, S., Iacopino, V., Grodin, M., & Danieli, Y. (1999). The role of health professionals in protecting and promoting human rights: A paradigm for professional responsibility. In Y. Danieli, E. Stamatopoulou, & C. J. Dias (Eds.), *The Universal Declaration of Human Rights: Fifty years and beyond* (pp. 357–369). Amityville, NY: Baywood Publishing. [Published for and on behalf of the United Nations.]

Smith, B., Agger, I., Danieli, Y. & Weisaeth, L. (1996). Emotional responses of international humanitarian aid workers. In Danieli, Y., Rodley, N., & Weisaeth, L. (Eds.), *International responses to traumatic stress: Humanitarian, human rights, justice, peace and development contributions, collaborative actions and future initiatives* (pp. 397–423). Amityville, NY: Baywood Publishing. [Published for and on behalf of the United Nations.]

Weine, S., Danieli, Y., Silove, D., Van Ommeren, M., Fairbank J. A., & Saul, J. (2002). Guidelines for international training in mental health and psychosocial interventions for trauma exposed populations in clinical and community settings. *Psychiatry, 65*(2),156–164.

3

From Veterans of War to Veterans of Terrorism: My Maps of Trauma

CHARLES R. FIGLEY

It rained almost every day in January in Vietnam. Being on the periphery of the sprawling marine base camp in Da Nang, hostile fire was rare. However, one evening there was an apparent attack. Sirens, floodlights, shouting, and the roar of jeeps and trucks awakened everyone in our battalion. The next day I learned from some amused Vietnamese workers that what started the fuss was a single shot from a single Vietnamese man (I forget his name) who was in his late fifties (my age now). Rather than trying to kill someone, he had hoped to "scare the Americans off his farm." Planting season would soon begin and he did not want to miss the opportunity. From that day forward I was concerned about his welfare and that of others like him. By then it was clear to me that the Vietnamese people did not want us there, were skeptical of the South Vietnamese government, and just wanted to be left alone.

I volunteered to go to Vietnam. I was already a noncommissioned marine officer with considerable responsibilities for a 20 year old. But after this it was no longer possible for me to view the war in black and white, us against the bad guys. Up to that point I viewed the war and my role in it as one of honor and commitment. The fear I felt was fleeting. I was not afraid to die for a just cause. But the more I learned about

47

the complications of this war, the more ambivalence I felt toward this and every other war. I was far less interested in being in an offensive combat role. I began to volunteer for far more risky assignments, such as courier duty via helicopter. I would deliver messages and accompany critical communications gear from base camp to "down range," as they call the front lines these days.

AFTER VIETNAM

I did my duty and by the grace of God I survived to return home. I was numb for months. But gradually I found a way to work through my war experiences. I did not know it at the time, but having another year to serve in the Marine Corps probably saved my life. It provided structure, opportunities to talk with others who had seen combat, and no opportunity to join my generation in the fog of pot smoking and protesting the war. That would come later.

Once out of the Marine Corps and uniform, I shifted my focus to completing my undergraduate degree. I found that the busier I was, the less I thought about the war—both present and past.[1] Three years later I graduated with honors from the University of Hawaii and received a full fellowship for graduate school at Penn State University. Along the way, however, I was forced to come to terms with my growing frustration over the continuing war and its effects on the Vietnamese and the young working-class American patriots in uniform. Two events stand out and are discussed elsewhere (Figley, 2005). By the end of 1974, remarkably, I had received my Ph.D. from Penn State and was a new assistant professor at Purdue University, my home for the next 15 years.

PRINCETON UNIVERSITY 1982

The conference table was big and worn but solid. The scratches were like notches of knowledge acquired from years of use by academics assembled there, like us, to collate the accumulating knowledge in emerging public policy. I was on sabbatical in the summer of 1982 at Princeton University's Woodrow Wilson School of International and Public Policy working with Robert Rich, who directed a federally funded project on victims of trauma. Robert Rich, Debbie Cohen, Marilyn Reeves, and I were trying to make sense out of some recently acquired data on the immediate and long-term effects of traumatic events.

Princeton was a long way from Hue, South Vietnam, and the steps of the U.S. Capital, where I had made a commitment to understand the consequences of war. The war had, of course, ended more than 8 years earlier. The problems of Vietnam vets were becoming a national health issue. The DSM III (APA, 1980) had included posttraumatic stress disorder (PTSD) and confirmed that trauma causes mental illness. By now I had established the Consortium on Veteran Studies (in 1995), the precursor to the Society for Traumatic Stress Studies, organized or participated in panels about Vietnam vets at all of the major relevant conferences,[2] completed several studies of Vietnam veterans, and published two books[3] and numerous articles[4] that together were gaining some recognition and led to my being promoted to full professor in that year.

My sabbatical at Princeton, however, was a turning point. It gave me an opportunity to build upon my understanding of the traumatic effects of war and to construct a more generic model of the trauma induction and reduction process. This effort had already begun a few years earlier. I had established the Task Force on Families of Catastrophe[5] in December 1979 in response to a request from the U.S. State Department. Immediately following the conference, Dr. McCubin, Dr. Spanier, and I flew to Washington, D.C., to personally present the document of more than 600 pages to the State Department. This process of reviewing what is known about traumatized families led to several seminal reviews, including my next two books[6] and the conviction that what we needed was a journal and a learned society to support.

THE SOCIETY AND THE JOURNAL OF TRAUMATIC STRESS

Breakfast meetings at a conference are rarely productive. What with being drowsy and in need of coffee, arriving, ordering, eating, and taking away the meals, discussions are constantly being interrupted. For this reason I asked the dozen or so colleagues to a meeting after they had eaten breakfast. At that meeting, on March 2, 1985, the Society (later the International Society) for Traumatic Stress Studies (STSS) was formally established. Those who attended made up most of the Society's Founding Board of Directors.[7]

I recognized that I could use the resources of the Consortium on Veteran Studies to provide the critical initial support to start the organization. However, I also knew that the constituency for a new field, organization, and journal must include but not be limited to veteran studies. Indeed, by bringing together a large number of scholars and practitioners who worked with a wide variety of traumatized populations, the unifying theories, concepts, assessment tools, and treatment approaches would evolve quickly.

However, we reasoned that it was wise to first establish an organization to support a refereed scholarly journal. A journal for traumatic stress studies would not only promulgate research findings about trauma but also report on promising assessment and treatment approaches. Based on my knowledge of publishing, I knew that publishers would not be interested unless there was a substantial subscription base such as would be provided by an organization.

In 1983, I wrote to a large number of colleagues proposing the formation of the Society for Traumatic Stress Studies and the *Journal of Traumatic Stress*. The letter read, in part, as follows:

> I believe that an organization, tentatively titled the Society for Traumatic Stress Studies, would be a useful contribution. Moreover, that the central purpose of this society would be to sponsor a scholarly publication, tentatively titled *Trauma and Its Wake: The Journal of the Society for Traumatic Stress Studies*. Such a journal would publish important advancements in the field of traumatic and posttraumatic stress. A distinguished editorial board is already in place in connection with the book I am editing, with the same primary title. . . . How appropriate is such a society and journal, in particular, and the emergence of a separate field of traumatic or posttraumatic stress in general? (Figley, 1986a)

The response was positive and enthusiastic. I then sent another memorandum the following year to the people I had previously contacted, and finally, after the completion of *Trauma and Its Wake* (Figley, 1985a) and the birth of his daughter, Laura, in February 1985, I called for the breakfast meeting at NOVA.

It was agreed that the purpose of the society would be "to advance knowledge about the immediate and long-term human consequences of extraordinarily stressful events and to promote effective methods of preventing or ameliorating the unwanted consequences." The objectives of the organization were to: (1) recognize achievement in knowledge production; (2) disseminate this knowledge through face-to-face contact with colleagues; and (3) make this information available through other knowledge transfer media, especially print media.

I proposed that the group be named a "society," since the term connotes a learned group of like-minded colleagues. "Traumatic stress studies" was viewed as the name of the field at that time (what I now call traumatology), or "the investigation and application of knowledge about the immediate and long-term consequences of highly stressful events and the factors which affect those consequences" (Figley, 1986a, b).

We agreed that the first, founding conference would take place in Atlanta in September 1985 and that Bonnie Green, Yael Danieli, and I would serve as the first program committee. We agreed to approach Max Cleland, Secretary of State of Georgia and former head of the Veterans Administration, as the keynote speaker.

The conference was successful and the rest is history. I will spare you the details regarding the endless meetings, bickering, and untoward behavior that are part of the start of any new field, organization, and social movement, of which we were all a part. In the meantime, my major concern was the journal.

I knew from my experience in establishing the *Journal of Psychotherapy and the Family* (now the *Journal of Family Psychotherapy*) that the critical ingredients for a thriving scholarly journal were an excellent editorial board and other reviewers, a constant flow of excellent submissions, and a publisher who would increase the readership. And, as noted earlier, landing a contract with an excellent publisher required at least 300 subscribers. The society would supply the subscribers through membership dues. My first priority, however, was establishing the founding editorial board, which was composed of an international, diverse, and highly respected group of traumatologists. I started with the list of colleagues I had written to about the journal back in 1983. There were no e-mails in those days. All this took time, involving writing, mailing, and meeting with key colleagues. Their membership on the board would be an important endorsement for the legitimacy of the venture and attract the interest of both publishers and colleagues who might wish to subscribe or submit a manuscript for consideration.

The first and third issues of the journal would be devoted primarily to papers originally solicited for the third volume of *Trauma and its Wake*, a follow-up to the first two volumes (Figley, 1985; 1986). For the second issue, I turned to my friend and colleague at Purdue University Don Hartsough.[8] He was at the time director of clinical psychology training at Purdue. I asked Don to organize a special issue of the journal focusing on diagnosis and assessment, which was a critical need for this emerging field. By 1986, the *Journal of Traumatic Stress* was established. The following year I offered the journal to the society and began the search for a publisher. Contracts were signed the following year with Plenum Press. And in January 1988 the first issue was published; it included articles by David Spiegel and Susan Roth. I wrote the first article, "Toward a Field of Traumatic Stress"; it tried to lay out the mission of the journal as part of the larger field of traumatic stress studies.

THE TRAUMATIZED FAMILY

My exposure to orphans in Vietnam was the genesis of my interest in children and families, particularly traumatized families. It was also the first experience I had in social work. While others were getting drunk in Da Nang, I was volunteering to establish good relations with the community. Mostly, I ended up playing with the children residing at the Catholic orphanage near our base camp.

After the Marine Corps I focused my studies, including graduate training, on human development and the role of various systems and contexts, in part based on my experiences with Vietnamese children. I was always interested in intimate relationships and their special dynamics or systemic properties. The first person I interviewed (in 1971, in Washington, DC) was a corpsman named Joe. He was obviously traumatized and had combat-related PTSD from his 13 months in Vietnam. However, it was far more complicated than a simple cause-and-effect diagnosis. First Joe was traumatized primarily by secondary or vicarious trauma; by the pain and suffering he experienced from treating those in harm's way; by the guilt he felt each time one of his patients died; by being obsessed with reacting quickly enough to save lives—long after being on duty and long after the war. But it gets more complicated. Joe also suffered from the guilt of the suffering endured by his family as a result of his actions. These actions were manifestations or symptoms of his PTSD: screams and thrashing as he slept, his quick temper, his bouts of depression, his hours of sitting by himself staring into the distance. All of these things affected his family and the way they treated him. They were war veterans too, twice removed.

Every study I designed, every paper I wrote, and every lecture I gave on the topic of trauma had some connection to this kind of systemic resonance—the interpersonal implications of being traumatized and behaving like a traumatized person. For example, at least one chapter of each of my first two books (Figley, 1978g; Figley & Southerly, 1980) focuses on psychosocial adjustment. The book series to which both belong is the Brunner-Routledge (originally the Brunner/Mazel) Psychosocial Stress Book Series.

In 1980 I organized and co-chaired a national conference on stress and the family and coedited two books comprising the best papers from it (Figley & McCubbin, 1983; McCubbin & Figley, 1983). Follow-up volumes, *Treating Stress in Families* (Figley 1989a) and *Helping Traumatized Families* (Figley, 1989b) focused on the assessment, treatment, and prevention of unwanted stress in families. Just as these volumes helped to bridge the multitude of traumatizing contexts, so too did they emphasize the overlooked area of family studies and its importance in understanding the multitude of manifestations of stress, particularly traumatic stress.

By 1989 I had moved from Purdue to Florida State University to direct one of the oldest and most respected Ph.D. programs in family scholarship, the Interdivisional Ph.D. Program in Marriage and Family, which had been established in 1950. Located in the Sandels Building, the program included a focus on family therapy and comprised a clinic designed to train students in that major. This provided an excellent opportunity for me to begin to study traumatized families. From 1991 to 1996, I attracted $1.2 million to the program, much of which focused on understanding and helping traumatized families. The first Gulf War[9] and the Oklahoma City bombing[10] provided the context for several major contributions that included but were not limited to helping traumatized families.

TERRORISM AND THE PROFESSIONALIZATION OF TRAUMATOLOGY

The Oklahoma City bombing on April 19, 1995, also provided the context for a major paradigm shift for me. I was in my office at the clinic that morning, and Mike Barnes, my research assistant (who would go on to focus his dissertation on families traumatized by an injured child), asked me, "Did you hear about the bombing?" As the reality of the situation became clear and the circumstances of the 1993 New York City terrorist attack were linked, it became immediately obvious to me that the response must be fundamentally different from all others in the past. In the following year, based on the expressed needs of Oklahoma mental health and policy professionals, we established the Green Cross and a five-course training program leading designation as a registered (later certified) traumatologist. More than 1000 individuals completed one or more courses. By the following May, nearly 60 had completed all requirements and became the founding members of the Green Cross Projects.[11] Thus, out of the ashes of the Alfred P. Murrah Federal Building emerged a new humanitarian organization dedicated to serving communities affected by terrorism or other traumatic events through those who had experienced such an event themselves and who had acquired the necessary training to help others.

Such professionalization had already begun through the Association for Traumatic Stress Specialists (ATSS, originally called the International Association of Traumatic Stress Specialists), which offers several certifications. However, their certifications were more for those who wished to exclusively specialize in work with trauma; they do not address the educational and professional standards of most who work with the traumatized. Moreover, ATSS does not have a humanitarian response structure, nor does it have a set of standards of practice.[12]

For this reason I established the Academy of Traumatology in 1997. I approached 40 of the leading traumatologists throughout the world to come together to determine such standards.[13] These founding members would be joined only by others they would elect.[14] The same year, with considerable assistance from Florida State University, we established the Traumatology Certification and Accreditation Program (Figley, 2004), and the same set of courses developed for Oklahoma City.[15] The vision was for the academy to take over the program and the accredited programs to take over the training. This vision was completed October 1, 2004.

The Green Cross Foundation was established in 1997. It[16] provides a home for the academy and its certification and accreditation program in traumatology as well as the Green Cross Assistance Program and the international journal *Traumatology*.

These vital resources were in place on September 11, 2001, when New York and other locations were struck by terrorists. My wife, Kathy, and I had just finished our monthly meeting with the Parent-Teacher Student Organization at our daughter's high school and were having breakfast at a local diner. Returning from the men's room, I heard only Kathy's calm voice saying "You won't believe this: A jet just hit the World Trade Center." I stared blankly at her. For the next half hour we sat there in shock as the second plane flew into the other tower. Kathy calmly squeezed my arm and said, "We need to get back to the [Green Cross] office, we could get a call at any time, so we'd better get ready." I knew she was right. I felt the dread of knowing what was in store for us, for our fledgling organization, and for our country. My concerns were well founded. Kathy and I worked long hours for the next 60 days. We were called upon by the New York local of the Service Employees Union International to help. We arrived the Sunday following the attack (September 16, 2001). The work of the Green Cross later received considerable praise (Figley, Figley, & Norman, 2002).

SECONDARY (VICARIOUS) TRAUMA AND COMPASSION FATIGUE

The reports that emerged from our research of 9/11's effects included the secondary effects on corpsmen, medics, chaplains, nurses, physicians, social workers, psychologists, and others who were traumatized by working with the traumatized.[17,18] It was confirmation of a concept, "compassion fatigue," that I had helped to invent and develop over the 1990s (Figley, 1992, 1995, 1998). I started this program of research by running ads in mental health newsletters that said, in part: "If you have ever been 'burned out' or depressed about working with the traumatized, please write me." This was part of an ad that I ran in the newsletters going to a majority of psychologists, social workers, psychiatrists, counselors, and family therapists.

The response was excellent. I received more than 100 letters over an 8-month period. In addition, I ended my various lectures and workshops by asking for the same information. Also, my students conducted a series of focus groups with the pediatric critical care unit at the nearby regional hospital. The purpose was to determine whether the work got to the hospital's staff. If it did, how did this manifest itself and what did people do about it that helped or hurt? From these various sources I developed the initial draft of the compassion fatigue questionnaire (Figley, 1992). It continued to evolve (Figley, 1993, 1994) from various research projects, leading to my first book on the topic (Figley, 1995). Subsequent forms of the instrument have evolved (e.g., Figley, 1999), especially the version that includes subscales for burnout and satisfaction, as suggested by Beth Stamm (Stamm & Figley, 1999; Stamm, 2002). Beth has gone on to develop her own instrument, the ProQual (Stamm, 2003), which builds on the previous compassion fatigue scales but does not include the subscales.

Also in the 1990s, I began to notice the erroneous disconnect between the study and treatment of the traumatized versus the grieving. This and other important contributions are found in two books, *Death and Trauma* (Figley, Bride, & Mazza, 1996) and the *Traumatology of Grieving*

(Figley, 1999). Together they made a powerful argument that the theoretical and conceptual separations between traumatology and thananatology were not research-based and obstructed progress in both fields.

TODAY AND TOMORROW

I continue to feel blessed by my family, friends, and colleagues who inspire me and protect me from compassion fatigue and discouragement in my work with the traumatized. I continue to be interested in the effects of terrorism. Joe Boscarino at the New York Academy of Medicine and I continue to study the survivors of the 9/11 attack, including social workers who were in harm's way, and to offer help to them and those who sought their services (Boscarino, Figley, & Adams, 2004). Through the leadership of Andrew Weaver, we have looked at the role of spirituality in coping with trauma (Weaver, Flannelly, Garbarino, Figley, & Flannelly, 2003) and how chaplains working on 9/11 were affected (Roberts, Weaver, Flannelly, & Figley, 2003).

Through a recent Fulbright Fellowship, I was able to study the way Kuwait has recovered from its invasion by Iraq in 1990 and the 8 months of occupation, particularly how this recovery was affected by the capture of Saddam Hussein in 2003. Spending time in Kuwait again (I was there in 1992 and 1993) primarily as a researcher forced me to shift my plans and go about the question in a different way. It was clear that we would not be able to replicate the research we did in the early 1990s in Kuwait or in New York. We were convinced that few would admit that they were traumatized out of fear that they would be perceived as weak by their enemies (e.g., Iraq). Our approach shifted to looking at the presence of "al Raha" or personal comfort, the most culturally pure manifestation of the absence of traumatic stress reactions. We are preparing to conduct a national survey of Kuwaiti citizens to determine the extent to which they are experiencing al Raha and the major factors that appear to covary with this state. Through a series of focus groups, we plan to determine the major factors that account for and are the consequence of al Raha and to test these factors in a second national survey.

As an extension to this approach, my colleague Ozlem Karaimak, a visiting scholar from Turkey, and I are testing the concept of resiliency as a personality trait, in contrast to the more typical version of resiliency as a state, a function of the situation. We are conducting a longitudinal study of the entire population of students at Florida State University enrolled in a social work course. Our findings may have implications for a program of research to confirm that we are all blessed or cursed with a certain level of "ego resiliency" (Figley & Karairmak, 2004) that remains the same across various situations, contexts, and levels of adversity. If so, these findings have important implications for the way we select, train, supervise, and care for professionals who work with the traumatized. Doc would be pleased.

CONCLUSION

What were the events in your life that led to your interest in trauma? The events, as noted above, were first being with the U.S. Marine Corps in Vietnam in a war that I learned to hate and a country I learned to love. The second event was being exposed to traumatized war veterans while demonstrating against the war in which they and I fought. The third event was the 1979–1981 Iran hostage crisis, an incident that transformed my interest in war to the broader issue of trauma and was related to my constant interest in families and psychosocial stress. The fourth event was the suicide of a friend and colleague, which led to concern about work-related stress and compassion fatigue. The fifth event was the 1995 bombing in Oklahoma City, which led to the founding of the Green Cross and the Academy of Traumatology, and to being fully engaged in the study and response to terrorism that shook this country on that fateful September 11th.

What have been your greatest achievements and contributions to the field? In summary of what I have already written, my greatest achievements and contributions have been (1) helping to create and understand the concept of PTSD, especially war-related PTSD; (2) helping to initially quantify the traumatizing stimulus as a stressor; (3) positing testable theories and models associated with the trauma induction, reduction, and resiliency of individuals, interpersonal relationships, and the secondary effects of trauma; (4) having cofounded the Society (International Society) for Traumatic Stress Studies; (5) having founded and been the first to edit the *Journal of Traumatic Stress* and given the journal to the society; (6) serving as founding editor of the book series on psychosocial stress starting in 1983; (7) producing the books *Stress Disorders Among Vietnam Veterans* (Figley, 1978), the *Stress and the Family* series (McCubbin & Figley, 1983; Figley & McCubbin, 1983), *Helping Traumatized Families* (1989), *Compassion Fatigue* (1995), The *Traumatology of Grieving* (1999), and the present volume; (8) having helped to establish the Traumatic Stress e-mail–based mailing list; (9) having cofounded the Green Cross Projects (1995); (10) serving as founding editor of the international journal *Traumatology;* (11) having been cofounder of the Green Cross Foundation and its Academy of Traumatology (in 1997); and (12) having given voice to the practitioner who must struggle with extremely challenging trauma clients who do not respond to the mainstream, evidence-based treatment approaches.

Who were the people who most influenced you to make these contributions? First of all, particularly my mother, Geni, who has always been my biggest advocate and supporter. Certainly John Kerry and the hundreds of other Vietnam veterans camped out on the Mall in Washington, DC, in

April 1971, particularly Doc and the others I interviewed. Ted Huston, my major professor for my doctoral program, who taught be how to think like a scientist. Throughout my career there have been so many upon whose shoulders I tried to make my small contributions. These include Chaim Shatan, Sarah Haley, Bob Lifton, Joe Wolpe, and Carlfred Broderick. Along the way my close connection with several special people taught me much and made me laugh. They include Shad Meshad, Joel Brende, Jack McClosky, Bonnie Green, Bob Lifton, Bessel van der Kolk, Frank Ochberg, Zahava Solomon, Ray Coward, and Graham Spanier. Now, my wife, Kathy and my daughters Jessica and Laura, and my mother and my sister, Sandy Elliott, are the love and support that keep me going.

How would you hope current and future trauma scholars will build upon your work? Always be skeptical but with the intention of getting it right for the traumatized who are suffering needlessly. Never be satisfied with effectively helping only one population of traumatized people and always be concerned about children and practitioners who help them and others. Always consider the further consequences of trauma beyond the individual to consider her or his family, friends, community, and acquaintances. Finally, I would hope that those who read my work will consider that I was (1) always open to criticism as long as it was offered as helpful, (2) always did all I could to assist other scholars, practitioners, or members of the public understand and apply my work or help them with theirs; (3) tried to be a good, decent human being who cared deeply about preventing trauma, injustice, intolerance, and despair.

Charles R. Figley, 1974

REFERENCES

Figley, C. R. (1975). Interpersonal adjustment and family life among Vietnam veterans, a general bibliography. *Congressional Record,* February 19. (Entered by Senator Vance Hartke.)

Figley, C. R. (1975). Review of Willard W. Waller on the family, education, and war. W. J. Goode, F. Furstenburg, Jr., & L. R. Mitchell (Eds.) *Family Coordinator, 24,* 104–105.

Figley, C. R. (1978a). *Delayed combat stress disorders: Contrasts among Vietnam veterans, Korean Veterans, and World War veterans recently inducted into the American Legion. A final report.* Indianapolis, IN: The American Legion.

Figley, C. R. (1978b). Frustrations remain. Vietnam vets: Still not forgiven (invited essay). *Indianapolis Star,* July 2.

Figley, C. R. (1978c). The residue of Vietnam (invited essay). *American Legion Magazine,* September, 1978.

Figley, C. R. (Ed.) (1978d). Stress disorders among Vietnam veterans: *Theory, research, and treatment.* New York: Brunner/Mazel.

Figley, C. R. (1978e). Tactical self-presentation and interpersonal attraction. In M. Cook & G. Wilson (Eds.), *Love and Attraction: An International Conference* (pp. 91–99). Oxford, UK: Pergamon, 1978.

Figley, C. R. (1978f). Introduction. In C. R. Figley (Ed.), *Stress disorders among Vietnam veterans: Theory, research and treatment* (pp. xii–xxvi). New York: Brunner/Mazel.

Figley, C. R. (1978g). Psychological adjustment among Vietnam veterans: An overview of the research. In C. R. Figley (Ed.), *Stress disorders among Vietnam veterans: Theory, research and treatment* (pp 57–70). New York: Brunner/Mazel.

Figley, C. R. (1979). The Vietnam veteran—a thoughtful look. *The Purdue Alumnus,* March.

Figley, C. R. (1979). Confusing the warrior with the war. Guest editorial. *American Psychological Association Monitor,* March, p. 2.

Figley, C. R. (1980). From hostages to heroes: The trauma of coming home (invited essay). *U.S. News and World Report,* November 10, 35–36.

Figley, C. R. (1980). The glory and the gore, an introduction to section I. In Figley, C. R., & Leventman, S. (Eds.) (1980). *Strangers at home: Vietnam veterans since the war* (pp. 1–6). New York: Praeger.

Figley, C. R. (1980). Confused, hated, ignored and dishonored, an introduction to section II. In Figley, C. R., & Leventman, S. (Eds.) (1980). *Strangers at home: Vietnam veterans since the war* (pp. 79–85). New York: Praeger.

Figley, C. R. (1980). Unpaid debts to unsung heroes, an introduction to section III. In Figley, C. R., & Leventman, S. (Eds.) (1980). *Strangers at home: Vietnam veterans since the war* (pp. 196–200). New York: Praeger.

Figley, C. R. (1980). A postscript: Welcoming home the strangers. In Figley, C. R., & Leventman, S. (Eds) (1980). *Strangers at home: Vietnam veterans since the war* (pp. 334–351). New York: Praeger.

Figley, C. R. (1980). The Iranian crisis: Caring for families of catastrophe. *American Association for Family Therapy Newsletter,* September, *11,* 5.

Figley, C. R. (1980). Psychosocial adjustment of recently returned veterans. *Strangers at home: Vietnam veterans since the war,* 214–254. NY: Praeger.

Figley, C. R. (Ed.) (1980). Mobilization I: The Iranian crisis. *Report of the Task Force on Families of Catastrophe to the US State Department.* West Lafayette, IN: Purdue University Press (Abridged version in the appendix of Figley & McCubbin, 1983).

Figley, C. R. and Southerly, W. T. (1980) Psychosocial adjustment of recently returned veterans. In C. R. Figley and S. Leventman (Eds), *Strangers at Home: Vietnam Veterans Since the war,* 167–180. NY: Plenum.

Figley, C. R. (1981). Working on a theory of what it takes to survive. *American Psychological Association Monitor, 12*(3), 9.

Figley, C. R. (1984). Treating post-traumatic stress disorder: the algorithmic approach. *American Academy of Psychiatry and the Law Newsletter, 9*,3 (December).

Figley, C. R. (1988). Partners in politics: Initial research findings and celebrity family syndrome. Invited papers presented at the Annual Meeting of the American Association for Marriage and Family Therapy, New Orleans, October.

Figley, C. R. (1992). Compassion fatigue and other hazards of family assistance work. Invited keynote address, Second National Training Workshop, Agent Orange Class Assistance Program, Washington, DC, November.

Figley, C. R. (1993). Compassion fatigue. *Family Therapy News*, January.

Figley, C. R. (1993). Compassion stress: Burden of the social worker. *Florida ASW Newsletter,* May.

Figley, C.R. (1993). Compassion Stress: Toward Its Measurement and Management. *Family Therapy News*, February, 1–2.

Figley, C.R. (1993). Compassion fatigue and social work practice: Distinguishing burnout from secondary traumatic stress. *Newsletter of the NASW Florida Chapter*, June, 1–2.

Figley, C.R. (1996). Review of the compassion fatigue self-test. In B. H. Stamm (Ed.). *Measurement of stress, trauma, and adaptation*. Baltimore: Sidran Press.

Figley, C. R. (1999). Police compassion fatigue (PCF): Theory, research, assessment, treatment, and prevention. In J. Violanti (Ed.), *Police trauma: Psychological aftermath of civilian combat*. Springfield, IL: Charles C Thomas.

Figley, C. R. (2000). Foreword. In . Mercy Warriors: Saving Lives Under Fire by John "Doc" Combs. Tallahassee, FL: Green Cross Press.

Figley, C. R. (2001). The history of trauma practice, part I. *Journal of Trauma Practice,*1:1, 3–18.

Figley, C. R. (2005). Strangers at home: A commentary on the secondary traumatization in partners and parents of Dutch peacekeeping soldiers. *Journal of Family Psychology.* 19:2,183–187.

Figley, C. R., & Leventman, S. (1980). Introduction: Estrangement and victimization. In C. R. Figley & S. Leventman (Eds.) *Strangers at home: Vietnam veterans since the war* (pp. xiii–xxiv). New York: Praeger.

Figley, C. R., and Leventman, S. (Eds.) (1980). *Strangers at home: Vietnam veterans since the war*. New York: Praeger.

Folsing, A. (1997). *Albert Einstein: A biography*. New York: Penguin Books.

Hogancamp, V., & Figley, C. R. (1983). War: Bringing the battle home. In C. R. Figley & H. I. McCubbin (Eds.), *Stress and the family: Volume II. Coping with catastrophe*. New York: Brunner/Mazel.

McCubbin, H. I. & Figley, C. R. (1983). Bridging normative and catastrophic stress. In H. I. McCubbin & C.R. Figley (Eds.), *Stress and the family: Volume I. Coping with normative transitions* (pp. 218–228). New York: Brunner/Mazel.

Schilpp, P. A. (1940). *Albert Einstein: Philosopher-scientist*. Evanston, IL: Living Philosophers, Inc.

Stanton, M. D., & Figley, C. R. (1978). Treating the Vietnam veteran within the family system. In C. R. Figley (Ed.), Stress disorders among Vietnam veterans: Theory, research, and treatment (pp. 281–290). New York: Brunner/Mazel.

ENDNOTES

1. I was able to get out of the Marine Corps early to enter Ohio State University in March 1967 but transferred to the University of Hawaii the following year.
2. American Psychiatric Association (Figley, 1977), American Psychological Association (Figley, 1978), American Sociological Association (Figley, 1979), American Orthopsychiatric Association (Figley, 1979), the National Council on Family Relations (Figley 1975), the American Association for Marriage and Family Therapy (Figley 1980).

3. *Stress Disorders Among Vietnam Veterans* (Figley, 1978) and *Strangers at home: Vietnam Veterans Since the War* (Figley & Leventman, 1980).

4. Among others, these included *Military Medicine* (Figley, 1977), *Marital and Family Therapy* and Figley, C. R. & Sprenkle, D. H. (1978). Delayed stress response syndrome: Family therapy implications. *Journal of Marriage and Family Counseling*, 4, (1) 53–60.

5. Among the illustrious experts who assembled at Purdue University were Graham Spanier (current president of Penn State University), Park Diets (the renowned forensic psychiatrist), Ann Burgess and Frank Ochberg (both contributors to this volume), Hamilton McCubbin (a dean at the University of Wisconsin and former director of the Center for POW Studies Section on Families), Raymond T. Coward (currently an endowed professor and dean at Penn State), as well as the wife of a POW, an FBI agent, Douglas Sprenkle (internationally renowned family therapist), and others.

6. Two volumes of *Stress and the Family* (Figley & McCubbin, 1983 and McCubbin & Figley, 1983).

7. Those attending the meeting became members of the founding board of directors: Ann Burgess (Vice President), Yael Danieli, Charles Figley (President), Bernard Mazel, Robert Rich (Secretary/Treasurer), and Marlene Young. Scott Sheely was selected as Executive Director.

8. Don was one of the founders of the crisis hotline movement in the early 1970s.

9. The Psychosocial Stress Program, along with the Program's Center for Marriage and Family Therapy, sponsored numerous conferences and training programs for military family professions in the region. Also, the program organized a panel at the 1990 annual meeting of the American Association for Marriage and Family Therapy, which brought together military family and family therapy experts to discuss what was needed (by way of policies, programs, and direct support) to help these families.

10. The program acquired special permission from the funding source and, at the invitation of Laura Boyd, Ph.D., Oklahoma State Representative for Oklahoma City, conducted a needs assessment. This led to the establishment of the Green Cross Traumatology Training and Certification Program, noted elsewhere in this chapter.

11. The history of the GCP is described elsewhere (Figley & Figley, 2001; Figley, Figley, & Norman, 2002).

12. Such standards were attempted by ISTSS but were connected to one of the twelve most popular trauma treatment approaches. Much to my dismay, the learned society I helped to establish continues to resist specifying the standards of care for professionals–researchers, practitioners, and volunteers who work with the traumatized.

13. In the ensuing 6 years there would be three deaths, eight new members, and five modifications of the Standards of Practice (see http://www.traumatologyacademy.org/SOC.html).

14. Now they are academy fellows, joined by regular members who have earned one of the several certifications recognized by the Academy of Traumatology.

15. Based on the first full year of the Traumatology Certification Program, the University Continuing Education Association named it the "Best (non-credit) Program of the Year" at its annual meeting in San Diego in 2000.

16. The Green Cross Foundation's mission is simply "to help the traumatized through research, education, and professional development."

17. Among them are Boscarino, Figley, & Adams, 2004 and Roberts, S., Weaver, A.J., Flannelly, K. J. and Figley, C. R. (2003). Compassion Fatigue Among Chaplains and Other Clergy after September 11th. *Journal of Nervous and Mental Disease*, 191:11, 756-758.

18. Boscarino, J. A., Figley, C. R., and Adams, R. E., (2004) Evidence of Compassion Fatigue following September 11 Terrorist Attacks: A study of Secondary Trauma among Social Workers in New York. *International Journal of Emergency Mental Health* 6:2, 98–108.

4

Making It Up as I Went Along

MATTHEW J. FRIEDMAN

My story is about a man who didn't have the foggiest idea what he wanted to do when he grew up. As he was rejecting and backing away from the obvious personal and professional options within reach, he stumbled upon a small path. He didn't recognize it as a path, but in his own erratic fashion followed it for 15 years. Finally, at the age of 49, he realized that this was indeed the right direction to follow. And he has followed it ever since.

In 1973, thirty-two years ago, I was an urban refugee who had turned my back on exciting prospects in academic psychiatry at Harvard and the Massachusetts General Hospital. I had come to northern New England ostensibly to complete my psychiatric residency at Dartmouth but personally to join the hippie community in Cornish, New Hampshire. I tried to embrace the counterculture scene as much as possible: growing my own food, maintaining goats for milk, raising pigs (named Erlichmann and Haldemann) for food, heating my house with wood I had hewn in the forest, reading and writing by kerosene lantern rather than electric light, and attending psychiatric grand rounds in my bib overalls.

Other factors were also at play, some of which were clearly recognizable despite my pervasive confusion about personal identity and future goals. There was my devout belief in Maslow's doctrine of self-actualization manifested as a moral obligation to do the best I could with whatever capabilities I possessed. My fascination with human behavior led to undergraduate studies in psychology, which in turn led me to discover neuroanatomy and neurophysiology. My doctoral dissertation in pharmacology was on neuroplasticity, how environmental changes can alter brain structure at the synaptic level. Having grown up within the Jewish subculture of Newark, New Jersey, during the 1940s, I had experienced anti-Semitism at first hand and had been personally, familially, and culturally affected by the genocide of the Nazi Holocaust. Finally, the traumatic death, by suicide, of my only sibling, my younger brother, Dick, 8 years earlier had created an enormous loss, punctuated by poorly understood feelings and questions with which I continued to struggle unsuccessfully.

HOW I GOT INTO THE FIELD OF TRAUMATIC STRESS STUDIES

Having left the Massachusetts General Hospital in 1972 to complete my psychiatric residency at Dartmouth during the following year, the only thing I knew for certain was that I needed a job to support my growing addiction to Vermont and New Hampshire. A position as staff psychiatrist at the Veterans Administration (VA) Hospital in White River Junction, Vermont, seemed best. I had no particular knowledge or interest in veteran-related psychiatric issues, but it provided an opportunity for an appointment to the Dartmouth faculty and a potential opportunity for clinical research. As I told myself and anyone else who cared to know, "I'll do this for a year and then find something interesting to do." Having recently completed my 32nd year as a VA psychiatrist, it is amusing to recall how wrong I was. Indeed, each year has been more interesting, challenging, and fulfilling than the last, and I am sure that the best is yet to come.

The Vietnam War was winding down. Combat veterans were flooding our clinics, occupying inpatient beds, and demanding that we do something to alleviate their angst and distress. We didn't know what to do for them. Although they were sometimes depressed, guilt-ridden, and suicidal, their problem certainly wasn't classic melancholia. They reported vivid, emotionally riveting reenactments of war-zone scenarios that bore little resemblance to psychotic hallucinations. They were often extremely mistrustful about the U.S. government, including the VA hospital system. Because of their overwhelming fears about personal safety, many carried firearms for protection wherever they went. And their rage at the government and the American public fueled hair-trigger tempers that, not infrequently, erupted into sudden, unexpected aggressive outbursts that were potentially dangerous to clinical staff.

At that time, I met and later fell in love with Gayle Smith, RN, MS, an in-country vet who had spent a year at the Third Surgical Hospital, a tiny MASH unit in Binh Thuy in southern Vietnam, not far from the Cambodian border. Gayle had recently joined the VA staff as a medical-surgical clinical specialist. Before we became emotionally involved, I thought she was the best nurse I had ever met. She helped me listen to the veterans so that I could hear their sorrow, guilt, and despair. I can't tell you how much I was personally moved as I began to appreciate the enduring emotional impact of their traumatic experiences during the war.

Fortified by Gayle, emotionally hooked by the veterans, and clinically alerted by the psychological pain saturating their stories, I decided to start a group for any veteran who wanted to join. In fact, we started two groups, one of which met in the hospital, which I led with Doris Brown, the psychiatric head nurse. Gayle led the other group, which met in our apartment. This was to provide a place for veterans whose distrust of any government facility, including a VA hospital, was so great that they were unable to "get past the bricks." I was later told that these were among the first groups offered to Vietnam veterans under the aegis of a VA facility. At that time I was unaware of the rap groups offered in the late 1960s by Vietnam Veterans Against the War. My actions were completely motivated by the urgency of the clinical demand I saw all about me.

MY CONTRIBUTIONS TO THE FIELD

That's how I got started. I continued to work in relative isolation at White River Junction for the next 4 or 5 years, challenged by the local veterans who came to see me. I slowly began to discover that I was not alone. Others around the nation, motivated no doubt by the same observations that had impelled my own actions, had also initiated clinical programs for Vietnam veterans inside and outside the VA system. I also gradually became aware of the gathering momentum to install PTSD as an official American Psychiatric Association diagnosis in the third edition of the *Diagnostic and Statistical Manual* (DSM-III). From that beginning, there were five experiences that now stand out as turning points in my career: establishment of the first Vet Center in the nation in 1979; my appointment as chairman of the (VA) Chief Medical Director's Special Committee on PTSD in 1984; my appointment as executive director of the National Center for PTSD in 1989; my involvement with the International Society for Traumatic Stress Studies; and the September 11, 2001, terrorist attacks on the World Trade Center and the Pentagon.

Establishment of the First Vet Center

In 1979 Congress authorized VA to establish "storefront" outreach centers nationwide for Vietnam veterans. This approach, inspired by the community psychiatry movement of the 1960s and 1970s and fueled by veteran community distrust of the VA hospital system, was the beginning of the current Vet Center program. I discovered that the plan was to select five initial sites as demonstration projects to test whether such a national initiative was feasible. I was determined to make White River Junction one of those initial sites. Having worked with traumatized veterans for 5 years and having also successfully established community-based programs in Vermont and New Hampshire as an innovative rural mental health initiative, I believed that I was uniquely qualified to set up such a center. Fortunately, my zealous presentation of this argument met with a favorable response from Don Crawford, the head of VA's Readjustment Counseling Service. Therefore, on October 1, 1979, I celebrated the establishment of the first Vet Center in the nation, in Williston, a small town a few miles south of Burlington, Vermont. I recognize that some Californians and Washingtonians may contest my claim that Vermont beat them to the punch, but the record is clear. We were first.

Establishment of the Vet Center generated more excitement and many new opportunities. First, it provided a headquarters around which the dynamic Vermont Vietnam veteran community could unite. Second, it enabled me, as chief of psychiatry at the White River Junction VA Medical Center, to create a continuum of outreach and clinical options, from Vet Centers to community-based clinics to hospital-based specialty care and finally to intensive inpatient treatment. Third, it gave me an effective base of operations from which to network with the growing nationwide community dedicated to understanding and treating PTSD and other war-related problems.

Because of my emerging profile as a trauma specialist, I began to receive invitations to speak at a variety of extraordinary meetings, often to challenging audiences full of passionate veterans, newly interested clinicians, and outraged skeptics. Since I was a biological psychiatrist and clinical pharmacologist, my assigned topic was frequently to discuss the pathophysiology of PTSD and pharmacologic treatment for this disorder.

It was actually through preparation for these speaking engagements that I discovered that the scientific questions pertaining to PTSD were as compelling as the clinical challenges. The important insights of Abram Kardiner in 1941, suggesting that war stress could develop into a "physioneurosis" with both physiologic as well as psychological components, influenced me greatly, as did the efforts of Larry Kolb, John Mason, Earl Giller, and Bessel van der Kolk to move the field in a neuroscientific direction. Others, such as Terry Keane and David Foy, helped me recognize that classic experimental psychological theory was also a useful theoretical context for understanding the uncontrollable stimulus-driven behavior and symptoms exhibited by these veterans.

The Chief Medical Director's Special Committee on PTSD

Dissatisfaction with the VA's limited willingness and capacity to meet the needs of Vietnam veterans with PTSD impelled the U.S. Congress to take an unusual action. In 1984, it established the Chief Medical Director's (CMD's) Special Committee on PTSD. What made this committee so "special" was its mandate to report directly to the Senate and House Veterans Affairs Committees with or without the concurrence of the CMD or other top VA leaders. Another unusual feature was that rather than empaneling an oversight committee of external experts, all special committee members were to be selected from within the ranks of VA professionals.

Looking back, this was a dangerous assignment, since the Special Committee's charge was to tell Congress the truth about the VA's inadequate clinical, research, educational, and veterans benefits activities pertaining to PTSD-related programs. In such a highly politicized atmosphere, an accurate account of the VA's performance was sure to incur the wrath of VA leadership.

I have always wondered why I was chosen to chair this select committee. I was an obscure psychiatrist from a small hospital in a remote part of the country. There were many better-known and more distinguished VA experts who were clearly more qualified for this assignment. Therefore I have always believed that many others were offered the chairmanship before me, and they all wisely declined because they recognized the impossibility of satisfying both VA leadership and congressional committee members at the same time.

It was an easy decision for me. I was too young to worry about job security, too naive about politics, too delighted to have been selected, and too motivated to make the most of this opportunity. So I accepted the chairmanship without hesitation.

Our initial meeting, held in December 1984, was a memorable event. It was my first opportunity to meet an extraordinary group of people who were to change my life. There were 12 of us: Art Arnold, Bob Baker, Spencer Falcon, Joan Furey, Joe Gelsomino, Fred Gusman, Terry Keane, Larry Kolb, Steve Petty, Ted Podkul, Jack Smith, and myself. All had made unique contributions and all were chafing at the bit to address the unmet needs of veterans. Larry Kolb was especially impressive. One of America's most respected psychiatrists, rounding out his career as a VA Distinguished Physician, he brought wisdom, tactical advice, and an unwavering commitment to tell Congress the truth about deficiencies in VA programs. He inspired us all.

I could easily devote an entire chapter to the Special Committee, which I chaired for 5 years, until 1989 (when I stepped aside to assume leadership of the newly established National Center for PTSD). From the beginning we established two crucial guiding principles for all the work that followed: (1) that treatment of war-related PTSD should be one of the highest priorities of the VA system and (2) that all Special Committee recommendations would be based on the best data available. These were unassailable principles and enabled us to avoid getting seduced by rhetoric or bogged down in politics. It also gave us license to investigate all data available on clinical utilization, research funding, educational initiatives, and disability claims. We even instigated a massive 4-week survey that monitored more than 450,000 outpatient mental health visits to VA hospitals and Vet Centers to assess clinical utilization for PTSD-related problems. As expected, we detected enormous differences from one hospital to another regarding access to care for veterans with PTSD. Similar inequities were found regarding PTSD disability awards. Prejudicial bias against funding of PTSD research projects was also uncovered by the Special Committee.

Our annual reports to Congress unquestionably nudged VA policy toward a more favorable perspective regarding PTSD programs. Our first recommendation, considered outrageously expensive at the time, that every one of VA's 172 hospitals receive funding for a special clinical program dedicated to PTSD treatment, helped influence Congress to allocate millions of additional dollars to meet such a goal. Finally, we were able to transform what was initially a contentious and uncomfortable relationship with VA leadership into a productive and mutually respectful working alliance without compromising our commitment to improve VA PTSD programs.

Chairing the Special Committee was an exhilarating and demanding experience that changed my professional and personal perspectives. Professionally, it forced me to think and act in a national rather than a local context. And personally, it helped me recognize my potential as a leader who was able and willing to take on difficult challenges and, more important, to get others to follow.

The National Center for PTSD

In 1989, after a national competition, our five-part consortium became the National Center for PTSD. Having determined that no single site could meet the congressional mandate to advance PTSD research and education (both within and without the VA system), we proposed a multisite organization to achieve these goals. The concept was simple. We sought to bring under one administrative roof a spectrum of VA academic programs that excelled in different key aspects of PTSD research and education.

Terry Keane and Fred Gusman, both Special Committee alumni, became the directors of the Behavioral Science Division at the Boston VA and the Education Division at the Palo Alto VA, respectively. Dennis Charney and Bob Rosenheck assumed directorship of the Clinical Neurosciences and Evaluation Divisions both at the West Haven, Connecticut, VA Medical Center. As executive director, I remained at White River Junction, where I established the Executive Division.

In the same way that a group medical practice consists of different specialists, such as internists, surgeons, pediatricians, psychiatrists, and so forth, we built the National Center for PTSD around preexisting VA areas of strength that enjoyed strong local support from the affiliated medical school. Terry (at Tufts and later at Boston University) had already emerged as a top expert in psychological assessment and treatment. Fred (at Stanford) presided over the largest inpatient PTSD program in the world. Dennis (at Yale), a well-known biological psychiatrist who had made major contributions to our understanding of pathophysiological and brain function abnormalities in depression and panic disorder, had begun to turn his attention to PTSD. Bob (also at Yale) as director of the Northeast Program Evaluation Center, was in charge of PTSD program evaluation throughout the entire 172-hospital system of the VA. In setting up my Executive Division, I took advantage of the renowned on-line bibliographic capability of Dartmouth's Baker Library to establish the National PTSD Resource Center.

Most people think that I took the lead in creating the national center. It isn't so. Terry, Fred, Dennis, and Bob were the ones who actually set it in motion. Then, quite unexpectedly, they asked if I would be willing to serve as executive director. I think they wanted me to deal with all the administrative headaches and responsibilities so that they could devote themselves to academic pursuits. Of course, I was eager to do it, but not if it meant returning to an urban environment. Expecting a negative reaction, I told them that I'd be willing to direct the national center only if I could stay in Vermont. To my delight and amazement, they agreed to let me do so. And that's how the Executive Offices for the National Center for PTSD came to be situated in rural White River Junction.

We achieved our present complement of seven divisions several years later with two new additions. Jessica Wolfe took charge of the newly created Women's Health Sciences Division while Ray Scurfield became director of our Pacific Islands Division in Honolulu, which was to be dedicated to cross-cultural research and education.

Our leadership has been remarkably stable, thanks in great measure to the vision, resourcefulness, and commitment of Paula Schnurr, who has served as deputy to the executive director since 1989. Other talented leaders who have emerged from within the ranks include Danny Kaloupek, Steve Southwick, Patricia Watson, Joe Ruzek, and Lynda King. As a result, disruption to the center's operations was minimized when Dennis Charney, Jessica Wolfe, and Ray Scurfield left for greener pastures some years ago. Since that time, John Krystal and Patti Resick have become directors of the Clinical Neurosciences and Women's Divisions, respectively.

Since space is limited, I'll give a brief summary of the national center's accomplishments before returning to more personal information. Our mission has been to advance the clinical care and social welfare of America's veterans through research, education, and training in the science, diagnosis, and treatment of PTSD and stress-related disorders. The breadth of our activities has extended from genetic research and brain imaging to multisite randomized clinical trials to large-scale epidemiologic surveys to program evaluation of every PTSD clinical program within the VA system. Our work has identified abnormalities in behavior, sleep, cognition, memory, physiological reactivity, and hormonal regulation as well as in brain structure and function in association with PTSD. We have developed some of the major instruments currently utilized in PTSD assessment, diagnosis, and treatment research. Our website www.ncptsd.va.gov has emerged as the most comprehensive Internet source of information on PTSD and stress-related disorders. (It is also the site at which many more details about the national center can be found.) *The Published International Literature on Traumatic Stress* (PILOTS), accessible on our website and developed by Fred Lerner, is acknowledged as the largest and most comprehensive computerized bibliographic database on traumatic stress in the world. Clinicians, scientists, and others have benefited from our two newsletters, the *PTSD Research Quarterly* and the *Clinical Quarterly*. During the past 15 years, the national center's authors have published more than 1,700 articles, chapters, and books; made more than 3,000 scientific or educational presentations; and obtained approximately $122 million in extramural funding for more than 400 peer-reviewed research projects. The national center's staff have been active in supporting clinicians through formal presentations, training programs, and the development of evidence-based practice guidelines. The center has provided consultation to top VA leadership and developed effective collaborative relationships with many partners within the public and academic sectors, most notably with the National institute of Mental Health (NIMH), the Department of Defense (DoD), the Substance Abuse Mental Health Services Administration (SAMHSA), the Centers for Disease Control (CDC), the National Child Trauma Network (NCTN), and others. In short, the National Center for PTSD has become the world's leading center of excellence dedicated to generating and disseminating knowledge concerning PTSD and other stress-related disorders.

Besides the joy and honor of directing the center, leadership has brought me unexpected challenges and opportunities. My major responsibility has been and continues to be the creation of a virtual center that transcends the local history, culture, momentum, and academic climate at each site. With a multisite consortium extending from Boston to Honolulu and incorporating five different VA hospitals and affiliated academic centers (e.g., Boston University, Dartmouth, Hawaii, Stanford, and Yale), we have had to balance the dynamic tension between center and local priorities. It has been an instructive and creative struggle to promote a national center identity among our professional staff that comfortably complements local academic and clinical allegiances.

When I accepted administrative leadership of the national center, I understood that my primary responsibility was to make it succeed. That meant subordinating my own academic interests to the center's priorities. Therefore I had to instigate projects or undertake tasks that no one else cared to tackle. My selection of such initiatives was often based on my belief that such projects filled important gaps either in the national center's academic portfolio or in the trauma field as a whole. In some cases, I believe that these activities helped to open new areas of traumatic stress studies. As a result, I have been involved in a wide variety of fascinating activities with many gifted collaborators. These include a comprehensive book on neurobiological aspects of PTSD (with Dennis Charney and Ariel Deutch); a conference, book, and epidemiologic survey on cross-cultural aspects of PTSD (with Tony Marsella, Marie Ashcraft, Spero Manson, and others); research on the consequences of United Nations peacekeeping missions (with Brett Litz), formulating the hypothesis that PTSD was a risk factor for medical illness (with Paula Schnurr); convening three national conferences to promote integrated primary care/mental health treatment (with Fred Gusman and Greg Leskin); cochairing multisite randomized clinical trials on cognitive-behavioral group and individual treatment for PTSD (with Paula Schnurr and Chuck Engel); a multiyear partnership with SAMHSA's Center for Mental Health Services and with DoD to develop evidence-based best practices following mass casualties or large scale disasters (with Patricia Watson, Fran Norris, Cam Ritchie, Joe Ruzek, Bruce Young, and Jessica Hamblen); ongoing efforts to establish a national VA/DoD brain bank regarding stress and PTSD (with Bob Ursano, John Krystal, Beth Osuch, and Terry Keane); monitoring the impact of traumatic stress on pregnancy (with Leslie Morland and Deb Goebert); and currently coediting a comprehensive handbook on the science and practice of PTSD (with Terry Keane and Patti Resick).

As I write this chapter, American troops, previously deployed to Afghanistan or Iraq, have begun to seek assistance for war-related psychological problems. The National Center for PTSD has been very active in advising national military and VA leadership as well as clinicians in the trenches on the best early interventions and evidence-based treatments for our newest veterans.

To summarize, stewardship of the national center has forced me to develop my own conceptual map of the trauma field as a whole; enabled me to influence the national academic, clinical, and policy agenda; and inspired me to identify conceptual and clinical goals for the future.

The International Society for Traumatic Stress Studies (ISTSS)

In 1995, I became president of ISTSS, having served on the board of directors in previous years. I had been welcomed by the young organization during my days with the Special Committee and sought a much closer relationship after the National Center for PTSD was established. For me,

ISTSS was the indispensable hub of a small but growing international community of scholars and clinicians through which I could meet other Americans working with traumatized civilians as well as trauma specialists from Europe, Scandinavia, Australia, Israel, Japan, South Africa, and elsewhere. With regard to my personal growth, ISTSS has been immensely important. It helped transform my American veteran frame of reference into a global perspective incorporating concerns about the full spectrum of traumatic stress among adults and children. Three projects exemplify the variety of new opportunities made possible by ISTSS.

During the heat of the "recovered memory" controversy of the mid-1990s, ISTSS resolved to address the inflammatory and polarizing rhetoric swirling about this topic by documenting the current state of the art in scientific understanding about memories of childhood trauma. Susan Roth invited me to coedit the pamphlet *Childhood Trauma Remembered: A Report on the Current Scientific Knowledge Base and its Applications*, which was published by ISTSS. Our strategy was to recruit eminent scholars on both sides of the controversy, to identify areas of agreement, and to provide recommendations for clinical practice based on the best available scientific information. Although it was hardly a simple assignment, we did succeed in cutting through the rhetoric on both sides and providing evidence-based conclusions to guide practitioners in the field.

My second memorable ISTSS assignment was the development of evidence-based practice guidelines for PTSD treatment. Edna Foa, who led this initiative, asked Terry Keane and me to help her direct this ambitious project. More than 40 colleagues worked with us to review the empiric literature on 12 distinct clinical approaches to PTSD treatment. It was the first comprehensive attempt to synthesize the evidence from empiric research in order to guide clinical practice. It has had a major impact on the field.

A book published in 2003, *Trauma Interventions in War and Peace: Prevention, Practice and Policy*, was the culmination of a complicated 4-year collaboration between the United Nations and ISTSS. Facilitated by Ellen Frey-Wouters, ISTSS's UN representative, and instigated by John Langmore, Director of the UN's Division for Social Policy and Development, and Martin Barber, Director of the UN's Office for the Coordination of Humanitarian Affairs, it involved approximately 50 trauma experts and UN officials from all corners of the globe. Our goal was to demonstrate how traumatic stress adversely affects people exposed to social deprivation or humanitarian crises and why recognition of this fact might improve UN efforts to alleviate distress. Bonnie Green served as principle editor. With the book as a launch pad, we now hope to promote official changes in UN policy.

Participation in the UN/ISTSS project is emblematic of my growing international orientation. Most notably, I have made six trips to the former Yugoslavia in recent years to assist with reconstruction efforts in Kosovo, consult on PTSD among Croatian veterans, advance traumatic stress studies in Romania, and cochair a NATO conference in Ljubljana, Slovenia (with Anica Mikus Kos) to develop guidelines for psychosocial interventions to promote recovery and well-being among children exposed to war and mass terrorism.

September 11, 2001

September 11, 2001, is a date that needs no introduction. The National Center for PTSD responded rapidly in a number of ways. Within hours of the terrorist attacks, Jessica Hamblen, Patricia Watson, and others posted dozens of fact sheets on our website, www.ncptsd.va.gov, regarding normal human stress reactions, advice to parents, guidance to clinicians, and effective early interventions. Demand for this information was so great that we logged more than 45,000 unique visitors to the website in a single day. We provided consultation to VA facilities in the New York area. Terry Keane developed a research protocol with the New York Fire Department to monitor mental health outcomes. Fred Gusman and his Palo Alto staff were the only civilians permitted to assist military officials dealing with the aftermath of the Pentagon attack. Steve Southwick and John Krystal in West Haven worked with Connecticut mental health disaster officials.

Patricia Watson and I (later joined by Fran Norris and Jessica Hamblen) began to consult closely with the New York City/State Office of Mental Health on effective early interventions for the millions of people affected by the 9/11 attacks. Through these efforts we have become part of a federal network dedicated to improving the nation's ability to meet the mental health needs of Americans exposed to mass violence or terrorism. These efforts are ongoing and have fostered exciting, productive collaborative initiatives with colleagues from SAMHSA, NIMH, DoD, CDC, NCTN, and elsewhere.

The 9/11 aftermath has also stimulated major scientific efforts to reexamine what we know about the acute response to traumatic stress, to understand the psychological and biological processes that mediate these reactions, and to carry out rigorous research on early psychosocial and pharmacologic interventions. I have played a leading role in stimulating research through a series of national conferences on science and practice during the acute aftermath of mass violence and terrorism.

The 9/11 experience has produced an important shift in my thinking. It has forced me to acknowledge the limited applicability of traditional clinical approaches and the need to emphasize preventive measures, pubic education, and societal preparation for future catastrophic events. I now advocate a public mental health approach to the threat of terrorism that emphasizes the promotion of wellness and resilience rather than the amelioration of mental illness and symptomatic distress.

My post-9/11 scientific concerns have also shifted. I strive to learn more about the difference between resilience and vulnerability. I believe it is of the utmost importance to understand how most humans react to catastrophic events, what genetic and acquired characteristics will enhance their capacity to cope with overwhelming events, and what acute psychosocial and pharmacologic approaches will provide effective early interventions. From a public health perspective, it is important to develop techniques for identifying vulnerable individuals during childhood and to develop psychological and biological "vaccines" that might immunize them from the impact of traumatic stress later in life.

WHO WERE THE PEOPLE WHO INFLUENCED ME MOST?

As chronicled throughout these pages, events and circumstances have been my primary influences. The Vietnam veterans who refused to take no for an answer and demanded that I learn how to help them were a decisive early influence on my career. Gayle Smith—RN, MS, in-country Vietnam vet, former MASH unit nurse, colleague, collaborator, and now my wife of 28 years—has remained a major influence. The emerging community of clinical revolutionaries who responded to veterans' distress, tried to understand the source of their suffering, effectively challenged the psychiatric establishment, and succeeded in getting PTSD accepted as an official diagnosis by the American Psychiatric Association influenced me greatly. Their example made it possible for me to move forward despite the relative isolation in which I was working. These include Robert J. Lifton, Chaim Shatan, Jack Smith, Art Blank, Sarah Haley, Charles Figley, John Wilson, and others.

When I began to chair the Special Committee on PTSD, I became a part of this dynamic community of scholars, clinicians, and advocates who were determined to further the understanding and treatment of PTSD. Larry Kolb was especially inspiring because of the combination of erudition, experience, and fire he brought to this mission. Others who were especially influential were Terry Keane and Spencer Falcon, who had already carried out research on PTSD assessment and treatment, as well as Fred Gusman, who showed me what could be accomplished in a clinical program if you had the courage, tenacity, and tactical skills to make it happen.

It was through Larry Kolb that I was introduced to the seminal work of Abram Kardiner, through John Mason and Earl Giller that I was first exposed to hypothesis-driven neurohormonal research, and through Bessel van der Kolk that I discovered the possibility of understanding PTSD through a biological model. I rediscovered the work of Walter

Cannon and Hans Selye as I began to conceptualize PTSD as a failure of adaptation to overwhelming stress. Larry Kolb, Terry Keane, and David Foy sent me back to my psychology textbooks to review classic work on Pavlovian and operant conditioning paradigms underlying fear, avoidance, and stimulus-driven behavior. Other major influences include Edna Foa and Patti Resick's elegant, conceptually driven cognitive-behavioral treatment approaches, Dennis Charney's translation of basic neuroscience into clinical practice, and Bruce McEwen's fundamental work on stress allostasis and neuroplasticity. Finally, Bob Ursano has helped me appreciate the important differences in preparing for normal versus pathologic reactions following acute catastrophic exposure within both civilian and military contexts.

Thanks to these influences, I believe that the scientific foundation of PTSD rests on the pillars of three distinct scientific traditions: learning theory, neuroscience, and stress and adaptation. I further believe that effective clinical approaches need to be grounded in such a conceptual and empiric context.

HOW DO I HOPE FUTURE SCHOLARS WILL BUILD ON MY WORK?

I have always maintained that the trauma field cuts across the entire spectrum of basic, clinical, and social sciences. We can consider everything from molecular mechanisms to public policy in the same breath. The national center exemplifies this perspective. At the molecular level, ongoing research has focused on genetic mechanisms, neurocircuity, neuroplasticity, and brain structures. At the public policy level, post-9/11 initiatives have focused on the development and implementation of interventions at the society/community level to prevent adverse posttraumatic reactions among veteran, military, and civilian populations exposed to catastrophic events. In between is a rich tapestry of scientific and educational activity addressing basic information processing, cognition and memory, the psychobiology of the human stress response, the pathophysiology of PTSD, epidemiologic and cross cultural variations, descriptive clinical phenomenology, development of diagnostic and assessment instruments, randomized clinical trials of psychosocial and pharmacological treatments, research on the relationship between traumatic stress and medical illness, and much, much more.

In my opinion, we have created a large footprint on which others can build. There is plenty of room for a multitude of scholars who wish to investigate traumatic stress from many different perspectives.

My dream for the future is easy to describe but will be difficult to achieve. First, it is to advance our scientific understanding of traumatic stress and its aftermath as far as our conceptual and technological tools will allow. Second, such scientific progress needs to inform clinical practice so that patients will benefit from evidence-based treatments. Third, we need to efficiently translate science into practice and disseminate such information to clinicians in the field. Fourth, translations of practice into science must guide basic research. Fifth, new discoveries about prevention and resilience should inform a proactive public mental health policy in order to prepare society for the inevitable impact of traumatic stress.

My final hope is directed toward politicians and policy makers rather than scholars and clinicians. Most PTSD is preventable. All we have to do is stop war, rape, genocide, child abuse, interpersonal violence, and the perpetuation of other human-made traumatic events. I hope that politicians and policy makers will begin to take more and more notice of the compelling scientific evidence that traumatic stress can ruin brain function, human potential, and the social fabric. I hope that they will be moved to take effective steps to protect the world's population from PTSD and related disorders.

Matthew J. Friedman, 1978

REFERENCES

Foa, E. B., Keane, T. M., & Friedman, M. J. (2000). *Effective treatments for post-traumatic stress disorder: Practice guidelines from the International Society for Traumatic Stress Studies*. New York: Guilford Publications.

Friedman, M. J. (2000). *Post-traumatic stress disorder*. Kansas City, MO: Compact Clinicals.

Friedman, M. J. (Guest Ed.). (1999). *Psychobiological aspects of PTSD*. Seminars in Clinical Neuropsychiatry. Philadelphia: W. B. Saunders.

Friedman, M. J. (2005). *PTSD and acute post-traumatic reactions*. Kansas City, MO: Compact Clinicals.

Friedman, M. J., Charney, D. S., & Deutch, A. Y. (Eds.) (1995). *Neurobiological and clinical consequences of stress: From normal adaptation to post-traumatic stress disorder*. Philadelphia: Lippincott-Raven.

Friedman, M. J., Keane, T. M., & Resick, P. A. (in press). PTSD: Science and practice. New York: Guilford Publications.

Friedman, M. J. & Mikus-Kos (in press). *Promoting the psychosocial well-being of children following war and terrorism*. Brussels, Belgium: NATO.

Green, B. L., Friedman, M. J., de Jong, J., Solomon, S., Keane, T., Fairbank, J. A., et al. (2003). *Trauma interventions in war and peace: Prevention, practice, and policy*. Amsterdam: Kluwer Academic/Plenum.

Marsella, A. J., Friedman, M. J., Gerrity, E., & Scurfield, R. M. (Eds.) (1996). *Ethnocultural aspects of post-traumatic stress disorder: Issues, research, and applications*. Washington DC: American Psychological Association Press.

Mental Health and Mass Violence—Evidence based early psychological intervention for victims/survivors of mass violence: A workshop to reach consensus on best practices. U.S. Department of Defense; U.S. Department of Health and Human Services; the National Institute of Mental Health, the Substance Abuse and Mental Health Services Administration; Center for Mental Health Services; U.S. Department of Justice, Office for Victims of Crime; U.S. Department of Veterans Affairs, National Center for PTSD; and the American Red Cross. NIMH Report, 2002.

Norris, F. H., Friedman, M. J., Reisman, D., & Watson, P. J. (in press). Clinical research in the wake of disasters and terrorism. New York: Guilford Publications.

Ritchie, E. C., Friedman, M. J., & Watson, P. J. (in press). Mental health intervention following disasters and mass violence. New York: Guilford Publications.

Roth, S., & Friedman, M. J. (1998). *Childhood trauma remembered: A report on the current scientific knowledge base and its applications*. Northbrook, IL: International Society for Traumatic Stress Studies.

Wilson, J. P., Friedman, M. J., & Lindy, J. D. (Eds.) (2001). *Treating psychological trauma and PTSD*. New York: Guilford Publications.

Young, B. H., Ford, J. D., Ruzek, J. I., Friedman, M. J., & Gusman, F. (1998). *Disaster mental health services: A guidebook for clinicians and administrators*. Palo Alto, CA: National Center for PTSD.

5

My Life and Work

JUDITH LEWIS HERMAN

EARLY INFLUENCES

My parents are first-generation Americans who lived in New York City. They are the children of Jewish immigrants from Central Europe. My father was a child of working-class parents; his father worked in the garment industry. My mother was the daughter of a family doctor who practiced among the immigrant community on the Lower East Side. Both parents were raised in a secular, socialist tradition; or, I should say, my mother was, and my father found his way to it from his father's pious Orthodoxy. They both became intellectuals—my father a professor of classics, my mother a psychologist—who instilled what I would call Enlightenment and progressive values in their children.

My grandfather, John Block, for whom I am named Judith, was my mother's role model. If she'd been in my generation, I imagine she'd have become a physician. That was not unheard of, but it was very unusual for women of her generation. She went to Barnard College and then did her doctorate at Columbia and started on an academic track to become a research psychologist. Then she was blacklisted because of a short period of membership in the Communist Party. So in the early 1950s, when I was around 10, I was introduced to the reality of political persecution and learned in a very personal way about what people do under those circumstances. There were a lot of dinner table conversations about who was going to testify, who was going to inform on others, who was going to defend the people who refused to inform, and so forth. Both my

77

parents had a keen sense of irony and indignation about all the weaseling, all the fancy excuses that people made to compromise with something that was morally reprehensible. That was a formative experience for me.

My father had never been a member of the Party, so when called to testify before Senator McCarthy, he could answer the key question ("Are you now or have you ever been ...?") and still keep his job. "You're barking up the wrong tree, Mister," he said. My mother refused to testify, invoking her constitutional right under the Fifth Amendment. After that, of course, she knew that she was never going to get an academic position anywhere, so she went a different route and got clinical training. When I was growing up she had a private analytic practice. But she always kept her hand in as a researcher by collaborating with colleagues in the university, and in her later work she tried to bridge the divide between academic research and clinical practice in a way that became a model for me. I should also say that her righteous indignation, her expectation of personal integrity, and the value she placed on standing up for your beliefs came out of actual experience. She also had a keen understanding of power dynamics in social relationships. When I told her that I was interested in psychology and wanted to follow in her footsteps, her advice was "Go to medical school. You'll have more power." She was right.

I left New York in 1960 to go to Harvard, little knowing that I would remain there for most of my professional life. At college I was lucky enough to find a mentor, an anthropologist named Laurence Wylie. He had done a study of a village in France, where he employed the methods of participant observation usually applied in so-called primitive societies. He and his family had lived in the village for a year, and then he had written about his experiences in a deceptively simple manner that was actually very sophisticated. The book had a kind of lucidity and warmth in its storytelling, and it gained a lot of recognition. As a result, Wylie was recruited to Harvard as the C. Douglas Dillon Professor of French Civilization, which was an odd fit for him, because he was so modest and unpretentious.

I don't know if he ever lived up to the grandeur of his endowed chair, but he was a wonderful teacher. He taught his students to keep their concepts very close to direct observation and direct experience. In his seminar on village culture, we read all the classics, but then we immersed ourselves in primary data in the form of field notes, and eventually a group of us went to the village. Our assignment was to keep a journal and to record our observations at first hand and then to see what we could infer from those observations. He also taught cooperative learning. There wasn't a name for it then, but he ran his seminar in the spirit of a Quaker meeting, which was initially quite bewildering to a group of high-powered, competitive students. We would all spout forth to show how smart we were, and he would just listen quietly; then he would say things like, "That's such an interesting idea. And it sounds so much like what your fellow student so-and-so said. Why don't the two of you cooperate and see if you can develop this idea together." And we'd look at each other in horror, because that was sort of *cheating*, wasn't it? Through his actions and through his example, he modeled a different kind of learning and a different kind of intellectual enterprise for me. Later, for a time, I found the same spirit of cooperative inquiry and emphasis on direct experience in the women's liberation movement.

FEMINIST AWAKENING

I had just finished my medical internship when I joined a women's consciousness-raising group in 1970. For me, the women's liberation movement was a logical extension of the activism that was already a central part of my life. I had been involved in the civil rights movement in the early 1960s and then, as the Vietnam War escalated, in the antiwar movement. The term *consciousness-raising* was originated by a friend, Kathie Sarachild, of New York Red Stockings. She had been a classmate of mine at Harvard, and we had both been in Mississippi during Freedom Summer 1964. Like many of the "second wave" feminists who came out of deep immersion in the Civil Rights Movement, Kathie based her organizing method on the grass-roots work she had done in SNCC (the Student Non-Violent Coordinating Committee). This involved bringing people together in small groups to speak personally about the reality of their daily lives. Direct testimony was a way to understand our political condition.

Consciousness-raising was an empiric method of investigation. What one observes about human consciousness, behavior, and relationships is so embedded in a social and political context that it is sometimes hard to see the simplest and most obvious realities and even harder to talk about them. I think that's particularly true of phenomena related to power and control, because these issues are so intensely colored by the emotions of fear, resentment, and shame. It is hard even to pay attention to what women actually say and feel about sex, motherhood, and relationships unless you have a political movement that says: "Forget what everybody else thinks you *ought* to be feeling, what you *ought* to be saying. Get down. Tell the truth. What did you actually think and feel and notice in you body?" You need a safe place to be able to do that. You need a political context to be able to do that.

It was an epiphany for me and for many women of my generation, I think, to apply these methods not only to the overtly political issues of racism and war but also to the supposedly private issues of family life, love, and sex. We began to recognize that oppression takes many forms and that the subordination of women is in fact a profoundly political issue. That is the meaning of the slogan, "the personal is political." It's a very simple idea, but historically, in the 1960s and '70s it was a radical idea. In fact, it still is.

DEVELOPMENT OF INTEREST IN TRAUMA

I began my psychiatric residency in 1970, at the same time that I was participating in my consciousness-raising group. My eyes were opened to the profound and pervasive everyday sexism of the culture and the constant humiliation that women were expected to endure in silence. In my residency program, for example, derogatory remarks and jokes about women were standard fare. In the interest of preserving my own peace of mind and preventing total ostracism, I decided that I would let nine out of ten remarks pass in silence and would only object to every tenth insult. Even so, I was constantly speaking up. I got along really well with the nurses as a result.

I think I was able to listen to my women patients more openly because of this parallel experience. And what happens when you start listening, really listening, to women? They start unburdening themselves of their secrets. Two of my first patients were women who had come to the hospital after attempting suicide. In the course of therapy, both disclosed histories of incest. As my patients and I came to understand how their childhood experiences had shaped their lives, the shame lifted, and with it the despair. These women got better. Therapy was liberating.

When I finished my residency I went to work in a storefront women's clinic, where I saw more and more patients who reported histories of incest. I was meeting for peer supervision with Lisa Hirschman, a colleague, who had just finished her psychology training. She too was encountering many incest survivors. We kept wondering "What's going on here? Is this an epidemic? If so, why isn't anyone saying anything about it?" We kept waiting and waiting for someone else to write about it but nobody did, so finally we decided it was up to us. What gave us the courage was our relationship with each other; neither one of us would have attempted this alone. Also, we had both come out of consciousness-raising, having learned that it was permissible to trust our own direct observations even if we were beginners and even if what we saw contradicted the established wisdom.

At the time, the *Comprehensive Textbook of Psychiatry* estimated the prevalence of incest at one case per million. Yet in short order Lisa and I were able to collect 20 cases, just from our own local community network. We published our first paper in *Signs*, a women's studies journal, in 1976. Even before it was published, the manuscript was passed from hand to hand, and we started getting letters from women all over the country saying things like "I've never told anyone. I thought I was the only one." These are classic statements of oppressed people who need a movement and don't know it. At this point we knew we were onto something real. With Lisa's collaboration, I went on to write my first book, *Father-Daughter Incest*, which was published by Harvard University Press in 1981 and is still in print. The book contributed to the recognition of incest as a serious social problem.

After the book was published, I reentered the academic world. I went to work in the Department of Psychiatry at Cambridge Hospital, one of the teaching hospitals affiliated with Harvard Medical School. Here I had the good fortune to meet my colleague Mary Harvey, who had just moved to Boston from Washington DC, where she had worked at the National Institute of Mental Health. Mary had just completed a national study of exemplary rape crisis centers. As a community psychologist with a background of social activism, she had very clear ideas about what a model program should be. Cambridge Hospital offered us the opportunity to build a program to serve the mental health needs of crime victims. This was the birth of the Victims of Violence program and the start of our 20-year, ongoing collaboration.

Around this time also I had the good fortune to make the acquaintance of Bessel van der Kolk, who briefly joined the staff at Cambridge Hospital after having worked for several years at the Boston VA. In his work with combat veterans, he had observed many of the same phenomena that I had seen in my work with abused women. We were both intrigued by the commonalities and sought for ways to pursue this line of inquiry further. We formed a study group that met monthly in people's homes. Bessel, with his boundless energy, insatiable curiosity, and an international collegial network, was the principal organizer. The group brought together people who worked with survivors of many different types of trauma: combat veterans, prisoners of war, abused children, battered women. For several years, this group was one of my main sources of inspiration.

Bessel and I also collaborated on a study of Borderline Personality Disorder, a condition that mainly afflicted women. In the rage and self-hatred of the reviled borderline patients, I thought I recognized the features of the incest survivors I had come to know so well. Bessel agreed that the clinical picture looked to him like a complicated traumatic disorder. J. Christopher Perry, a colleague at Cambridge Hospital, was conducting an ongoing study of people with borderline and other personality disorders. He had gathered a great deal of in-depth information about his subjects but had never asked them about experiences of childhood abuse and neglect. Though skeptical of our hypothesis, he agreed to allow me and Bessel to interview his subjects, blind to their diagnoses. We found that Borderline Personality Disorder was strongly and specifically related to a history of childhood abuse. We published our initial findings in the *American Journal of Psychiatry* in 1989. These findings have since been confirmed by many other investigators.

With the Borderline study complete and the Victims of Violence Program well established, I thought it was time to attempt an overview that would delineate the common features of psychological trauma. I sought to unify a diverse body of knowledge and to develop concepts that would apply equally to the experiences of war and political violence, the traditional sphere of men, and to the experiences of domestic and sexual life, the traditional sphere of women. This was the genesis of my second book, *Trauma and Recovery*, published by Basic Books in 1992. The book has been widely read and has been translated into 14 languages.

MOST SIGNIFICANT CONTRIBUTIONS AND FUTURE DIRECTIONS

I believe that my main contribution has been to further the understanding of the psychology of oppression. My work has always followed the line of intersection between the social dynamics of power and the psychology of human relationships. I have attempted to elucidate the ways in which people are formed and deformed by relationships of dominance and subordination. These relationships are always imposed and maintained by violence; therefore it is important to understand the psychology of terror. Often, however, the violence is socially invisible; this is especially true when oppressive relationships are socially legitimated or condoned. In these circumstances, power is maintained by collusion and secrecy; therefore it is important to understand the psychology of shame.

I formulated the concept of Complex Post-Traumatic Stress Disorder to describe the pathology that results from experiences of prolonged and repeated exposure to violence. The concept was validated in the United States in field trials for the fourth edition of the *Diagnostic and Statistical Manual* (DSM-IV) and I believe it will turn out to be robust across cultures; a similar concept has been recognized in 10th edition of the *International Classification of Diseases* (ICD-10). Interestingly enough, this concept remains controversial for the same reasons that, to my mind, make it interesting. It doesn't fit neatly into established diagnostic categories. The DSM-IV committee didn't like it because they didn't know where to put it. Is it an anxiety disorder, a dissociative disorder, a somatiform disorder, or a personality disorder? Actually, it's all of the above, which, if you wanted to think about it, might tell you something worth knowing about the connections among body and mind, consciousness, and self.

Of course the phenomena I've described as Complex PTSD don't go away simply because we don't know how to categorize them. Investigators from very different backgrounds keep stumbling across these same phenomena and are finding the formulation of Complex PTSD to be useful. So I'm hoping that by the time DSM-V is complete, we will have official recognition of this concept within the diagnostic canon.

If traumatic disorders are afflictions of the powerless, then empowerment must be a central principle of recovery. If trauma shames and isolates, then recovery must take place in community. These are the central therapeutic insights of my work, and I believe they have held up well across cultures and over time. Certain principles follow regarding the appropriate roles of patient and therapist. It is most important to recognize that the patient is in charge of his or her recovery. The therapist is an ally, a witness, and a consultant. Treatment is not a protocol that we impose on patients. We are not looking for *compliance*; our patients have had quite enough of that already. At best, we serve as a bridge for our patients from social isolation to safe and supportive community. That's one reason among many why groups, self-help, and social action are all important components of recovery.

To me, the study of psychological trauma is and always will be an inherently political project, because it calls attention to the consequences of oppression. As the field of traumatic stress studies has gained legitimacy in recent years, scientific inquiry within the field has entered a more conventional phase. This is a mixed blessing. I continue to believe that the study of history and politics must go hand in hand with our studies in psychology and neurobiology. The most interesting questions tend to lie in those areas that we don't yet understand, areas that are murky and confusing, emotionally laden, and riddled with controversy. If you are a young investigator who wants to get ahead, you should probably avoid interesting questions like the plague. But if you really want to be a scientist, if you really want to figure out how the mind works or how society works, those are the places to go.

Judith Lewis Herman, 1977

6

A Life in but Not Under Stress

MARDI HOROWITZ

WHAT WERE THE EVENTS IN YOUR LIFE THAT LED TO
YOUR INTEREST IN TRAUMA?

I realize now more than I did at the time that I was alert to issues of trauma because of stressor events I experienced early in my own life. Some of these experiences included being sent off, as a 5-year-old child, to live at a school away from home; having a hemorrhage after a tonsillectomy; being in close proximity to a dog as he attacked and seriously injured another child; and being violently attacked by two older boys.

All these events occurred before I was 10 years of age. When I was 20, working as a patrolman for the Fish and Wildlife Service, I had a near fatal experience, induced by my own too-optimistic error of judgment. I had ventured by foot, in my waterproof hip boots, across a muddy bay more than a mile from my anchored boat, knowing that the tide was due in. There were immense tides, up to 18 feet in depth, and I had underestimated not so much the speed of the water coming in but how much it would slow me down, especially when it tipped over the top of my boots and filled them with water. I had long minutes to think this over as I took off my boots and clothes and swam through the cold water, and a few nightmares afterwards.

These were vivid experiences without sequelae other than occasionally intrusive memories and bad dreams. Every life has analogous events, and my life was less traumatized than many. I think the thing that influenced me was a kind of mindfulness about it all. I learned to observe the workings of my own consciousness, especially in review of my error in judgment.

The pathway that really led me into the field of psychological response to stress was similar to the movement of a crab crawling sideways. Before medical school, I had decided to become a researcher. I had assisted my high school chemistry teacher, Mr. Toon, in setting up demonstrations for classes. I also assisted my UCLA chemistry instructor, Professor Stone, who was doing research on new fire extinguisher chemistry. In psychiatric residency, Dr. Jurgen Ruesch steered me toward the study of nonverbal communication. I chose visual imagery as a mode of communicating with verbally uncommunicative patients. I was thinking about finding out more about conscious and unconscious mental processes.

I did the usual library research and felt there was no good theory about the psychology of visual cognition. I embarked on clinical studies of images and visual symptoms. I wrote position papers; these became my first book, *Image Formation and Cognition* (Horowitz, 1970; happily this is still in press, in a third edition called *Image Formation and Psychotherapy*). After residency, I served in the U.S. Navy and studied marine military advisors in Vietnam who were brought back because of mental problems. Some had intrusive visual imagery from combat experiences. After the Navy, I was awarded an NIMH Research Scientist Development Award to study visual imagery, especially the cognitive processes involved in dreaming. I also became a psychiatric consultant to local naval and military hospitals and a Veterans' Administration hospital, where the staff doctors presented cases to me.

My initial hypotheses about dreaming were contradicted by a series of subjects who were deprived of rapid-eye-movement (REM) sleep in the laboratory, so I shifted my stance and methods. I decided to study repetitive and intrusive visual images in waking life in psychiatric patients who presented such symptoms. I used the descriptive and multiexplanation qualitative case-study method: I observed everything I could about the patient's visual experiences. In addition to the method of repeated review of everything the patient associated with these visual experiences, I also added interventions and then observed their effect. That is, I tried various procedures to increase the patient's control, as in ability to shift attention in order to decrease the intrusive quality. I helped patients put the image in mind, dispel it, return it to mind, and change it by efforts of will and/or my directions. My effort was to start a less involuntary review of these experiences—in other words, I tried to shift the experiences from involuntary causation to conscious control.

I immersed myself in intensive methods. I tried psychological tests such as the Thematic Apperception Test (TAT) and the Rorschach. I interviewed with various degrees of directiveness and suggestions. I asked for dreams, fantasies, logical analyses, reveries, and the effects of drawing. For each individual case, I attempted to explain the repetitive unbidden image episodes and their mental contents. I sought every possible explanation, not just one, and its interactive motives. I looked for biological, social, and psychological causative mechanisms and their connection.

As I studied case after case, one explanatory principle stood out, and it operated in many cases: intrusive thoughts in the form of images were frequently derived from perceptions during a traumatic event. The post-combat and postaccident cases in military settings gave concordant observations. They also frequently involved fantasy elaborations and distortions of actual perceptions.

It seemed to me that stress responses after traumatic experiences would be a paradigmatic way to study emotion, memory, and cognitive processing. One would know the event structure and could trace the memories as they were transformed into meanings, into stories that related to self. I decided to focus on symptoms of intrusive thinking that recapitulated past traumatic events. That soon involved studying numbing and avoidance, the paradoxically connected opposite deflection of conscious experience.

I gained valuable information from my (1) series of intensively studied clinical cases, (2) systematic research on published studies of response to serious life events, and (3) laboratory methods of inducing stress in different contexts. I designed experimental and field research studies and received various government and university grants as well as private foundation awards to support my work.

Field studies allowed for the study of people with the same stressor experience who were not seeking psychiatric help. Continued clinical studies led me to open a research clinic for the treatment of people who had symptoms precipitated by stressor life events. This clinic allowed the selection of patients by particular and specific life events. The laboratory experiments allowed for the use of groups of subjects with control and contrast designs.

WHAT HAVE BEEN YOUR GREATEST ACHIEVEMENTS AND CONTRIBUTIONS TO THE FIELD?

I think my contributions have been theoretical, methodological, and empirical. My research findings looped back to improve theory. For example, from clinical studies I became impressed with how people commonly reported intrusive mental representations and demonstrated episodes of warding off, avoidance, and a numbing of emotionality. I developed methods for quantification of these experiences by reliable judgments that were made of videotapes, transcripts, and written self-reports. These content-analysis methods were used for studying time periods after stressors in patients, field subjects, and volunteers for stress-film experiments.

The quantification methods demonstrated the reliability and validity of clinical concepts about intrusive thinking. Intrusive phenomena increased with degrees of emotional subjective stress, intensity of stimuli, and prior traumas related in contents to current stimuli. Even when we induced a range of positive (desirable) and negative (undesirable) demand sets in subjects, it was clear that stressor events increased intrusive episodes. Reliability and validity of findings across clinical, field, and laboratory research modes helped push along the new proposed diagnosis of PTSD by 1980 (as summarized in Horowitz, *Stress Response Syndromes: Personality Styles and Intervention*, published in 1976, and as of 2001 in its fourth edition).

Part of the experiences in defining PTSD involved the sequelae of the Vietnam War. While consulting at a VA hospital, I found that the staff usually did not know if a patient they discussed had been in Vietnam. Because the war was widely regarded as a terrible mistake, the veterans concealed their combat history. Also, the military doctors of the time believed, too hopefully, that the early treatment, optimistic return to duty, and rotations off combat duty would prevent the stress reactions seen so frequently in prior wars. Another VA consultant and I reported our prediction of delayed stress response syndromes after we sought out and found enduring postcombat intrusive and avoidant symptoms (Horowitz and Solomon, 1975). We projected rates of clinical-level stress response syndromes in combat veterans of more than one-quarter of returning military men and women. There was enormous resistance to our findings and predictions, even though others, such as Robert Lifton, Henry Krystal, John Talbott, and Chaim Shatan, held identical points of view. Publications were delayed, for example. Nonetheless, studies of Vietnam veterans were finally conducted, with pressure from the U.S. Congress, and our predictions proved correct.

Many clinicians scoffed at efforts to collect reliable data on patients because mental-emotional processing was too rich and complex a tapestry of changing colors and forms; empiricists thought that the validation of more than a handful of variables was not possible. Investigative clinicians like me tried to bridge this gap. The bridge holds onto the complex subjective bank of mental-emotional processing and tries for objectivity.

It helps, in qualitative studies, to look at forms of conscious experience in addition to the contents. For example, intrusive thinking is a form of conscious experience, and there are many, many contents that could be represented in an intrusive image. A sudden pang of intense feeling is a form: that is, it has a wave of intensity: it could contain various different types of emotion and still be a pang. It is easier to quantify the fact of reporting an intrusive experience than to catalogue all its possible representations. Thus description of form leads to quantitative and more generalizable measures.

Once a general array of forms is identified, clinical syndromes and typologies of people are easier to recognize. Given a system of forms, different judges can examine the same recorded material and fill out the common format, remaining blind to the contents as inferred by other judges. New judges can compare the findings of the blind judges to see if they reach accord using the common format to organize their clinical inferences. In this manner, systematic formats such as configurations of role relationship models for case formulation can be shown. This will enable clinicians to reach a consensus. In the past, there were clinical disagreements as people followed theoretical authority figures without revising what they themselves believed in observing patients (for this sequence of studies see Horowitz, 1979; Horowitz & Eells, 1997; Eells & Horowitz, 1992; Horowitz, Eells, Singer, et al., 1995; Horowitz, 1991).

Through the development of useful tools for consensus, complex theories can be based on a series of single case studies. Qualitative understanding can be buttressed by selective quantitative measures of a few variables that are representative of larger arrays of qualitatively analyzed variables. In this way, theories of mourning and posttraumatic personality reschematization can be addressed (Horowitz, 1987, 1998). Diverse brands of psychotherapy can be put together for a common theoretical purpose (Horowitz, 2003). New definitions of important tenable but outmoded theories of how psychic defenses work can be advanced and supported by evidence of reliability and predictive statistical significance (Horowitz, Znoj, & Stinson 1996; Horowitz & Znoj, 1999; Horowitz, Stinson, & Milbrath, 1996).

Putting the methods together allowed my colleagues and me to use stress response as a way to reconsider cognition, emotion, and motives in a general theory of conscious and unconscious mental processing. Our revisions and additions included several key aspects. One was the use of an information processing model that could explain seemingly opposite phenomena, such as a person having intrusions on the one hand and inhibitions of processing on the other. The second was an effort at biopsychosocial integration. At each of these sectors of explanation, the effort was to avoid reductionistic thinking and to look for intercausalities. It seemed essential to understand multilevel processing, which could contain the contradictions so inherent in the human mind, with its modularity of subsystems. A stressor event could never be seen as acting alone; it occurred in contexts.

By advancing a cognitive-psychodynamic theory, which included person schemas present before the trauma, the assembled model could explain the symptoms of PTSD: why seemingly opposite deflections from ordinary consciousness occurred, with intrusions on the one hand and serious avoidances, numbing, or denial on the other. Moreover, individual variation and predispositions could be explained in terms of the individual particularized mismatch between new information, retained in active memory, and enduring attitudes, maintained as slowly changing schemas. A completion tendency kept processing going until either the new information was modified to fit enduring schemas or the schemas were modified. Until then, various defensive control maneuvers might be used to avoid dreaded, undermodulated states of mind such as searing shame, unending guilt, despairing sadness, or revengeful rage.

This cognitive-psychodynamic theory also provided ways for case formulation and planning treatment intervention. The complexity of layers of schemas, and pre-existing personality conflicts, allowed one to consider blends of approach, from systematic desensitization, graded exposure, to interpretations and support to permit posttraumatic growth through the transformation of personal meaning systems. It also allowed one to predict who and when might be retraumatized by recollections, and who might be helped by instructions to recollect traumatic memories.

My colleagues and I constructed a variety of scales for assessing intrusion and avoidance, or denial (denial requires a clinician's inference, avoidances can be self-reported). The most influential of these has been the Impact of Events Scale, because it is an easily repeatable self-report of subjective distress (Horowitz, Wilner, & Alvarez, 1979; see recent comparative statistics in Sundin & Horowitz, 2002, 2003). Other scales were diagnostic, as in the empirical demonstration of the reliability and validity of a new syndrome, Complicated Grief Disorder (Horowitz, Siegel, Holen, et al., 1997).

In review of clinical cases over time, it became clear that trauma and personality were inextricably linked. Identity and relationship patterns determined, in part, what would be traumatic, how it would be traumatic, and if and how mastery might be achieved. Trauma itself had an impact on identity: It could cause a shift from competent to incompetent images of self, from attractive to unattractive images, from a strong sense of strength to a sense of weakness or a return to childlike status, as well as a shift from having a coherent identity to depersonalization or dissociative experiences. Trauma, or better yet the course of coping with it, could also have a harmonizing effect, leading to posttraumatic growth in identity and relationship skills such as empathy.

The accumulation of cases and review of videotapes and transcripts led to several other contributions. One is a method of case formulation called Configurational Analysis (Horowitz, *States of Mind*, 1979; Horowitz, *Understanding Psychotherapy Change*, 2005. Another is the use of this cognitive-dynamic integration to develop a manual for brief therapy of stress response syndromes. This was, I think, important because, as summarized recently in the book *Treatment of Stress Response Syndromes* (Horowitz, 2003), a treatment technique that is useful in even a majority of cases can be harmful to a handful. As just one example, re-experiencing and exposure operations can help in both processing and desensitization, but such techniques can also retraumatize a patient and prolong the pathological condition.

A third contribution was developing a theory about achieving a positive change through the mourning process. A theoretical model of mourning helped us understand seemingly paradoxical findings (Horowitz, 1990, 2001). The avoidance of grief reminders is such an example. A conscious choice might be a sign of coping and mastery. Extreme denial and disavowal could lead to reduction in intrusive experiences and pangs of feeling but prolong the work of mourning. The result could be character constrictions and veiled sorrow. We remained attuned to the difference between *self-report* scales such as the avoidance measure of the Impact of Events Scale (which requires conscious recognitions to lead to ratings) and *observer reports* of denial. We attended to observation and measurement of topic inhibition, emotional dyselaborations, and other defensive control processes. Observers can score what is manifested on behavioral analysis of narratives but not "known" by the subject and so not assessed by self-report measures.

My study of mourning deepened a theory of how identity and affiliation beliefs are reschematized. Reschematization is a form of posttraumatic growth that has to occur if the person is to achieve accord between inner working models of self in the world. A slow process seems to be as fast as human beings can achieve such changes. The process is aided by insight but requires acceptance, coping choices, new decisions, and repeated actions to institute new behavioral patterns.

The theory is summarized in my book *Cognitive Psychodynamics: From Conflict to Character* (Horowitz, 1998). I hoped in this book to help clinicians to understand their patients more fully, to help them facilitate such silver linings to the dark cloud of a trauma as the following:

1. Advancing and priming the patient's more competent, attractive, mature, and coherent self-concepts
2. Advancing and priming his or her more harmonized, less ambivalent attachments to others
3. Helping the patient to acquire and enhance courage, empathy, and compassion as traits of character

WHO WERE THE PEOPLE WHO MOST INFLUENCED YOU TO MAKE THESE CONTRIBUTIONS?

The theoreticians who were most influential on me were Sigmund Freud on defense, Erik Erickson on identity, John Bowlby on attachment, Irving Janis on information processing, and Richard Lazarus on methods for experimental study of stress. Jerome Singer gave me generous advice and support and has been a friend and lifelong colleague from whom I have gained in every way. Betty Picket, Earnest Haggard, Bert Booth, and David Hamburg of the NIMH Research Scientist unit were tremendously supportive. Those who mysteriously "found me" have included the board of directors of the John D. and Catherine T. MacArthur Foundation, John Conger, William Bevan, Jonas Salk, and Murray Gell-Mann, who were most encouraging in helping me to form and lead their program on conscious and unconscious mental processes.

I will not list here my colleagues in the actual research, having done so elsewhere numerous times, but I must pay special tribute by naming Nancy Kaltreider, Charles Marmar, Daniel Weiss, Nancy Wilner, Sandra Tunis, Tom Merluzzi, Charles Stinson, Constance Milbrath, Mary Ewert, George Bonnano, Hans Znoj, and Eva Sundin. Robert Wallerstein, my department chairman, gave me the clinical resources to get the work started, leading to two NIMH Center grants and two 5-year awards from the MacArthur Foundation, in addition to various research grants.

HOW WOULD YOU HOPE CURRENT AND FUTURE TRAUMA SCHOLARS WILL BUILD ON YOUR WORK?

The field has had enormous growth and increasing breadth and depth. It does have a frontier that needs more work. At that frontier, I suggest we need to integrate therapies according to a general theory of change. We need to find out more about trauma and personality interactions. I do want to close on a note more methodological than substantive. I argue for more process-of-change research, more multivariable efforts at case formulation, and more readiness to get at conscious and unconscious complexity in how and why a trauma gets mixed into a life story, even into character itself.

So the bottom line of what I suggest to new investigators is this:

1. Use and develop an integrated theory that is open to emotional unconscious mental processing as well as conscious thoughts and expressed emotions.
2. Recognize that while standard measures are useful, we need new measures of newly conceived variables.
3. Consider that causation is usually multivariant; hence designs of one variable correlated with one other variable are limited.
4. Think through a sequence of studies before embarking on a time-consuming course.
5. Be suspicious of easy, ordinary variables such as demographic characteristics. I think matters are more complex than male-female, young-old, ethnic group, rich-poor, educated-uneducated, etc.
6. Even in a multiple-subject study, take a few subjects and record in-depth interviews with them. Review these records until you

practically memorize them. Understand how subjects developed what they reported on the scales you used in the big study. See where the intensive subjects fit on a scattergram of those group-measured variables.

7. Examine the items used in rating scales to derive the scores on your variables. Relate your in-depth understanding to the items and the array used to create variables into the big study. Now write out a theory of how correlations between variables might work.

8. Argue with existing theory until more truth comes out.

9. Grant review committees do not spark new ideas. Be bold anyway. Let new questions emerge, and then pursue a revised research design. Avoid the ruts. I wish you both good results and much serendipity.

Mardi Horowitz, 1976

REFERENCES

Eells, T. D., & Horowitz, M. J. (1992). Methods for inferring self- schematization. *Psychoanalytic Inquiry, 3*, 32–34.

Horowitz, M., & Znoj, H. (1999). Emotional control theory: A revision of the concept of defense. *Psychotherapy Practice and Research, 8*, 213–224.

Horowitz, M. J. (1990). A model of mourning: Change in schemas of self and other. *Journal of the American Psychoanalytic Association, 38*(2), 297–324.

Horowitz, M. J. (1998). *Cognitive Psychodynamics: From Conflict to Character*. NY: Wiley.

Horowitz, M. J., & Solomon, G. F. (1975). A prediction of stress response syndromes in Vietnam veterans: Observations and suggestions for treatment. *Journal of Social Issues, 31*, 67–80.

Horowitz, M. J., & Eells, T. (1997). Configurational analysis: States of mind, person schemas and the control of ideas and affect. In Eells, T. (Ed.), *Handbook of psychotherapy case formulation* (pp. 166–197). New York: Guilford Publishers.

Horowitz, M. J., Eells, T., Singer, J., Salovey, P. (1996). Role relationship models: A summation (response to eight separate journal invited commentaries on paper: Role relationship model configurations), *Archives of General Psychiatry, 53,* 633–654.

Horowitz, M. J., Siegel, B., Holen, A., Bonanno, G., Milbrath, C.,& Stinson, C. (1997). Diagnostic criteria for complicated grief disorders. *American Journal of Psychiatry, 154*(7), 904–911 (cover article).

Horowitz, M. J., Stinson, C. H., & Milbrath, C. Role relationship models: A person schematic method for inferring beliefs about identity and social action. In Colby, A., Jessor, R., & Shweder, R. (Eds.), *Ethnography and human development.* Chicago: University of Chicago Press.

Horowitz, M.J., Wilner, N., & Alvarez, W. (1979). The Impact of Event Scale: A measure of subjective stress. *Psychosomatic Medicine, 41*(3), 209–218.

Horowitz, M. J., Znoj, H, & Stinson, C. (1996). Defensive control processes: Use of theory in research, formulation, and therapy of stress response syndromes. In Zeidner, M., & Endler, N. (Eds.), *Handbook of coping* (pp. 532–553). New York: John Wiley & Sons.

Sundin, E., & Horowitz, M. (2002). Horowitz Impact of Event Scale: Psychometric properties. *British Journal of Psychiatry, 180*(3), 205–209.

Sundin, E., & Horowitz, M. (2003). Horowitz Impact of Event Scale: I. An evaluation of 20 years of usage. *Psychosomatic* Medicine, *180,* 205–209.

7

Fully Primed

LAWRENCE C. KOLB

Hearing the voice of Charles Figley, the editor of this volume, on November 30, 2003, was most enlivening. For some years, I had exchanged no information with any of my colleagues in the Veterans Administration (VA) or with any of the former patients whom I saw with the condition of posttraumatic stress disorder (PTSD). As soon as Professor Figley reintroduced himself, I knew what he would ask me. I knew he had the editing of a new book in mind and would I, if possible, contribute something to it. There was some doubt in my mind as to whether this could be done. But with encouragement from my children, it seemed to me that such a step might be most stimulating and perhaps informative. I recalled his great contributions and the organizations of the International Society for Traumatic Stress Studies (ISTSS). Dr. Figley informed me that he had called to learn whether I might make a contribution to a new volume on the history of research into PTSD. It was his hope that those who had received the Pioneer Award from the society or comparable distinctions would be willing to undertake the writing of autobiographical chapters that pertained to the development of the ideas in relation to the subject of the award.

Ever since that day, my mind has been occupied with memories of my experiences after I accepted an appointment in the office of the Chief Medical Officer of the Bureau of Medicine and Surgery of the Department of Veterans Affairs. This was Dr. Jack Chase. Dr. Chase proposed to me that I become the first distinguished physician in psychiatry. He described this senior group as one to provide information on the various specialties. He advised me that the appointees might make their own decisions as to the sites of their offices; that each would be supported by a full-time secretary and also annual travel monies to make visits throughout the system. Dr. Chase mentioned that many of the previous appointees had used these funds to conduct teaching operations in the system's various hospitals and clinics.

The proposal by Dr. Chase was one that I certainly felt I should consider, as I was about to retire from my commissionership of the Department of Mental Hygiene for the State of New York. However, it was my wish to discuss the issue of acceptance with Madeleine, my wife, and others. This would require a few weeks of consideration. Before leaving Dr. Chase's office, it struck me that in some way I was assuming an obligation. I wished to know more about his offer and inquire of Dr. Chase what his expectations were for my appointment. I inquired of Dr. Chase exactly what the expectations were from the appointee. His reply was simply "Do whatever you can for the veterans." After discussion with Madeleine, I returned to advise him of my willingness to accept the position the VA was offering.

MORE THAN JUST A WALK ACROSS THE STREET

It so happened that the offices of the N.Y. State Department of Mental Health were immediately across Holland Avenue from the VA's offices. On the morning of my departure, I visited my office on the south side of the avenue, saw my administrative staff there, and then moved from the offices on the top floor of one building on Holland Avenue to the midsection of the fifth floor in the Albany Veterans Medical Center. I introduced myself to the hospital director of the VA Medical Center on the north side of the street. Following our brief initial meeting, he escorted me to a small office on the fifth floor, where I was to be housed. The next morning, I was seated alone in a small office under a 25-watt light bulb.

Some feelings of doubt about my decision to retire to this new job were accompanied by a sense of depression. That seemed like a negative attitude and I commenced to consider how it might be modified.

Two thoughts crossed my mind. One was that I would consult the directors of the other medical and surgical services to ask about the ways in which my activities in that hospital would advance the collaboration between psychiatry and their specialties. The other was to become acquainted with the psychiatrists and psychologists to learn if there was any way I could be helpful.

The chiefs of the medical and surgical services were quite unanimous that it would be helpful to develop a pain clinic for the hospital. An effort along this line fitted well and promised a way in which I could be useful to the Albany Medical Center. Back in the 1950s my office, I being one of the newly appointed psychiatrists to the staff of the Mayo Clinic, seemed to be an unofficial pain clinic. This resulted from my being brought for several days to the bedside of a teenage boy who was in great and apparently uncontrollable pain following the amputation of his right leg, owing to the discovery of a malignant sarcoma in his tibia. My good fortune in being able to help control his pain quickly then led to frequent referrals to other patients. My pain studies led to a number of publications, the one entitled "The Painful Phantom" being most widely read.

The chief of the Psychiatric Consultation Service asked me to cover for him while he vacationed in the summer. He was teaching a senior class group and it was hoped that I would continue this for him. This was very agreeable to me, as in my many years on the staff of Presbyterian Hospital in New York City I had done such things while establishing the consultation service in that hospital.

While making consultation visits with the medical student group, one of the first patients seen was a young man on the orthopedic service. The request for the consultation was very cryptic. It merely stated that the patient was giving the nursing staff trouble in management. With no idea of what meaning that had, I advised my young friends that we would only learn by approaching, listening to, and talking with the nurses first. At the same time I once again gave the students my observations that the best information in the hospital as regards patient behavior generally came from the nursing staff, and that they should be seen in the course of most consultations.

We went down to the ward to find a young man lying in an orthopedic bed with his right leg suspended in a sling and extended upward and outward. Quite obviously, there was an infection to his thigh, as there was an open draining wound. I asked the nurse to remove the dressing. We saw that the wound was filled with maggots. He had an osteomyelitis of the tibia. It was not unusual in those days, when one had such a lesion, for the surgeon to implant maggots in order to clean the wound.

I introduced myself as a psychiatrist and told the young man that we had been asked to consult with him in light of the difficulties he seemed to be having with the nursing staff. He admitted that such was the case. When inquiries were made as to how he thought this happened, he told us he felt that the nurses' demand that he remain in bed during the night was difficult for him to comply with, particularly as he was having bad nightmares. When the nurses demanded that he return to bed, he often refused. He was then asked to tell us about his nightmares and his difficulty sleeping. He could not control his bad dreams.

My following questions came from a list that we regularly used in examining men who had come under fire while engaged with the enemy. This patient told us that he had served as a U.S. Navy medic with the marines assigned to a combat unit in Vietnam. He was the first Vietnam combat veteran I had seen. I asked him if it had been a gunshot wound and had this been received from the enemy. He looked at me and then began to cry. Imagine the scene! Five of us standing around the bed of this young man whom the nurses had found difficult to manage at night in the VA hospital. When he was able to control his crying, we asked him to tell about his dreams and about his experiences while in Vietnam. He described to us an unexpected ambush of the unit with which he was working. In the field, he experienced a great deal of fire from the Viet Cong. He heard one of the men screaming for help nearby and moved toward him. As he did so, he was hit in the leg. He was able to give himself some analgesic but nevertheless had a great deal of pain. The firefight continued for some time, with a wounded soldier still screaming for help nearby. He was very upset at being unable to get to him. The enemy eventually withdrew, but for 3 hours he and the other wounded man lay in a field, waiting to be picked up.

Then, taking the students aside, I related to them some of my past history in studying and treating "combat fatigue" in patients during World War II.

That brought to mind a number of my experiences at Johns Hopkins before I entered active duty in the Navy. At that time, I was appointed a fellow in neurology and my chief was Dr. O. R. Langworthy. He was professor of neurology and directed the research lab in that discipline. I was the first research fellow to be appointed to his department. He was a person who influenced me greatly. At Johns Hopkins, a number of other fellows in the neurosciences added to my education, and I am indebted to them for what they brought to me.

I had a number of years of training as a neurologic fellow at the Johns Hopkins Hospital. Here I became acquainted with the startle reflex, during a period when I learned of the Tennessee falling goats and their startle reflex. Early on as a neurologic fellow at Johns Hopkins, I had a roommate, an anatomist from Tennessee, who told me about an unusual condition in some herds of goats. When frightened, these goats would jump and fall head over nose. After a few moments of rest, they would get up and run on again. It happened that I had been telling him about the myotonic patients I had seen in the neurologic clinic some time before. Thinking about the Tennessee goats and the case of Thomsen's disease (myotonia congenita), it seemed to me that there was a similarity. I purchased a few goats and had them sent to Baltimore and ran an experiment in which we nested the goat in the sling for a couple of minutes. We had heard that the goats needed to be startled in order to induce the falling. There was no question that this was a case learning of then-recent discovery that quinine effectively relieved the tendency to have a myotonic reaction. I found that my goats were just the same. This was the first time I had heard of the startle reflex. These observations were later published (Kolb, 1928).

It was at Hopkins that I learned of Pavlov and conditioning (Pavlov, 1928). Just before my fellowship was completed, there was a year of study at the National Hospital Queens Square, London. There one of my mentors, Dr. Arnold Carmichael, put me on a team to study with him the transmission of nervous impulses in the sympathetic nervous system. This was where I learned to use and understand a polygraph (Carmichael et al., 1941). Thus I came well prepared to investigate PTSD.

On December 14, 1941, I was ordered to active duty with the Navy. My assignment was to the Naval Hospital at Portsmouth, Virginia, under Dr. George N. Raines. A few months into this posting, he detailed me to examine a young aviator from the Pacific fleet with a clinical problem new to me. I did not know that my driving interest in PTSD was about to begin.

The patient was a lieutenant aboard an aircraft carrier that had been sunk by Japanese kamikaze fighters. After struggling in the ocean for some time, he was picked up by a boat crew from another ship. The young man said, "I thought I was going to die." I went on to discover that he felt nervous and shaky, had trouble sleeping, and then dreamed of dive bombers descending on carriers. Later, he described to me his fearful dive bombing of a Japanese cruiser before returning to the aircraft carrier. This was my first patient with symptoms of what was then called "combat fatigue."

The young man stayed with us for only a few days, as commissioned officers are usually treated at another facility. Shortly after that, Raines put me in charge of the combat fatigue unit at the Portsmouth Naval Hospital. This was the name for the condition now called PTSD.

Being in the Norfolk Naval Hospital was in itself an education. Raines was a regular medical officer in the U.S. Navy, extraordinarily capable and fearless in his management of critical comments on the decisions made by his staff. He became my first major mentor. Raines and I published four articles on combat fatigue from the Portsmouth hospital (Raines & Kolb, 1948).

Another person of importance to me there was Robert A. Cohen, with whom I shared an office in an abandoned men's lavatory. Our two old oak desks faced each other, and the patients' interview chairs next to the desks made it possible for either of us to often be interrupted by the other. Bob Cohen was undertaking psychoanalytic training at that time. I admired his skill with patients and his capacity to describe their unusual behavior in such a way as to make it understandable.

My seeing the acute psychiatric casualties from the combat scene quickly interested me in reading what was available about the war neuroses. I read what I could find. I discovered Abram Kardiner, Grinker and Spiegel, and others (Kardiner, 1941; Grinker & Spiegel, 1945). The latter book describes treatment with intravenous sodium amytal as a means of rapidly clearing various disassociated states. I started to use this treatment method, called narcosynthesis, and immediately had quick and effective results.

My orders to report aboard a hospital ship came shortly, and I found myself, for the next year and a half, in both the Atlantic and Pacific largely transporting disturbed patients to stateside facilities for treatment.

Shortly after taking over the combat fatigue unit, we received a sailor just returned from the Mediterranean, where he had survived his ship's being torpedoed and sunk. This patient was one of the first to whom I gave intravenous medication for the purpose of therapeutic catharsis. It happened that as I commenced to prepare for him, my new assistant, an officer aboard one of the ships of the Mediterranean, entered the room to observe, as I had suggested he might do. As I proceeded to inject the sodium amytal, our patient leaped off the table and attempted to leave. He was apparently reliving an attempt to fight his way to the main deck and to get overboard. While I was attempting to restrain our patient, there was a dull thud behind me. I turned around and there was my assistant on the floor! Tommy told me later that he also had survived a ship sinking before being returned to Norfolk, and he was associating with the patient's trauma. Later, searching the literature, I could find no account of the production of cognitive dissolution on startle in those with PTSD. Usually our patients recovered consciousness completely within a half hour or so. Both of my patients did just that. Tommy, after being discharged from the Navy, later became a qualified psychiatrist and psychoanalyst and did very well.

After the war, I enrolled in the Washington Psychoanalytical Institute. My personal analyst was Freda von Reichmann. Harry S. Sullivan supervised me in the treatment of two patients. I read his work and heard him lecture on a number of occasions and came to know him personally. It was from the analyst that I sharpened my ability to listen and to detect the repetitive themes in what my patients were telling me.

Returning now to the medic who suffered a wound in his leg, it seemed that he was not particularly expressive of his emotional distress during our interview and indeed might be aided by catharsis under narcosynthesis. A complication of narcosynthesis was the fact that some patients failed to retain a clear memory of what they were doing and saying during an interview. For this reason, I videotaped the patient. Then, in discussing his behavior while under medication, we used the videotape as a confrontation to clarify any distortions in his recollection (Kolb, 1986).

We returned and I advised him of the nature of the treatment and the possibility that he might be somewhat better if he were to have the opportunity of catharsis of this dreadful wounding event. I advised our young patient that I could try this kind of treatment to see if it would help his sleep problems and continued restless anxiety. He was willing to proceed with the treatment.

VIDEO

Recalling that a major problem that patients had when recovering from a cathartic state was recalling what they had said and done while under hypnosis, I decided to seek the help of the VA's fine video laboratory to make a recording of the patient's behavior during treatment. The lab was willing to videotape his reactions, which, once recorded, could be shown later to the patient. This too was the subject of considerable discussion throughout the hospital. The medical students and nursing staff widely gossiped about the combat vet's televised emotional response. That there was someone in the hospital recognizing those with PTSD and also providing them with treatment became a matter of wide discussion. My office became an immediate focus for their referrals through their physicians on the medical or surgical divisions or by themselves if they could not obtain a referral through their own treatment team. We became the center for PTSD in that hospital.

WE NEED AND GET A LAB

Following the initial narcosynthetic trial, amytal was used initially to induce the flashbacks in the men with PTSD. In spite of that, I tried to record heart rate, blood pressure, and respiration during the drugged state. This was after I had decided to commence testing these men by attempting to induce the therapeutic flashback. In the weeks following our initial meeting with the PTSD vets, I listened to the histories of many men and noted a frequent theme in their reports—namely, their experiences of suddenly getting dizzy, short of breath, and hot when they heard a sudden sound or series of sounds that reminded them of gunfire. It seemed to me that we could easily develop a psychophysiologic test and record the reaction of the sympathetic nervous system following their exposure to sound effects reminiscent of the battlefield. This could be done omitting the verbal suggestion at the beginning of the session that the vet was back in Vietnam.

It was most fortunate that Edward Blanchard, then professor of psychology at the State University of New York, was available to collaborate with me. I had decided that my experience with a polygraph would not be sufficient. I needed to find someone who regularly used such an instrument and understood how to analyze the data coming from it. Alan Kraft, a professor of psychiatry at the State University of New York in Albany, spoke to me about professor Blanchard and his ongoing work in recording the responses of those with anxiety disorders in the civilian population. Kraft suggested to me that I meet Dr. Blanchard and inquire of him what to do next. By this time, I had concluded that the behavior of my patients was of reflex origin. It was about the time that I had my appointment to see Blanchard *that all my memories, experiences and meetings at the naval hospitals, and readings on psychiatry and psychology, including Pavlov's conditioning theory, fused.* From these thoughts, I prepared my explanations for the need for a lab as well as a research proposal to carry out research on the psychophysiology of PTSD. It was my hope then that we would develop a diagnostic test to support or make this diagnosis.

Phoning Ed Blanchard, I briefed him on my research and we arranged to meet. He thought it would be worthwhile to test a few patients in whom I had made a diagnosis of PTSD and to determine if they had a psychophysiologic response indicating a sympathetic nervous system arousal following a simulation of combat sounds. One of my patients agreed to be the subject of such a test, which was carried out by some of the doctoral candidates working under Blanchard's supervision. Shortly after the first test was completed, Ed phoned to tell me that indeed they recorded increases in a number of the parameters indicating sympathetic hyperarousal. He thought it would be worthwhile to continue with this work and compare the responses of the Vietnam veterans with those of other groups of young people serving as controls. We thought it vital to establish in the medical center a psychophysiologic laboratory similar to the one at the State University of New York.

We had to agree upon and prepare for the taking on of our first patient for psychophysiologic recording. Accordingly, I prepared a sound tape consisting of approximately 30 seconds each of a symphony orchestra, silence, and combat noises from Vietnam, including an AK-47 rifle, mortars, and some screaming at the end. This tape proved to be very effective and we continued to use it throughout the number of years we worked on this issue.

Ed Blanchard agreed to perform the psychophysiologic examination of combat veterans I had diagnosed as suffering from PTSD. He exposed them to my audiotape, simulating the combat sounds of Vietnam, and immediately after the test I received a telephone call telling me that the man examined had had a physiologic response to the war sounds.

This was a very fortunate arrangement in that there was little communication between the two teams, which operated in geographically distant locations. The needed contact was handled by Blanchard and me, assisted by our secretaries.

Later on, while my patients were still being sent to him, Ed explained the pressures on his clinic and suggested that it might be wise to have a psychophysiologic laboratory in the hospital where I was working. There Louis and I had continued to televise reactions in our patients who, following their exposure to the tape, we thought might have PTSD. These men were all under light barbiturate narcosis, having received intravenous medication from me.

Encouraged by our findings of physiologic arousal following the audiotape of battlefield sounds, it seemed to me we that were encountering evidence of conditioning in these men with clinical PTSD. I thought about the potential meanings and usefulness of this test to the veterans. I wrote to the chief medical officer requesting an interview to further our studies of the Vietnam veterans and to discuss our need for a laboratory for this purpose.

On the day I arrived in Washington, Dr. Earl Brown, serving as the acting Chief Medical Officer, met with me as Dr. Chase was away. I told him about our experiences with the combat veterans during the narcosynthetic treatments as well as the responses obtained by Professor Blanchard during the psychophysiological testing. I went on to state my belief that we had the opportunity to discover an important determinant of PTSD as well as to develop a biological/diagnostic approach to those with a chronic illness. He listened and agreed to do everything that might be done to support my wish. He was hopeful but not very encouraging.

Within 3 weeks, Dr. Brown's office let me know that they had found a polygraph machine and would arrange with the director of the Albany hospital to set up the laboratory. This was faster than any action taken for any research proposal from any grant that I had ever received.

THE RESEARCH

Louis Mutalipassi and I had been reviewing the initial data in the videotapes of the men first seen, whom we brought to therapeutic catharsis through the previously described audiotapes. We also had Professor Blanchard's reports, in which he noted evidence of sympathetic nervous system arousal following sound stimulation with our audiotape. His reports showed increases in various organ functions due to arousal of the sympathetic nervous system. It was at this time that we decided to publish our first paper on the conditioned emotional response (Mutalipassi & Kolb, 1981).

There were 14 responders to this stimulation. All underwent cognitive dissolution, loss of current reality orientation, and dissociation when taking on some earlier battlefield scenes. In addition to this material, Professor Blanchard had sent us the first reports of an analysis of the psychophysiologic recordings of 9 veterans. We also had available the earliest of Professor Blanchard's reports.

> Eleven combat veterans with the clinical symptomalogy of the post-traumatic stress disorder were re-exposed to the same soundtrack played at different intensities in a fully conscious state, while physiological assessment of heart rate, blood pressure, frontal muscle activity, peripheral skin temperature and skin resistance were monitored on a Grass Model 7D polygraph. Similar exposure and physiological assessment was made of 11 post-doctoral university students of the same age range. Both groups were also stressed with a mental arithmetic problem. The results of the analysis

of the physiological date show that both groups responded similarly when presented with the arithmetic stressor. However, when combat sounds were presented the veterans all displayed significant increases in heart rate, systolic blood pressure and forehead muscle activity whereas the control subjects exhibited not significant changes. One exception was a veteran then on Haldol who also stated that the sounds were unrealistic. This was the first paper on PTSD that came from my office. (Mutalipassi & Kolb, 1981)

We interpreted our findings as meaning that those men who responded to the tapes had an abnormal potential for arousal of the emotion associated with fear (Kolb, 1987, 1989). They had thus a perceptual abnormality with impairment of discrimination and a fixation through emotional conditioning to a startle arousal pattern. Those showing the abnormality did not extinguish the conditioning stimulus, as was usual according to conditioning theory. What had happened? To me it seemed that this deficit might be caused by impairment of the presynaptic neurons of the agonistic system of the brain. We knew that excessive stimulation caused blindness in the visual system and also that excessive sound stimulation caused deafness. It seemed to me that postsynaptic neurons might similarly suffer serious impairment or death. My thought was that this defect, which later we seemed to find existing throughout life in American war veterans, was consequent to cell damage and death in the brain. If malfunction existed in the brain's capacity to desensitize through relearning, as happens in animal experimentation, the system would be worsened by the taking of alcohol or other mind-altering drugs. This was in keeping with our medical findings that the arousal of perceptual disturbance with flashback was recurrent most frequently in those who drank or who were drug abusers. The intensity of the sound system we were using was modifiable, and it was possible to increase the intensity of simulation. In so doing, the patient recorded worsening of his subjective feelings, sweating, heartbeat, and respiration.

One of my patients with severe PTSD, a marine sergeant, told me this story. While trying to decondition himself alone, and in a state of angry frustration, he turned up the volume to the maximum on the recording. He went into a flashback to Vietnam. On coming to, he looked around and found he'd destroyed all the furniture in his room.

Kardiner (1941) identified startle reaction and the often-attending symptoms of anxiety and tension as the central features of the World War I patients. Consider the robot-like behavior that one might expect if a group of PTSD sufferers were exposed simultaneously to an intense, threatening sound, similar to one they may have heard at the time of their trauma. Such scenes have occurred. Dr. Theodore Lidz, who was a psychiatrist at the Guadalcanal Hospital as the campaign started to wind down there, had a way of turning up at various small professional meetings when I was presenting some of this material. Ted never failed to rise to describe the complete chaos in the wardrooms as the patients jumped from beds and rushed here and there to seek safety in hiding in one way or another.

Beyond the psychophysiologic assessment of those suspected of having PTSD, some other studies were commenced, unrelated to the diagnostic process.

Dr. Ralph Gerardi (Blanchard et al., 1986) developed a procedure for uncovering malingering in those with PTSD who were able to simulate responses to the sound stimulation. There were others who also worked on this test from laboratories other than Albany. This piece of work was important in that the test was accepted as proof of the presence of combat-induced stress disorder by the VA Board of Pensions and Disabilities. However, in my opinion, this privilege was sorely needed, for most of these men had grave difficulties in social rehabilitation, including the finding of work, adapting to their families, and so on.

Following the leads we had, from our work and from Mason et al., (1988) and his group, which uncovered evidence of unusually high levels of norepinephrine as well as a discriminating norepinephrine-cortisol ratio in some PTSD sufferers, there were also papers indicating that electroencephlographers were studying PTSD. It occurred to me that there was a need now to stimulate interchange between the various VA groups and laboratories that were engaged in these kinds of investigations. We suggested this to the central office of the VA, who engaged with myself and others in organizing such a conference in Albany.

Also, we commenced trials of treating patients with drugs known to suppress norepinephrine (Kolb et al., 1984). The drugs were proponol and clonidine. Another study along this line was that in which we investigated changes in norepinephrine to combat-related stimuli, comparing Vietnam veterans and Vietnam veterans with known PTSD (Blanchard et al., 1991). A third study along this line was terminated due to the ending of my tenure.

VIDEOTAPES AND EDUCATION

We developed a library of 18 videotapes of narcosynthetic interviews of veterans that were used from time to time for educational purposes. We used some of these tapes when requested. Several of these were shown by me to a subcommittee chaired by then-Congressman John Kerry. This was a House subcommittee on veterans affairs.

Later, the chief medical officer requested my services on a committee to investigate and resolve a public confrontation on the grounds of the VA Medical Center in Brentwood, California.

What had occurred was that one enraged veteran, when denied admission to the hospital, drove his jeep up the central staircase of the VA medical center and into the lobby, shouting many unflattering comments. Soon, vast numbers of veterans appeared in a park-like area around the hospital. There they pitched tents and staged a sit-down siege. Representatives of the group were seen and stated their demands to present their description of events about the reception they were receiving at various medical centers in the area. This was the first time such a confrontation had been arranged by disgruntled Vietnam veterans. The Department of Veterans Affairs was very distressed.

When I arrived in Los Angeles, the other members of the committee were gathering in a conference room that had an outlook over the hospital lawn in Rockwood. There we could see the neat tents as well as a large number of Vietnam vets wandering here and there. I listened to the comments of the committee members as I walked around. There were no introductions. The chairman of our group, who was a deputy administrative officer in the Bureau of Medicine and Surgery, talked a bit about Vietnam veterans. I got the impression that he had a very negative impression of them.

I introduced myself and advised them that I was the psychiatric representative there and that I had brought with me two videotapes. I then described the taking and utilization of televised videotapes in which we had recorded the behavior of men under a light barbiturate anesthesia. I went on to state that I had two such with me and that, if they watched them, they would gain an insight into the suffering of the men who had PTSD. I then gave them a brief history of the men's history and exposure to combat so they would understand what was being acted out. We showed the tapes. It was remarkable how silently attentive the group became as they watched the emotional agony of these two men as they recounted their situations.

When the investigating committee gathered the following day, the members were advised that those in charge had attended a meeting with the Vietnam veterans, heard their complaints about the medical care given them at some of the hospitals, and learned of the wishes of the group in regard to bringing this information to the administrator of the VA. We were then advised that it would not be necessary to remain and that it was expected that the confrontation would shortly be resolved. I returned to Albany and, aside from the newspaper reports of the resolution of the sit-down encampment, heard no more about this confrontation. It impressed me how powerful the showing of those videotapes was in changing some leaders' attitudes.

ACHIEVEMENTS

Our research showing that there exists an abnormal physiological disturbance in the brains of those with chronic PTSD is probably the most significant observation made in the laboratory. I think of the condition as a wound in the head with a physical break in the scalp. This wound that produces a scar is dependent upon repeated, intense, emotional stimuli driven by horrors of excessive exposure to terrorizing situations. These situations threaten the life of the individual and lead to fear-driven emotional states.

The recordings of the responses of the bodily organs on the polygraph are the indicators of the biological reaction. It is the evidence of the biological recurrent abnormality of perception that has been of major significance to those in the medical and psychological field as well as individual patients and the many others to whom they are related. The recognition of this abnormality has opened PTSD to become a medical subject. It has diagnostic, prognostic, therapeutic, and psychological implications. Recognizing PTSD as we do today has brought about a major change in the acceptability of our recent veterans as well as the treatment they receive, both by therapists and the public at large. As regards the latter, I see a great deal of that due to the educational activities of myself and others working in the field. A very great effectiveness of the teaching may have been achieved by the use of television and the presentation of the extraordinarily realistic, anguished behavior of suffering subjects. To me, on all occasions, the audience was caught up with this material. For years I have thought that the behavioral sciences are best illustrated by television. My lab deserves considerable credit for initiating this modern illustration tool to audiences.

Medically, PTSD patients are now managed with much more respect and consideration than before they attained a diagnostic status. The VA accepted the existence of abnormal physiological responses as support for the diagnosis of PTSD. Sick men have been able to obtain disability ratings and their pensions. Many of the social and family problems were relieved. The pharmacologic treatment was initiated and now is given along with the psychosocial treatment.

My support of the proposal for development of the National Center for PTSD, its subsequent approval by Congress, and later development is, to me, a matter of great significance as well. I served on the advisory committee until my retirement.

FUTURE EXPECTATIONS

It is my hope that PTSD as a disorder will become much more widely known. The medical profession and related aids should be at the front line of detection. They should place their questioning of life-threatening situations at the forefront of their clinical examinations. By so doing, preventative therapeutic prescribing in the acute phase might be used to alleviate the symptoms and prevent a progression to a chronic condition. Here I recommend the book on motor vehicle accidents by Blanchard and Hickman. The model of the examination that is laid out in their book could well be used by others (Blanchard & Hickman, 1997).

Preventative therapy is badly needed in the populations suffering natural disasters in the world. I read a report about World War II and of such worldwide catastrophes which informed me that the death toll in many of the primitive cities in Asia and China far exceeded that which we suffered in the 9/11 disaster.

In this vein, it would be my hope that an international consortium of study of natural disasters would arise, such as was established under the aegis of the World Health Organization. In addition to the funding for a central office, it should have monies to support a full-time disaster task force. This group would be sent to the site of an event for a period to study and assist survivors.

My hope is that the new knowledge emerging on synaptic transmission in the PTSD neurosystem will lead to development of drugs specifically designed to modulate the symptoms of startle and disassociation. Disassociation is often found deriving from the intense exposure to a fearful situation. It is indeed an amazing occurrence. In it, the individuals give up current reality and find themselves in an earlier, less fearful event. It is good to see that some of our neurochemists are now considering probing the neurochemical changes that perhaps produce this startling piece of pathology (Blanchard & Hickman, 1997).

Lawrence C. Kolb, 1943

REFERENCES

Blanchard, E. B., & Hickman, E. J. (1997). *After the crash psychological assessment and treatment of survivors of motor vehicle accidents.* 2nd ed. Washington: American Psychological Association.

Blanchard, E. B., Kolb, L. C., Prins, A., Gates, S., & McCoy, G. E. (1991). Changes in plasma norepinephrine to combat-related stimuli among Vietnam veterans with posttraumatic stress disorder. *Journal of Neurologic and Mental Disease, 179*(6), 371–373.

Blanchard, E. B., Kolb, L. C., Taylor, A. E., & Wittrock, D. A. (1989). Cardiac response to relevant stimuli as an adjunct in diagnosing post-traumatic stress disorder: replication and extension. *Behavior Therapy, 20*(4): 535–543.

Carmichael, E. A., Honeyman, W. M., & Stewart, W. K. (1941). Peripheral conduction rate in the sympathetic nervous system of man. *Journal of Physiology, 99,* 338–343.

Grinker, R. R., & Spiegel, S. J. (1945). *Men under stress.* New York: McGraw-Hill.

Kardiner, A. (1941). *The traumatic neuroses of war.* New York: Paul Hoeber.

Kolb, L. C., Harvey, A. M., & Whitehill, M. R., (1938). A clinical study of myotonic congenita and myotonia dystrophy with special reference to the therapeutic effect of quinine. *Johns Hopkins Hospital, Bulletin, 63,* 108–214.

Kolb, L. C., Burris, B. C., & Grifis, S. (1984). Propranolol and clonidine in treatment of post traumatic stress disorder in war. In B. Vander Kolk (Ed.). *Post-traumatic Stress Disorder: Psychological and Biological Sequelae.* Washington DC: American Psudriatric Association.

Kolb, L. C. (1986). Treatment of chronic post distress disorder therapies. *Current Psychiatric Therapies, 23:* 119–127.

Kolb, L. C. (1987). A neuropsychological hypothesis explaining posttraumatic stress disorders. *American Journal of Psychiatry, 144*(8), 989–995.

Kolb, L. C. (1989). Heterogeneity of PTSD. *American Journal of Psychiatry, 146*(6), 811–812.

Kolb, L. C., Ciccone, P. E., Burnstein, A., Greenstein, R. A. *Heterogeneity of PTSD [letter].* *American Journal of Psychiatry, 146*(6): pp. 811–812.

Kolb, L. C., Burris, B. C., & Griffiths, S. (1984). *Propranolol and clonidine in treatment of the chronic post-traumatic stress disorders of war.* In B. A. van der Kolk (ed.). *Post-traumatic stress disorder: psychological and biological sequelae.* pp. 97–105. Washington: American Psychiatric Press;

Mason J. W., Giller, E.L, Kosten, T.R., Harkness, L. (1988). Elevation of urinary norepinephrine/cortisol ratio in posttraumatic stress disorder. *J Nerv Ment Dis, 176*(8), 498–502.

Mutalipassi, L. B., & Kolb, L. C. (1981). The conditioned emotional response. a subclass of the chronic and delayed post traumatic stress disorder. *Psychiatric Annals, 12,* 970–987.

Pavlov, J. P. (1928). *Lectures on conditioned reflexes.* New York: International Publishers.

Raines, G. N., & Kolb, L. C. (1948). Treatment of combat induced emotional disorders in a general hospital within the continental limits. *Journal of the American Psychiatric Association 101,* 331–335.

8

Psychoanalytic Approaches to Trauma: A Forty-Year Retrospective

HENRY KRYSTAL

Sickness, insanity and death were the dark angels standing guard at my cradle and they have followed me throughout my life.

—*Edward Munch (Stang, 1977)*

Before the German invasion, my family lived in the southwest area of Poland, in Sosnowiec. In the winter of 1929, I developed pneumonia and puss in my right lung. Without antibiotics, this was a deadly condition. I was operated on and a rubber tube drain was inserted into my chest. I had to stay in the hospital for three months. This was my childhood trauma, which I survived only because my mother stayed with me all the time. In 1999 I wrote a paper on *resilience*, which won the Hayman prize of the International Psychoanalytic Association. As I write this essay I am reminded coincidentally that in that paper I started by discussing the essential function of "primary" childhood narcissism resulting from the "programming" of the child in a state of secure attachment to the mother that he was loved. This was the single most important asset in promoting survival in Holocaust victims. My mother's loving and caring response and her rescuing and "guarding" me helped me to turn the trauma experience into something that I could live with and reflect upon. Although I was a fragile and sickly boy, by 1939 I was 14 years old and had finished the 8th grade in a coeducational school.

A few months into the Nazi rule, my older brother was ordered to report to them. They announced that the whole group was to be sent "to the East for labor." My parents and brother panicked and escaped to the Soviet occupied part of Poland and made me stay with my grandparents in a "shtetl" in central Poland called Bodzentyn. A shtetl was a small town with a mostly Jewish population. In this way I got separated from my brother and parents and they all perished in the Holocaust.

I remained in Bodzentyn until Yom Kippur in 1942 when the whole Jewish population was eliminated. After surrounding the shtetl with the aid of their Lithuanian, Latvian, and other helpers, the Germans killed every Jewish man, woman, and child they found in their homes, sometimes while they were in their beds or hiding. The ones who followed orders, lined up in the central market place, and were not killed in the "Action" were stuffed into freight cars and shipped to their death in Treblinka. I was in one of two truckloads of young people that they selected for work assignments. I was sent to a labor camp in Starachowice. There were several camps like this in central Poland, where we were put to work in armaments and ammunition manufacturing. The particular camp branch I landed in was on top of a hill where there was absolutely no water, and of course we had no change of clothes. As a result of the consequent infestation with lice, an epidemic of typhus broke out. This was followed by weekly selections. People who could not run fast enough were shot, and the rest of us had to bury them in mass graves.

While I was working in a section of the plant in which we sandblasted artillery machine grenades, I learned to be a machine maintenance man. From that time on I listed my occupation as "schlosser." This means "locksmith," but in the German usage (at least at that time and place) it was meant to denote any metal skilled work, including tool and die making. This accident provided a survival opportunity later.

In the spring of 1944, as the Soviet armies were approaching, the Nazis liquidated this camp and sent us all to Auschwitz. In the months that followed, as we were submitted to the Auschwitz–Birkenau "routines," I did my best to survive one day or rather one moment at a time. We were marched out to work, mostly on roads, while the Capos and SS-man entertained themselves with beating and torturing us. In retrospect, about this time I was about to hit the skids toward a "musulman" death of emotional exhaustion. This was a pattern well known to us prisoners. The clue that reminded me of my desperate state at the time was that I recalled that I used to pray or plead with my mother to help me somehow. This happening reflected both my regression to my childhood trauma state in which my mother rescued me, and the common condition of being no longer able to pray to God after what I had witnessed. (I discussed this issue in detail in my paper on resilience in 1999.) By invoking my mother's image, I preserved my capacity to fight for my survival for some time. However, soon came a development that really tested my courage.

I discovered that I had developed scabies. Usually this is just a nuisance; but in Auschwitz it was a deadly condition because during selections, the sick were sent to their death, and people with skin diseases were their favorite. I had terrible alternatives: to ignore it, and hope for a miracle, or to take the terrible chance of reporting for the sick call. I decided to take a chance. The doctor diagnosed me immediately and sent me to the hospital camp. Every two weeks this place was emptied and the patients were sent to their death in the gas chamber followed by the crematorium. After I was settled down in the hospital bed, a doctor helped me to recover and luckily I got back to my barrack in time.

When I returned to my previous camp in the morning, I realized that I was being identified by my tattoo number and taken with a group of men to a separate barrack. There must have been more then a thousand men taken aside all of whom had arrived the day before in a vehicle from Slovakia. We were taken one at a time for an interview and testing by a Herr Bunsius, the head engineer from the Siemens factory. The tests and quizzes were designed to identify the qualified tool and die makers. At the end of the day the prisoner camp commander announced that 16 people (15 Slovak tool and die makers and I) were selected.

Finally, we were transferred to the Siemens Company "Lager" in Bobrek, a branch camp of Auschwitz. I was not really a qualified tool and die maker, but fortunately there were people in this camp from my hometown, who knew me and/or my family, who had been there for over a year, and they took me "under their wings." I remained there until we were marched out on the death march westward on January 18, 1945. In the middle of a winter night we were marching while we could hear the Soviet artillery quite close by. While marching and freezing in our inadequate clothing, I realized that whoever could not keep up the pace was killed and left by the side of the road. After some time, one of my two buddies weakened and was ready to give up. We took him by his arms and walked on. It is very remarkable that even though I tried to tell this story, and even when I tried to describe it in a paper, I have not been able to regain the memory of what happened after this point. How long we held on to each other, or when and why we stopped I do not remember.

Much later, just before dawn, I seem to have been walking all alone. The marchers, the SS-men with their wagons, even the horse and buggies that were part of the convoy disappeared. They were absolutely all gone, without a trace. I recall some thoughts about hiding or escaping at this point. I cannot really explain why I did not, except that we were already in the German part of Upper Silesia, and I felt that I could not expect any help from anyone. As I kept walking, I encountered an old German soldier. He was leaning against a fence, and carrying his rifle. I do not recall any conversation between us. The next thing I remember is walking with him in a city, with very busy military traffic, controlled by a military policeman at the intersection. Next, I found myself in a camp where the prisoners were "stored." By struggling with others who were packed together on the ground, I "won" a place on the floor to lie down. I took off my coat and wrapped the loaf of bread we were given as we were leaving our Bobrek camp. When I was awakened and ordered to get on the train, my bread was gone. This is when I experienced the worst despair because, in my rage and disappointment about not having escaped or hidden during the night, and after discovering this last blunder, I lost my confidence.

I ended up in the Buchenwald camp where prisoners from all the evacuated camps in the east were kept. This was a bedlam beyond description. Everything was out control. The struggle for survival was down to a struggle for a spot to lie in. After a week or so, the Siemens company representatives sent a list, and had all us surviving former "Bobrek" tool and die makers rounded up and shipped to Siemenstadt, (a suburb of Berlin) to work in tool making in their enormous armaments and ammunition factories there. We did, until one day when there was an air raid. When we came out of the shelter, the factories and the entire town was gone—bombed out. After a short time the Bobrek survivers were shipped away, apparently with the intent to send us to a factory they still had operating somewhere. We never "made it" and after some time we were delivered to Sachsenhausen, one the original Nazi concentration camps. I remained there until April 22 when, on my twentieth birthday, I was put on the last death march westward—again away from the advancing Soviet army. Each day we marched all day and just before darkness set in the SS-men would put our unit in small woods that they had surrounded. Usually they handed out one or two raw potatoes to each of us as they counted us, and we'd lie down on the ground for the night. On May 4, in the morning we discovered that the SS-men disappeared. Slowly, we inched out of the forest till we got to a road where we beheld the Germans giving up their weapons and they were marching to prisoner-of-war camps. A few allied officers were standing by the road supervising the operation. I walked up and spoke to an officer: We were Liberated!

Retrospection. The Genetic view of emotions shows a gradual and orderly development of the human capacity to experience emotions, and a gradual learning to use them as signals in information processing. The are three infantile affect precursors: 1) a state of well being, 2) a state of distress, and 3) "freezing" (or "playing possum"). This last pattern is universal in all animals, but in the human infant it disappears at about two months of age. (Papousek & Papousek 1975). This is the reason why it is often overlooked. However, it needs to be highlighted because it returns in trauma. These affect precursors fulfill then-potential through specific developmental lines: affect *differentiation, verbalization and desomatization*. Out of the state of distress evolve the painful feelings such as anger, guilt, jealousy, shame, anxiety, fear and so on. Our memories and representations of ourselves must be consciously accepted, tolerated and hopefully utilized as signals to ourselves, in the service of successful adjustment. Otherwise they must be handled by repression, isolation, projection, and other (fantasy) defenses. These tend to be experienced as externally imposed "symptoms" Contrary to our subjective experience, we cannot "express" our emotions in the sense of *riddance*. **Emotional self-continence** is a self-evident truth.

Adult Catastrophic Trauma is signaled by fear. When one is confronted with danger that is estimated to be unavoidable and inescapable, one surrenders to it. This view is in harmony with Freud's (1926) statement that "the essence and meaning" of the cause of trauma is the subject's estimation of his own strength and his admission of helplessness in the "Erlebte Situation:" that is the subjective recognition and admission of helplessness in the face of unavoidable, inescapable danger, and a surrender to it.

Once an individual surrenders to his/her subjectively evaluated inevitable fate, the affect changes from fear to the **catatanoid** reaction. This is the point of *onset of the traumatic state*. The individual gives up most or all of his/her initiative and obeys orders. This is a powerfully hypnotic state. The more the subject obeys "the deeper one goes under" and the progression cannot be stopped until one reaches a cataleptic or "robot" state. Being able to establish and maintain the constricted state is a life saving operation.

If the attempt to arrest the progression of such an "automaton-like" state fails, the deepening traumatic state manifests itself in a growing numbing of pain and painful affects, followed by a total loss of self-reliance, initiative, and agency. There is a loss of empowerment and of any assertiveness. The right and the capacity to say "no" and carry out self-defense are progressively paralyzed. At some point the traumatic self reaches a malignant state of progressive blocking of all mental functions. Finally just a vestige of these functions and some capacity for self-observation are retained.

In this state, most normal narcissistic functions, i.e., self-preservation, self-regard, self-defense, self-respect and self-concern collapse and the person is "frozen." Silently present is a massive and dangerous diminution in self-reliance and capacity to maintain self-caring. If the trauma continues to progress it may reach a point when all <u>vitality</u> is suppressed, and the individual dies of psychogenic death, with the heart stopping in diastole (Krystal, 1984). This process is universal in the entire animal kingdom. (Seligman, 1975).

For those who manage to arrest the traumatic progression in the "robot" state, and who must live in such condition for a significant amount of time, there are consequences that last the rest of their lives. The survival in the situation of impasse, or "no exit," occurs in a state of psychic closing off. Survivors undergo a temporary symbolic death in order to avoid physical or psychic death. I have described the traumatic experience in order to prepare us to recognize a number of aftereffects, as direct continuations of some component reactions of trauma. The surrender pattern may be continued with an inability to assert oneself in any later life situation from major to trivial ones. The situation that triggers the trauma response may also produce "primary repression." The percepts (ideas) not compatible with survival of the self are not registered at all, but create a "hole in the associative networks." They are not repressed but repudiated. (This corresponds to Freud's use of the term Verwerfung vs. Verdrängung.) Very commonly there develops a pattern of life-long startle reactions, consisting of the "jump" pattern, not only physically but also in terms of behavior patterns such as a tendency to blunder when scared. The startle is accompanied by *blocking of cognition* experienced as *"freezing"* in stressful situations. In some cases, having identified the symptoms of trauma we are confronted with situations in which we find the *clinical picture of posttraumatic states with alexithymia, and related problems* but no matter how we try, we get no history of trauma. We must assume that this picture represents the aftereffects of infantile trauma.

Considering the aftereffects of psychic trauma: the existence in a chronic state of closing off the affective responses, in a hopeless situation in which the "agitated" anxiety reaction had ceased causes the development a chronic disturbance of affects. Traumatized individuals overreact physically to anxiety and depression. Most become conscious of mostly somatic symptoms of their affects only. The survivors show an *affect regression* in which the affects come up in a *dedifferentiated, deverbalized,* and *resomatized* way. About 1970 I made contact with Sifneos and Nemiah who were working with psychosomatic patients in Boston. There followed a period of mutual stimulation as reflected in many conferences and papers. Eventually the following concepts were evolved, beginning with alexithymia, a term which Sifneos coined (1973).

Alexithymia involves a diminution of the usefulness of affects for information processing. It is recognizable by disturbances in three areas: impairment in the patient's ability to name and localize emotions, and to recognize and use emotions as signals to themselves. The affects are experienced as vague and confusing, and remain undifferentiated and unverbalized. Object representations are characterized by a lack of individual attachment and appreciation. Instead, there tends to be an exploitative quality. The capacity for self-caring, self-comforting and self-regulation are seriously impaired, sometimes to life threatening proportions. The blocking of the normal development of the transitional process causes lifelong impairment in the capacity for "solacing" (Horton, 1981).

Analytic psychotherapy treatment of traumatized patients who show various degrees of alexithymia and psychosomatic diseases or addictions cannot be done successfully with the principles developed for the *neuroses* alone. There is need for preparatory work in the opening phases of the analysis during which one may start demonstrating and explaining the nature of the patient's emotional, affective, and cognitive disturbances (Krystal 1982, 1982-83; McDougall 1972, 1974, 1984). In this process the patient's thoughts of and reactions to having emotions are attended to. One is trying to find out what the patient's conceptions of emotions are. Their "color blindness" about emotions needs repeated attention. Next is the matter of the reaction to "having an emotion" which may reveal deep-seated convictions about what ought to be "done" with affects. Eventually, the analyst may be able to understand and demonstrate the regressions, deficiencies, and arrests that these patients have suffered in the genetic development of affect.

Promoting affect differentiation involves the naming of effects, "interpreting" the story behind the affects, and use of elucidation, confrontation, and interpretation, in order to highlight the differences between adaptive mature responses and the patient's infantile affective responses. The "idolatrous transference" causes the patients great difficulty in receiving and discovering in their analysis, the message about their own powers. They cannot register the possibility and permissibility of overcoming their inner dissociations and blocks. The healing message to the alexithymic patients which is very hard for them to experience and feel, is that *love is real, and that it works*. They have a difficult time imagining that idea. They cannot believe it. They demand instant wish fulfillment. Their view on this matter is: "If you loved me, everything would feel perfect. Since it does not, then you too are offering me "counterfeit nurturance." And: "This I have been getting all of *my* life." The above-mentioned impairment in the capacity to grieve successfully, and thereby to achieve self-integration and the capacity for mutuality, interdependence, and intimacy requires belated attention here. Trauma throws one into the often insoluble dilemmas of "connection or separations," integrity vs. disintegration, and activity vs. stasis. Such conflicts demand our attention in these analyses to a degree that is not as central or essential for "good neurotics." It is clear that these patients are definitely not talented for the psychoanalytic cooperative efforts. In this context it is useful to recall that Sifneos (1972–1973) cautioned that an accurate interpretation, which might produce good results in a "good neurotic" may produce a life-threatening exacerbation in a psychosomatic patient.

If psychosomatic, addictive, alexithymic patients stay in treatment until they become able to understand and feel what the therapist is talking about, it is necessary to deal with their inhibitions in self-care, self-soothing, and self-regulation. They need to start questioning why they treat themselves as robots, and have no empathy for anyone. By this time it should be possible to interpret their transference, dominated by the wish for the therapist to take over the operation of all their vital and affective functions. The interpretations of the idolatrous transference must wait until the patients are able to use their emotions effectively. They cannot give up the infantile views of themselves until they are able to use the analysis for effective grieving (Wetmore, 1963). These patients have been using substitutes for the primal object as "placebos" making it possible for them to take care of themselves, and simultaneously deny their self-caring. In order to succeed with such patients, the analysts cannot not expect to conduct therapy while sitting there like wooden statues, but they must more freely express emotions experienced. Sometimes it is necessary to admit to such a patient that his or her perceptions of the analyst's reactions are accurate. One may even have to reveal countertransference reactions and empathic failures (Maroda, 1999). Such a confirmatory admission may occur at a crisis point of the treatment. This openness on the part of the analyst may enable the patient to trust his or her feelings in key object relations for the first time ever.

Henry Krystal, 1972

REFERENCES

Browning, C.R. *Ordinary Men. Reserve Police Battalion 101 and the final solution in Poland.* NY, HarperCollins 1993.

Freud, A. Comments on trauma. In: *Psychic Trauma.* Ed. S. Furst NY, Basic Books, 1967.

Freud, S. *Inhibition, Symptom and anxiety.* In: Standard edition vol. 20, London Hogarth Press, 1959.

Krystal, H. *Psychotherapy with alexithymic patients.* In A.J. Krakowski and C.P, Kimball (eds.) Psychosomatic Medicine. NY Plenum Press, pp. 737–745, 1982.

Krystal, H. Trauma and the stimulus barrier. *Psychosomatic Inquiry* 5: 131–161, 1985.

Krystal, H. *Trauma and Aging.* In C. Caruth, (Ed.) Exploration in trauma. Baltimore, Johns Hopkins Press pp. 65–100, 1995.

Krystal, H. Resilience. *Psyche.* 9/10: 389–859, 2000.

Krystal, H. And Niederland, W.G. *Psychic Traumatization.* Boston, Little, Brown 1971.

Maroda, K.J. *Seduction, surrender and transformation.* Hillsdale, NJ Analytic Press, 1999.

McDougall, J. *The antianalys and in Analysis.* In Ten years of psychoanalysis in France. NY, IUP, 1972.

McDougall, J. The Psychosoma and the Analytic Process. *International Review of Psychoanalysis* 1: 437–454, 1974.

McDougall, J. Alexithymia: a psychoanalytic viewpoint. *Psychotherapy and Psychoanalysis,* 38: 81–90, 1982.

Niederland, W.G. The Problem of the survivor. *Journal of the Hillside Hospital,* 10: 233–261, 1961.

Papousek, H. and Papousek, M. *Cognitive Aspects of preverbal social interaction between human infants and adults.* In: Parental Interaction. (Ciba Symposia), NY, Associated Publishers, 1975.

Rappaport, D. *On the psychoanalytic theory of affects.* In M.M. Gill (ed.) Collected Papers pp. 476–512, NY, Basic Books.

Seligman, M.E.P. *Helplessness. On depression, development and death.* San Francisco, Freeman, 1975.

Sifneos, P. Is dynamic psychotherapy contraindicated for a large number of patients with developmental disease? *Psychotherapy Psychosomatics* 21: pp. 133–136 1972–1973.

Sifneos, P. The prevalence of "Alexithymic" characteristics in psychosomatic patients. *Psychotherapy and Psychosomatics* 22: 255–262, 1973.

Stang, R. *Edward Munch: the man and his art.* NY, Abbeville Press, 1977.

Stern, M. M. Pavor Nocturnus. *International Journal of Psychoanalysis:* 32, 302–306, 1951a.

Stern, M.M. Anxiety, trauma and shock. *Psychoanalytic Quarterly,* 20: 179–203, 1951 b.

Stern, M.M. Trauma and symptom formation. *International Journal of Psychoanalysis,* 20: 202–218, 1953.

van der Kolk, B. A. Biological Considerations about emotions, Trauma, Memory and the Brain. In: *Human Feelings.* Ablon et al. (eds) Hillsdale, NJ. Analytic Press, pp. 212–256, 1993.

Wetmore, R.G. The Role of Grief in Psychoanalysis. *International Journal of Psychoanalysis,* 44: 92–103, 1963.

9

Some Reflections[1]

ROBERT JAY LIFTON

MY FORMATIVE PLACE

Every insight expressed by a healer or investigator, every use of the eyes of understanding, is a function of his formative place, of all that goes into his special relationship to history. My formative place was Brooklyn, New York, where I spent most of my childhood. My parents were second generation. They were born in America, but barely—their parents had been born in shtetls in Russia. My father, in particular, stood for progressive principles that I think affected me and others in my family. He made his way in this society by attending the City College of New York. It's kind of interesting that I somehow made my way back to the City University, which is an outgrowth of City College.

As a kid I was fascinated by sports—I loved sports more than anything else. The first books I read were about sports, like books about Baseball Joe, as one baseball hero was called. I remember feeling that almost all that adults did was boring because it didn't involve a ball or some kind of sports play. This kind of imagery is still very much in my mind, and it's part of whatever mental or creative process I may have expressed.

---

[1] This chapter is drawn from several interviews with Dr. Lifton and retains a spoken style. Much of the chapter derives from an interview by Harry Kreisler of the UC-Berkeley Institute of International Studies.—Editor

Later, maybe in my early teens, I became very interested in history. I read William Shirer on the Third Reich and various books about contemporary history. Freud once said that he spent all of his professional life making his way back to his original interest, which was ancient cultures. Well, I could say that I have spent a good deal of my professional life making my way back to what was a very early interest, that of history and the historical process.

THE WAR YEARS

I've publicly, in my writing, made a confession that, in a sense, I've been trying to live down ever since. When I heard about the dropping of the atomic bombs on Hiroshima and Nagasaki, especially the first one, I was stunned but pleased, because I thought it would end the war; then I wouldn't have to go, and other people wouldn't have to go, and America would win a glorious victory. Later, I felt very ashamed about this, but I mention it because of the attraction that large-scale destruction can have if it seems to be on your side, and for what we take to be virtuous purposes.

World War II had an enormous impact on me. The Nazis were very much in my lenses, all the more so as a Jew. And I had the idea, which many people had at that time but most of us have lost over the decades, that our government and our country stood for decency and progressive policies. That was all very important for me. At the same time, I got from my parents and my father especially a kind of critical sense that the government and people in power can do wrong things, and that one should contest those. That was an early feeling of mine.

It's hard for me to gauge exactly how my sense of ethics developed. It wasn't out of any religious conviction. Again, I was influenced by my father, who was very much an atheist and took pride in combating the traditional or orthodox forms of Judaism, which his parents and my mother's parents were very steeped in. That orthodoxy felt very suffocating to me as a kid growing up and witnessing it, though not really entering into it. Yet my parents conveyed to me the ethical idea that human beings ought to be treated well. It was vague in its source and has been largely secular for me, but it has a spiritual component.

I was enormously shocked to learn of the Holocaust in the aftermath of World War II. Like other middle-class Jewish families, mine had complicated, almost guilty feelings that we had been so privileged in not having undergone that ordeal. At the same time, we were terrified and outraged because it had been directed at Jews like ourselves. It wasn't talked about a lot in my family as it was happening; maybe we didn't want to know all that was happening. Soon after the war, I remember seeing pictures that were shocking, doubly so in that people were murdered in this way because they were Jewish, as I was.

MEDICAL SCHOOL

When I was young, I was very unclear about what I wanted to do. I was interested in history but didn't know where that would take me. And I had a somewhat vague interest in both medicine and what was to become, in my mind and in my work, psychiatry. I had read some books about "healers of the mind," as they were called.

I was rushed through my early education, much of which took place during the war, but I was an intense student, interested in my work and very committed to it. I spent just 2 years at Cornell University, covering more than 3 years of work. I then went to medical school and became interested in psychiatry, even helping to form a kind of psychiatry club. It's sometimes said that psychiatrists are doctors who are frightened by the sight of blood. I might have fallen into that category. I never quite envisioned myself as a proper doctor under that white coat, but I was interested in the idea of healing and in the psychological dimension.

MILITARY SERVICE

When I was in my psychiatric residency training in New York City during the early fifties, at the time of the Korean War, I was subjected to the doctor draft. I was first sent to Westover Field in Massachusetts, but there was a request for somebody to be sent overseas, and I was chosen. And of course, like any red-blooded American lad, I asked to be sent to Paris. They sent me to Japan and then quickly to Korea. I often say that the military saved me from a conventional life in the United States and I've never really thanked them for it, because I haven't exactly been promilitary in my work. But I did make wonderful discoveries while living in Japan for almost a year and a half with my wife. We immersed ourselves in Japanese life. We never lived on the base but rather among the Japanese, and we formed groups with them, including a discussion group my wife created, in which we met a lot of young Japanese students who later became ambassadors or other leading national figures.

In the Air Force I was always stationed in the rear and was never in any kind of combat. But as my last assignment I was sent back to Korea, along with other Air Force and Army psychiatrists, to interview GIs returning from North Korea, where they had been in Chinese Communist custody and had been put through what later came to be known as thought reform, which is a direct translation of what they called their process.

THE EARLY YEARS

I arranged to be discharged from the military in Japan so that my wife and I could embark on a trip around the world. We had only reached our second stop, Hong Kong, when I began to hear stories of people who had been subjected to a more intense version of thought reform. I was able to obtain some research support to stay in Hong Kong for another year and a half, interviewing both Westerners and Chinese coming out of China. That work on thought reform, or so-called brainwashing, was my first real research study.

I did that first study because, while in the military, I had been exposed to something that I took to be important: the thought-reform process. In Hong Kong I saw a chance to study it more broadly and systematically, unencumbered by any military limitations. The work interested me enormously, and I thought it would be useful to the world. That central problem of ideological totalism has entered into all of my subsequent work, just as it has beggared the world at large.

I began to recognize that you can study people who have been under some kind of duress in connection with a significant historical event, which strongly affected them or which they helped to create.

Through the influence of various anthropologists, some of whom I got to know, like Margaret Mead, who was very supportive of my work, and Ruth Benedict, through her writings, and then through Erik Erikson's work in psychoanalysis, I came to a kind of tripartite idea: the people I studied were creatures of the immediate historical process that had brought me to them; at the same time, they were part of a long cultural tradition and history that made them who they were in many ways; and they were human beings with universal psychobiological struggles. This has served as a rough model for looking at people I've studied in different cultures, in Japan, China, Germany, and the United States.

In the late 1950s, at Harvard, I became a close younger friend of the remarkable sociologist David Riesman, who was the first American faculty person to be an adviser to an antinuclear group. Under his leadership we started a little newsletter in which we talked about the American shelter-building craze and some of the absurdities of strategic declarations about fighting and winning nuclear war. One of the major moral questions of that time was, "If you saw your neighbor coming toward your shelter, where he might use up some of its valuable oxygen, should you shoot him?" And we thought that there's something wrong with a society where that's one of its main ethical questions.

It was my deep concern about nuclear weapons that took me to Hiroshima, where I did my second major study. My wife and I had traveled there to look into what had happened in that city, and I was astounded to find that nobody had really studied it—which was an insight in itself. People resisted it. And the Japanese were overwhelmed by it. Some came to help, but it was hard to study it in that kind of atmosphere. I had just received an appointment to Yale. I'm eternally grateful to Fritz Redlich, who was the chair of the department. When I wrote to him, saying, "I've come upon this situation in Hiroshima that nobody has studied; I really want to stay here and study it," he replied almost by return mail, saying that he'd arranged for a modest research grant. And I stayed there for 6 months and did the work.

My earlier study of thought reform had also addressed an extreme historical situation. I knew something about Japan. I was concerned about nuclear weapons questions. I had a little experience. Though I wasn't without doubts, I felt I could do it. So one builds a sense of self that includes the idea that one is the kind of person who just might be able to do this kind of work. And that's how it happened, with a lot of anxiety along the way about whether I could carry it through, or sometimes in response to others who thought it seemed a little crazy for a psychiatrist to be out there doing such things. But for me such things—these studies—became a version of self and world.

ASPECTS OF PSYCHIC NUMBING

Prior to my study of Hiroshima, I had benefited from the influence of Erik Erikson, whom I met very early in my work and who took an interest in what I was doing. I used his concept of identity, or ego identity, as a central focus in my book on Chinese thought reform. But when I went to Hiroshima, people were talking about death all the time, about people dying all around them, and about their own fear of death. And I realized that neither in Erikson's work nor anyplace else in psychoanalytic or psychiatric theory was there much about death-related concepts. Freud had been greatly concerned about death, but it didn't fit into his particular conceptual structure except in a very broad, vague way in connection with the death drive.

So I began to try to formulate a new but also very old kind of paradigm of life continuity, or of death and the continuity of life, as a basic model within which all of us live. In doing so, I realized that the symbolization of life and death is what we're all about, not just Hiroshima survivors. And I see that as the most useful kind of model or paradigm for any kind of historical work, because all historical groups experience some sort of struggle that has to do with life and death rather than with the more classical Freudian model or concept of instinct and defense. I came to the idea of what I call "psychic numbing" (which at first I called "psychic closing off") in trying to understand what Hiroshima survivors were describing to me. They would say such things as "I saw this array of dead and dying people around me … but suddenly I simply ceased to feel." Some used the metaphor of a photographic plate that was overexposed. It was as though the mind was shut off.

I began to wonder not just about those who were exposed to the atomic bomb but also about those who made the nuclear weapons. And I thought about the psychic numbing involved in strategic projections of using hydrogen bombs or nuclear weapons of any kind. I also thought about ways in which all of us undergo what could be called the numbing of everyday life. We are bombarded by all kinds of images and influences, and we have to fend off some of them if we're to take in any of them or to carry through with our ordinary day's work, or give depth to whatever we have to do or say. So it isn't all negative. Take the example of a surgeon who is performing a delicate operation. You don't want him or her to have the same emotions as a family member of the person being operated on. There has to be some level of detachment where you bring your technical skill to bear on it. And from that I formulated a model for professional work, which is a combination of advocacy and detachment. The detachment may involve what I call "selective professional numbing," while the advocacy consists of the ethical principles one brings to the work. In Hiroshima I tried to combine rigorous exploration of the effects of the atomic bomb with my profound concerns about nuclear weapons.

SYMBOLIC IMMORTALITY, HIGH STATES, AND NUCLEAR WEAPONS

It became clear to me by the 1970s that all of us, not just religious people or people who think philosophically, need a sense of being part of something larger than ourselves, something that precedes and extends beyond what we know in some part of our mind to be our limited life span. As human beings, we are the creatures who know that we will die, but we fend off that knowledge. Being part of something larger than ourselves is what I call the symbolization of immortality. And that can be done biologically through our children and grandchildren; or through our works, our influences in the world; or through some sort of religious belief system; or through being bound up with eternal nature. But all of these are in some way called into question, both by the rapidity of historical change, where we lose a clear sense of value structures or belief systems, and by the existence of ultimate weapons, and what I call the "imagery of extinction" that accompanies them.

Every adult has the sense that he or she might be obliterated at any time by these weapons that we have created. While that doesn't destroy our need for symbolic immortality or our ways of expressing it, it does cast doubt on them. That's why we tend to embrace what I took to be a fifth mode of symbolic immortality, the experience of transcendence or high states, whether through meditation or drugs or anything that takes us outside ourselves into something like ecstasy, whether in quiet or dramatic ways. The experience of transcendence is called forth in all cultures, and we saw much of it in this country in the sixties and seventies. I think that nuclear weapons have something to do with our intensified embrace of high states, and so does the speed and confusion of historical change. That confusion and quest are intensified by the mass-media revolution, which feeds us with so much in the way of contradictory images that we become ever less certain of which structures we want to retain or believe in.

WHAT VIETNAM VETERANS TAUGHT ME

I learned a lot from Vietnam veterans, especially from those who turned against their own war. Many of these young men—they were all men in the groups that I worked with—had been used to the idea that, when your country calls you to the colors, you go. They were patriotic. And they had a kind of macho feeling that war was a testing ground for manhood. Many of them had literally sat on their fathers' knees—fathers who had been veterans of World War II—and been told about that glorious victory, and they wanted their moment, too. But when they experienced their first death, whether of Vietcong—the enemy—or of a buddy shot up next to them—when they were in some way involved in a death encounter, their conviction in all of this was shattered. Many of them simply could no longer justify their being there. Everything there seemed strange and bizarre—there was something wrong or dirty about that war. And there were atrocities that they witnessed or participated in.

An encounter with death can threaten one's entire belief system. One then has to struggle with what has been learned, to reorder the images from that encounter, and to put them back into some kind of inner form that one can use, which is a whole restructuring of the self. There can then be a process of renewal. That's what a number of Vietnam veterans, with whom I and others worked in what we called rap groups and in individual exchanges, were struggling to do.

Any experience of survival, whether of large-scale disaster, intimate personal loss, or, more indirectly, severe mental illness, involves a psychic journey to the edge of the world of being. The formulative effort—or quest for meaning—is the survivor's path of return. I've been preoccupied with the survivor all through my work. When we talk about this in retrospect, it all sounds very logical, as though one just wafted through it—but it doesn't happen that way at all. I struggled with each of these studies and was often confused and uncertain about what they meant. As I tried to put together what I had observed, the survivor became a very important and ubiquitous leitmotif.

The concept of the survivor is really double-edged. Having touched death, survivors can close down and remain numbed and be incapacitated by what they've been through. Or they can confront their experience and derive from it insight and even wisdom, which informs their lives. Or they can do both. Great achievements have occurred in relation to survival, including spiritual and religious movements. There are many dimensions to the survivor.

In my work on what I call the "protean self," which is both very early and very recent, I've tried to evolve a concept of self-process that can move from survival or a death encounter into many different images and forms, absorbing seemingly contrary dimensions. The general idea is that a death encounter can be used to re-create oneself in relation to it. I've seen this happen in various people whom I've interviewed. I wrote my first essay on the protean self way back in the late sixties, derived largely from my early work on Japan. But I wasn't ready to write the whole book until I'd thought it through much more. And that book was published in 1993, a long time later.

The Vietnam veterans were striking in this way. Over the course of the rap groups, we could see them undergoing changes—about their views of the war and war making, about Machismo and maleness, and about their lives in general. Though they did not change entirely, important aspects of themselves changed within months or even weeks, and much of this change could be lasting. The Vietnam veterans I worked with were both perpetrators and victims. They were in some cases responsible for atrocities in a war that should never have happened. But at the same time they were victims in that they were sent there ignorantly, thrust into what I call an "atrocity-producing situation," and they suffered and had all kinds of psychological aftereffects. And they taught me a lot about the capacity for change. From that process one could see genuinely new kinds of self taking shape. All this was important for me to grasp, and it influenced everything I did subsequently.

THE NAZI DOCTORS

A rabbi friend once pointed out that my work on Hiroshima was my path as a Jew to the Holocaust. I think if I had heard this at a lecture it might not have made an impact on me the way that it did coming from someone sitting next to me. I had a complicated reaction to his statement. On the one hand, I was annoyed by it because it seemed pontifical, even for a rabbi, who perhaps is supposed to pontificate. But I didn't entirely disbelieve it either, and actually I came to see that the combination of my being a Jew and the influence that the Holocaust had on my life very early on affected how I responded both to nuclear weapons and the Hiroshima experience. Though these were very different events, each was massively destructive and deeply dangerous to humankind—to the continuity of all human life. So in that sense they blended. And I came to think that my friend was more than a little correct in what he had said. And the fact is that years after the Hiroshima work, I came to my study of Nazi doctors.

I embarked on that study because, increasingly, I had the feeling that I wanted to do a Holocaust study and that I wanted it to be about perpetrators, as I thought this was more needed. A lot of work had already been done on survivors, while there had been very little on the psychology of perpetrators. Then the person who had been my editor for my book on Hiroshima survivors called to tell me that he had been sent interesting material on a trial in Frankfurt involving doctors, which he wanted to show me. Those physicians had been actively involved in the killing process, and I jumped at the opportunity to study them. The Nazis, especially Hitler and his inner circle, viewed their movement as mainly biological. One Nazi doctor whom I interviewed said: "I joined the Nazi Party the day after I heard a speech by Rudolph Hess in which he declared National Socialism was nothing but applied biology."

For the Nazis, this meant finding some way to heal or cure the Nordic race. Hitler wrote that the Nordic race was the only one that could create culture; the other races could sustain but not create it. And he said that the Jewish "race" was culture-destroying and had infected the Nordic race, so something had to be done to get rid of that infection. This was, in a sense, a biological kind of process, and in my work I called it the "biomedical vision" at the heart of Nazism. That was a major reason why the Nazis focused so centrally on doctors as a group; Hitler emphasized, early on, that doctors were especially important to the Nazi project. And I found this to be true.

One dimension of the study was the psychohistorical aspect we just talked about, the biomedical vision. Another dimension was the nitty-gritty way in which a doctor who is trained to heal instead becomes part of the killing mechanism. There's a process that can be called "socialization to evil," and it is all too easy to accomplish. Doctors joined the Nazi Party, embracing the promise of revitalization that Hitler offered; they joined the medical profession, which is a group of its own, and then the military, and then they were sent to a death camp. All of these were groups that they became part of and were socialized to. These doctors had not killed anybody until they got to Auschwitz, so they weren't extraordinary killers to start with; they were ordinary people who were ultimately corruptible.

A key mechanism in socialization to evil was what I came to call "doubling." These Nazi doctors were at the heart of the killing process in Auschwitz; they made "selections" of prisoners for the gas chambers and were in charge of declaring people dead. In a sense, they ran the killing process, although their assistants generally did it for them. So when they were in Auschwitz, they functioned from an Auschwitz self, which was responsible for doing all of this, as well as for the very vulgar life that one led in Auschwitz: heavy drinking and coarse jokes—the whole combination of things that made up Auschwitz. But they would go home to their families, from Poland to Germany, for weekends or leaves, and they would be ordinary fathers and husbands who functioned in a relatively ordinary way, calling forth a prior, relatively more humane self, even though, of course, both "selves" were part of the same overall self.

Doubling has more to do with the work of Otto Rank, one of the early psychoanalysts, than with Freud himself. Doubling is a form of dissociation and became a mechanism of socialization to evil in Nazi doctors. Identifying such a mechanism in no way diminishes a Nazi doctor's responsibility for his behavior.

A similar process was present in many members of Aum Shinrikyo, the destructive and murderous cult that I studied in the mid- to late nineties. The process can occur in anyone as a form of socialization to evil. They don't necessarily call it doubling, but that's what happens, in effect.

DESTROYING THE WORLD TO SAVE IT

No individual is inherently evil, murderous, or genocidal, but under certain conditions virtually anyone is capable of becoming all of these things. Aum Shinrikyo wasn't, at the beginning, clearly a terrorist group, but rather one of the Japanese so-called new religions. There have been an extraordinary number of new religions ever since the middle of the nineteenth century, especially after World War II, during what has been called the "rush hour of the gods," and again intensely after 1970. Young and not-so-young people were drawn to Aum Shinrikyo because it gave them strong religious satisfaction. Shoko Asahara, the guru of Aum Shinrikyo, was a very talented religious teacher and a gifted teacher of yoga, as well as a self-promoting con man. One can be all these things in the same overall self. Some of these disciples, with the help of various forms of meditation, including sustained rapid breathing, which brings about deoxygenation and vulnerability to high states and mystical experiences, became extremely attached to the guru and to this kind of religious practice. They could, in a sense, turn the other cheek, or numb themselves to evidence of violence within the cult that they didn't want to see because they were so drawn to the cultic experience. In that way, they could form both an Aum self, which thrived within the cult, and a non-Aum or anti-Aum self, which had doubts and even antagonisms that had to be suppressed because, within the guru-dominated cult, they were taboo.

But these young people were not inherently evil any more than the Nazi doctors were. Rather, they were socialized into a group that became murderous. Most of them didn't know that Asahara, with the help of his trusted high disciples, was stockpiling chemical and biological weapons and was attempting to obtain nuclear weapons. All disciples were drawn into Asahara's world-ending prophecies and expected a great battle in which Aum Shinrikyo would play a decisive role and then survive that world destruction in order to initiate a new spiritual perfection. But very few disciples knew that Asahara intended to make use of weapons of mass destruction to bring about great catastrophes that would initiate World War III and bring about a biblical Armageddon.

LESSONS LEARNED

In my psychiatric residency, I was trained in a kind of modified psychoanalytic interview method in which you evoke the life experiences of the person you're talking to. So for me, early on in my work, the interview was a central kind of instrument. As I've continued to use it over the years, I've found it to be a beautiful instrument, and I think that it's underused. It can be used by almost any kind of researcher, in the humanities as well as in psychology or the social sciences.

I also found that I wanted to modify the interview process. These weren't people who came to me for help because of my having been trained as a clinician. Rather, I went to them, seeking some knowledge of their experience. So I tried to make it more of a dialogue, a give-and-take in which they could ask me questions about my life while I was probing their experiences. I think it requires kind of a dual level of function in which one is a human being in a dialogue and is not immune from very human questions, as you might be if you're distancing yourself as a doctor who's on a level above the patient. At the same time, I tried to bring to bear my professional and psychological knowledge in order to grasp what they were telling me.

In my book on Hiroshima, I describe how, in the first days of those interviews, I was stunned and overwhelmed by the stories that people told me; I thought, yes, this is a worthwhile study, but can I really do it? Then after a few days or a week, I found myself less intensely affected and more able to think about the categories of response that I was hearing. That was a version of the selective professional numbing I mentioned earlier, which I needed to be able to do the work at all. But I also came to realize that it was a potential danger, because in professional practice the balance is usually overweighted toward numbing rather than intense emotion. Either extreme can be problematic for this kind of research and for therapeutic work as well.

The interview has to be, above all, a kind of human exchange. It's a chance for people to examine their own lives. That was true for former Aum Shinrikyo members, whose trust I had to gain as they were working their way out of the cult psychologically. Most of them said that they derived value from the interviews because they could explore what they had been through in ways they hadn't otherwise been able to do.

CAPACITY FOR EVIL

My work is full of the study or recording of evil. Evil seems to be called forth all too frequently; people are readily socialized or are able to adapt to it. I've also seen the other side of it; survivors may be able to gain knowledge from their ordeal, and to re-create themselves with the help and love of those around them. So I'm careful not to insist on a single kind of lesson being drawn from all of this. I consider myself neither an optimist nor a pessimist, but to simply confront and make my way through these dreadful events is an act of hope, as is the recording of what people are sometimes able to do in spite of their exposure to these events.

So I consider myself a hopeful person. I think that all of us have to work to combat these events and take steps to prevent their recurrence in some kind of spirit of hope. That's what I try to convey to my students and to others I talk to.

One looks into the abyss in order to see beyond it. You don't want to be stuck there; otherwise your imagination is deadened and defeated by the very event you're studying. If you don't look into it you are ostrich-like. If you get stuck there you are incapacitated. So you want to look beyond it to other human possibilities.

SUPPLEMENTAL INTERVIEW WITH ROBERT JAY LIFTON, SEPTEMBER 2004, BY CHARLES FIGLEY

What were the events in your life that led to your interest in trauma?

No specific events led directly to my interest in trauma. The military in a way was responsible for my opening out to issues of trauma, first in Japan and then in Korea. And from there I began to see myself as one who could engage these issues in an historical context. My earliest study, on thought reform, or "brainwashing," certainly involved a form of trauma. From there I thought that I could go on to study Hiroshima—a very different situation—because I now had some experience in studying an extreme environment. The work on thought reform, and then my Hiroshima study, marked the beginning of my approach to psychology and history, and to individual interviews with people under duress. It seemed a natural sequence for me to undertake.

It then became a question of identity and sense of self—I do, and can do, this work; no matter how difficult, I can bring some order and under-standing to these events. Thus, in my work on trauma and my work in general, Hiroshima was a major turning point because it combined everything I had become concerned with: a large and historical event, and advocacy in confronting and combating nuclear weapons.

What have been your greatest achievements and contributions to the field?

This is largely for others to determine, but I would point to my Hiroshima work and to my work on Nazi doctors—two books and two personal immersions. One of my relatively less known books, *The Broken Connection: On Death and the Continuity of Life*, is also worth mentioning. It is a systematic and conceptual statement of my ideas and approaches to trauma. It also places all of my work on large-scale trauma into a model for those in the trauma field. Collectively, my work speaks to the study of mass trauma and to the focus on the survivor in the face of such trauma.

If I were to list some of the concepts found in these books, I would mention psychic numbing, doubling, and the symbolization of immortality. Also, I would point to my emphasis on the overall psychology of the survivor, including the potential for pain and immobilization on the one hand and for illumination and renewal on the other.

Who were the people who most influenced you to make these contributions?

Erik Erikson had the greatest overall intellectual influence on my work. I learned from him that it is possible to bring depth psychology into history, to bring a psychoanalytic perspective to the world at large. And from Erikson's work I also could find ways to make use of the psychoanalytic tradition while at the same time deviating from it. Erikson's ideas about identity were crucial to my early work on Chinese thought reform. Subsequently I moved toward a somewhat more radical view in developing the concept of a many-sided and more fluid protean self. My Hiroshima study also led me away from Erikson as I struggled with ideas about the death encounter and various aspects of trauma.

As a young man I was fortunate to become very close to David Riesman, and from him I learned a great deal about American society and how societies work in general. All of my work places considerable emphasis on collective and social influences on behavior, and Riesman also taught me much about the nuances of collective behavior. Riesman conveyed to me some of the precariousness of American society and its inclinations, when threatened by change, toward dangerous waves of angry backlash. And I learned a great deal from him about genuine intellectual exchange and the deep pleasures of real dialogue.

I never met Albert Camus, but his writings had a powerful impact on me early in my work. In the late 1950s his explorations of the general subject of totalism—and especially his book *The Rebel*—spoke directly to my struggles with Chinese thought reform. His novel *The Plague* also had much to say to me about ways of confronting death, about the nature of evil, and about trying to live the ethical life. I can remember the morning in January 1960 when, while sitting at breakfast with my wife, I read in the *New York Times* that Camus had been killed in a car crash. I suddenly found myself in tears, overwhelmed by a sense of loss.

Suzanne Langer and Ernst Cassirer were extremely important to me in their focus on the broad principle of symbolization. This was a radical idea, because it made clear that no perception—certainly no trauma—is received nakedly, so to speak, but rather must be re-created by our brains, our gray matter. That is the basis for a dynamic view of trauma, and of psychological experience in general.

Working with Erich Lindemann at the Massachusetts General Hospital in the late 1950s gave me a broad perspective on psychoanalytic theory. And his pioneering work on the effects of the Coconut Grove nightclub fire in Boston had much to say about the lasting impact of psychological trauma, and about survivors' struggles to give their experience some form or meaning.

At this time I became close to Leslie Farber, an idiosyncratic psychoanalyst who taught me much about overcoming dogma in favor of close observation and sensitivity to fiction and literary criticism as sources of insight.

In my early work on massive trauma, I also learned a great deal from the searing writings of such Holocaust survivors as Primo Levi, Elie Wiesel, Jorge Semprun, and Piotr Rawicz.

And of course we are all children of Freud. When, after my Hiroshima research, I worked on death-related theory, I went back to Freud. And in writing *The Broken Connection* I found myself in a sustained dialogue with him in which I would translate his instinctual ideas into the symbolizing principles I was trying to develop in connection with death and the continuity of life.

My wife, Betty Jean Lifton, has had a different kind of influence on my work, also of enormous importance. She has helped me see the potential for larger meanings in my explorations, which has enabled me to make bold decisions even in the midst of uncertainty. Her personal support has included a sense of intellectual perspective.

How do you hope that current and future trauma scholars will build on your work?

What future scholars take from one's work is always unpredictable and sometimes unidentifiable. Having said that, I hope that they would build on my studies of large and terrible historical events, and on my attempts to bring psychological depth to these events. These are areas that scholars have often avoided. Also, I hope that others will see the affirmation in these confrontations with the forces of darkness, an affirmation that can only be expressed by means of full immersion into such forces. In that and other ways I want my work to be seen—as many have told me they see it—as hopeful. And my wish is that others will continue my efforts to combine scholarship and advocacy—to apply careful study to a commitment to combat destructive forces. Finally, I hope that they will combine my historical forays with empirical work with real people. I have been a kind of missionary for the interview method, as I see it as inherently humane and able to provide the kind of information that no other approach can. The ideal here is that of combining historical imagination, human encounter, and conceptual boldness.

Robert Jay Lifton, 1975

REFERENCES

By Ribert Jay Lifton:

Thought Reform and the Psychology of Totalism: A Study of "Brainwashing" in China, 1961 (Durham: University of North Carolina Press, 1989).
Death in Life: Survivors of Hiroshima, 1968 (Durham: University of North Carolina Press, 1991).
The Broken Connection: On Death and the Continuity of Life, 1979 (Washington, DC: American Psychiatric Press, 1996).
The Protean Self: Human Resilience in an Age of Fragmentation. 1993 (Chicago: University of Chicago Press, 1999).
Home from the War: Learning from Vietnam Veterans, 1973 (New York: Other Press, 2005 [with a new preface on the war in Iraq]).
The Nazi Doctors: Medical Killing and the Psychology of Genocide (New York: Basic Books. 1986).
Destroying the World to Save It: Aum Shinrikyo, Apocalyptic Violence, and the New Global Terrorism (New York: Metropolitan Books, 1999).
"Americans as Survivors." *New England Journal of Medicine* (2005) 352:2263–5.

By Others:

Camus, Albert: *The Rebel* (New York: Knopf, 1954).
Cassirer, Ernst: *An Essay on Man* (New York: Doubleday Anchor, 1944).
Erikson, Erik H.: "The Problem of Ego Identity." *Journal of the American Psychoanalytic Association* (1956) 4:56–121.

Erikson, Erik H.: *Young Man Luther* (New York: Norton, 1958).

Farber, Lesile: *The Ways of the will* (New York: Basic Books, 1966).

Langer, Suzanne K.: *Mind: An Essay on Human Feeling* (Baltimore: Johns Hopkins Press, 1967, 1972).

Levi, Primo: *Survival in Auschwitz* (New York: Collier, 1961).

10

There Is Reason in Action

FRANK OCHBERG

1968

Bobby Kennedy was shot and killed that year and I was shattered. It was only a few months after the assassination of Martin Luther King and not that long after President Kennedy was gunned down in Dallas. These were vital young leaders, reaching the prime of life, moving many of my generation to political awareness and public service. I was 28, married to Lynn, living in Palo Alto, and halfway through a psychiatry residency at Stanford. I had no idea how young I was—how uninformed and undirected. Surely it was the triple slaying of those particular men, JFK, MLK, and RFK, at that particular time of my life, mid-20s, that focused my emotions and my attention on human cruelty and tragic loss. The whole decade was tumultuous, and 1968 was the darkest year, with race riots at home, battlefield deaths in Vietnam, and drug use turning from playful experimentation to hard-core abuse and dependence.

The day after Robert Kennedy died, Dave Daniels called and said, "Frank, we have to do something." Dave was an untenured assistant professor, somewhat of a maverick on the faculty who partnered with the more activist residents and med students, steering us into extracurricular, self-defined assignments. Some of us worked at a drop-in center in East Palo Alto, the other side of the tracks. Some organized study groups on community mental health and deinstitutionalization. We met at Dave's house for mentoring and mutual support. Although considered an activist, I was unprepared for action when Dave called. He was ready to organize committees and write articles, and he wanted me to cochair an effort within the Stanford Department of Psychiatry to address the issue of human violence. I recall saying something like, "Dave, I'm still in a state of shock. I need to think about this. Let me call you back."

This was long ago and I cannot remember exactly how I felt, but I know I talked to Lynn, describing how Dave was off and running when I was stunned and still digesting what had happened. I wanted to let things sink in, to absorb the blow, because I certainly felt like I had been hit and all the air was out of me. And I knew that cochairing a committee would be a full-time job on top of everything else that a resident does.

Lynn had no hesitation. "You should call him back and get going," she said. It helps to have a spouse who wants you to tackle tough assignments. She didn't push, but spoke her mind and encouraged. She still does.

Within the hour I was on the phone with Dave and we agreed to call a meeting that week, open to any residents or faculty who cared to attend. We'd offer a few ideas about symposia and articles and events, and we'd listen and take stock afterward. We didn't envision a final product, but we knew we could mobilize a dozen or more colleagues to create something of value.

And we did.

We met that week and blocked out a group of topics and procedures and a management plan. The department chairman, David A. Hamburg, was on sabbatical, away for the year. The acting chair, Herb Lederman, was genial and supportive but occupied with his own research and disengaged from the residents and junior faculty. Erich Lindemann, professor emeritus and former chair at Harvard—my clinical supervisor—said, "You are all denying your grief." I remember that clearly, a distinguished psychoanalyst who interpreted action as denial.[1] No one in authority led us. No one stopped us.

More than half the residents in my year signed on, along with a slightly smaller number from the following year and several faculty members. Together we wrote a book published by Little, Brown, titled *Violence and the Struggle for Existence* (Daniels, Gilula, & Ochberg, 1970). We also conducted seminars, symposia, and classes under the banner The Stanford Committee on Violence and Aggression. Lloyd Cutler, Executive Director of the National Commission on the Causes and Prevention of Violence, flew out to interview us as he organized his group, larger and far more prestigious than ours, but informed by our approach nevertheless.[2]

As a group of volunteers, we learned that our motivation was high but our abilities mixed. Some had trouble meeting deadlines. Some felt every word was precious and resented editing. Some wanted to write chapters that were already assigned to others. Nobody wanted to write about gun control, so I took on that topic with my pal Chris Gillin, who was equally uninformed and uninterested. Our wives, Lynn and Fran, helped with the research, and after a month we were dangerous experts, ready for combat with the National Rifle Association.

Others wrote about media and violence, drugs and violence, presidential assassination, the biology of aggression, the sociology of aggression, the connection (and the lack of connection) between major mental illness and acts of violence. We learned together and we shared ideas among ourselves. A general theory emerged: Aggression is a fundamental part of our species-specific behavior, innate and adaptive. Our capacity for aggression allows us to organize ourselves and attain needed resources in ways that are historically and biologically human. But violence, by our definition, is needlessly destructive aggression. Violence has never been adequately prevented and it threatens our existence. While we are not evolving into a more neurologically aggressive animal, we certainly are not overcoming our brutish heritage. And overcome it we must, because our impulse to hurt and harm affects so many more victims and potential victims as our weaponry grows more deadly and our deadly knowledge spreads.

I learned a lot at Stanford: how to be a psychiatrist, how to work with peers, how to manage a productive committee, how to edit a book, and how to think about our violent species. David Hamburg, our chairman, helped with his presence and his absence. He is a remarkable scientist, humanist, and leader who went on to become president of the Institute of Medicine, runner-up in the search for president of Harvard, then president of the Carnegie Foundation of New York. He and his wife, Betty, also a professor of psychiatry at Stanford, took a personal and professional interest in many residents' careers, including mine. Both stressed scientific method, critical thinking, and fact-based argument. Both were eclectic in applying several disciplines at once to the understanding of complex human issues. And both were outspoken advocates of progressive politics. Although they were diplomatic and discreet, you knew where they stood on the issues of the time.

Dave Hamburg was pleasantly surprised to return from abroad to find a significant fraction of his department at work on a book and advising a presidential commission. He joked that it might not have happened had he been there.

That could be true. Dave Daniels was the faculty member who got down in the trenches with me and sorted out personality disputes, who worked overtime to polish bad prose, who pushed to get a decent publisher, and faced down the nay sayers who thought we were overreaching. Dave Daniels had his difficulties with Dave Hamburg. I do not know all the details; I think the young professor went too far for the older professor's sense of decorum in arranging '60s-style seminars and scolding the faculty for lack of engagement in social issues. Several years later, after being passed over for advancement, Dr. Daniels left the department.

I deal with this sort of issue all the time now and I find it worth mentioning in a chapter on coming of age as a trauma expert. I paid a lot of attention back then to the behavior of alpha males. My role models were not physically aggressive. But they used science to advance humanity by organizing, motivating, and leading others. It is a rare group of primates that tolerates more than one alpha male.

A decade later I discovered the alpha female.

GOVERNMENT SERVICE

During the Vietnam era, young doctors were drafted one way or another. We could be deferred until we completed our residencies and serve as specialists, or we could be conscripted right after internship and end up near the front lines. My internship was in the U.S. Public Health Service, in uniform, in San Francisco. That made me ineligible for deferment. Very fortunately for me, I was accepted into an elite group, the Mental Health Career Development Program (MHCDP), which took a half-dozen members a year, gave us commissions in the Public Health Service, paid our way through any approved psychiatric residency, assigned mentors from the National Institute of Mental Health (NIMH), brought us to national meetings throughout our residency years, and groomed us for national leadership positions in the federal government. We were not sent to Vietnam.

By 1973 I had moved up the ranks to become director of the Services Division of the NIMH and was responsible for the federal components of community mental health in America. The position was a blend of politics, policy, personnel, budget, and law. President Nixon had nothing against community mental health; he just didn't want the feds to fund it. My job was to get Congress to fund it fully without getting my boss or me fired by the president. I had a maestro as a mentor. Bert Brown is 9 years older than I, a psychiatrist, a concert pianist, a raconteur, and a drafter of President Kennedy's first Community Mental Health Act. He was my boss when I first moved from Stanford to NIMH in 1969. As his assistant, I learned the machinations of mental health administration. When he moved up from deputy director to director of the NIMH, I moved up, too. He appointed me director of the Services Division in 1973.

Although my purview included just about everything that crossed the director's desk, my special assignments were combinations of his interests, my interests, and the jobs that had to be done. I assisted with the first Surgeon General's Report on Television and Violence. (Back then there was no reliable evidence that television caused criminal behavior; now the data tell a different story.) I designed, with others, the NIMH Minority Center and assisted in a book on racism and mental health, explaining how that minority center was conceived and organized

(Willie, Kramer, & Brown, 1973). When Stan Yolles was fired as NIMH director and replaced by Bert Brown and the two felt that they would rather not meet face to face, I ferried messages between them. This reminded me of shuttle diplomacy as a kid in Manhattan and the Bronx, dealing with estranged Jewish relatives.

For the life of me, I cannot remember how I met Jerry V. Wilson, the Washington D.C. Chief of Police, but we were well acquainted during this period in the 1970s. So it didn't surprise me when he called and said in his Arkansas drawl, "Frank, will you be my token shrink on the National Terrorism Task Force?" The attorney general had asked Jerry to head up a national panel to set standards and goals for law enforcement agencies—federal, state, and local—as they faced the emerging threat of terrorism. Although I was the principal federal official in charge of community mental health, I became also—thanks to the enthusiastic support of my boss, Bert Brown—the only mental health voice on the National Task Force on Terrorism and Disorder.

COPS AND SHRINKS

I couldn't believe it. The FBI representative on our task force, Con Hassel, had read the book we wrote at Stanford. Nobody read that book other than relatives of the authors and Conrad V. Hassel. We became best friends.

Con took me down to his office in the basement of the FBI Academy, where he had a picture of J. Edgar Hoover on one wall and a picture of Emily Dickinson on the other. "Hope is a thing with feathers," he quoted, and appeared to have a tear in his eye.

We spent a weekend with Frank Bolz and Harvey Schlossberg of the NYPD. Both were detectives, but Harvey had a Ph.D. in psychology and a Park Avenue practice as a moonlighting job. Some genius put Frank and Harvey together and they invented the modern era of hostage negotiation. To hear them tell it, with Brooklyn accents and salty expletives enlivening the science of calming homicidal desperados, is to learn advanced psychiatry from a vaudeville team. Harvey gives a briefing on the biochemistry of stress, noting how the urge to urinate increases with time and with the fluids supplied to the siege room by the crafty NYPD. Frank confides, "So we give them a pot to piss in and they give us a hostage. We are in business."

Harvey reminds Frank of the time he asked a uniform officer on surveillance, "Is the hostage ambulatory?" and the beat cop replied, "No. He's walking around."

That was my overtime job in the mid-1970s. I traveled the country with Con and the task force. I learned all I could about hostage scenarios. I interviewed people who had been held hostage. And when I had a chance to extend this study to Scotland Yard, Con told me, "Study the victim, Frank. We know enough about perpetrators. Nobody studies the victim of terrorism."

My day job—getting Congress to renew the Community Mental Health Centers Act—was done. The president couldn't have cared less. Watergate had exploded, the tapes were revealed, the liars were exposed, and those who menaced the Kennedy mental health legacy were facing prison time.

I landed a plum assignment in 1976. It was called the Work-Study Program Abroad and was available, by competition, to one or two USPHS officers a year. I had to write a detailed essay, line up institutional support, and have letters of reference. Con Hassel and Bert Brown helped. I would study hostage negotiation, victims of sieges, and the way psychiatry and law enforcement could combat terrorism. I'd have a faculty slot and a desk at the Maudsley, London's premier psychiatric teaching hospital. This would be a year's assignment at full pay, with a generous allotment for travel and full shipping charges for the family—now five of us. The kids were 12, 9, and 6 years old.

ROOTS

I'll back up a bit now because the story is rolling along, and it sounds as though everything fell into place easily. That isn't entirely true.

None of us come to the clinical practice of victim care without intimate personal experience.

When I was 16, my mom died. She had been ill most of her life with Crohn's disease—regional enteritis—a painful inflammation of the small intestine that required surgery and periods of bed rest, dietary restriction, and a lifestyle limited by constant physical discomfort. Crohn's disease is not supposed to become cancerous, but in her case it did. She wasted into a skeleton before my eyes. Mirrors were removed. Relatives spoke in whispers. She asked me to find out what was being said because no one would tell her. I was a high school kid. My brother was 6. My Dad, a shopkeeper, was at his wit's end. He didn't want me to know that this was cancer, not Crohn's, but he blurted it out one day when I had made too much noise doing something adolescent and exuberant: "Quiet! Don't you know your mother has cancer?" He regretted it as soon as he said it. Both of us were stone silent. I cried.

A decade later, recovered, married, serving that USPHS internship, I was on a surgical rotation, assisting in a knee repair. A nurse tapped me on the shoulder and said, "You have to scrub out. There's been a family emergency."

I don't like writing about this. I don't like remembering.

It had to be bad. You don't pull a surgical assistant off a case for anything trivial.

When I pushed through the OR doors, still in my greens, the hospital chief of psychiatry Dan Beittel was there. He said, "Your baby boy was killed in an accident," and he drove me home. Little Alex, 9 months old, had been in a crib. The side came down while Lynn was asleep and he crawled out and was strangled between the bed and a dresser.

Our daughter, Billie, was 2. She had no idea what had happened. Before I heard the news, between the operating table and the hospital hallway, I had a fantasy that everyone was dead—wife and both children. The fact that only one died was a relief.

Some relief.

There were awful calls to relatives, a coroner's inquest, a week of leave, and then back to finish the internship. I did not have PTSD. But I did have a fear of further loss and grief. And I'm sure something hardened in me. I didn't want to be too close to any one person. The idea of grief counseling or any form of therapy appalled me. I wanted to share feelings with whom I chose, when I chose.

Back in college I studied English history and literature and read all of Shakespeare and most of the Romantic poets. There were lines and images and cadences that came back to me in my personal posttraumatic state, stoic and poetic at once. This was not a mature or healthy path and the marriage was chaotic until we talked, with help, several years later. Even then, I had a lot of growing up to do.

I don't believe the tragic death of my mother and the traumatic death of my son made me a PTSD pioneer. But I wouldn't be who I am and I wouldn't resonate with those who survive had I not experienced my own losses and my own clumsy steps afterwards.

The combination of science and literature was part of my formative years. I grew up in New York City and attended the Bronx High School of Science. I loved science and completed several college courses before getting to college. But at Harvard I discovered the liberal arts and would have become a Shakespeare scholar had I not flunked something called "the junior generals." This 2-hour essay exam was a hurdle in the honors program of my department. Pass it and you are almost guaranteed a summa or a magna. Fail and you graduate cum laude in general studies. I wrote a miserable exam and knew it. I figured that without highest honors in history and lit, I'd never get a scholarship to the right grad school. Professor Rueben Brower, my adviser, consoled me. "So you don't go to graduate school in English literature. You go to medical school. William Carlos Williams went to medical school."

Johns Hopkins gave me a full scholarship, although I lacked organic chemistry (I took that at summer school at Fordham). Hopkins had been censured for taking too many science majors and turning out doctors who were "not well rounded." They couldn't have found an applicant with fewer college science courses.

ENGLAND

By the time I landed at Heathrow, age 36, I had experienced heights and depths, yins and yangs, but nothing beyond the borders of America (Tijuana doesn't count). It took a while to settle in, make friends, learn to drive on the other side of the road, and handle pounds and pence, but that all fell into place soon enough.

I had a scare when the assistant commissioner told me I couldn't take their hostage negotiators course because it was limited to a carefully selected group of officers. "But you can help us teach it," he said. That made me gasp and smile at once. I had a spot in the room; I'd have to teach Sherlock Holmes.

It all worked out—principally because they got me roaring drunk one day and told me the most outrageous jokes with Scots and Irish and Welsh accents and I laughed until my sides split; after that I was either "the Yank" or "the shrink," but I was OK. And I learned far more than I taught. In fact, between my time with them and a few weeks in Holland—when a group of Moluccans held hostages on a train and in an elementary school and I ended up in the command center assisting the chief negotiator—I figured out something now known as the Stockholm syndrome.

STOCKHOLM SYNDROME

Today it is common knowledge, but back then we were all surprised and intrigued by the strange case of Kristin, the bank teller who was held hostage in a vault at the Kreditbank in Stockholm for several days in August 1973. Kristin became enamored with Olsson, the armed assailant, broke off an engagement with her fiancé, and lambasted Olaf Palme, the Swedish prime minister, during and after her captivity. According to the police investigator who discussed the case with me, she had sex with her captor in the vault (although conflicting accounts make that assertion unreliable).

Kidnap and hostage experts knew that in certain cases an unexpected bond forms between captor and captive. Anna Freud called a similar situation, observed in concentration camps, "identification with the aggressor." But what I saw at least a dozen times after Stockholm, and what I learned from a year of interviewing persons held hostage, was not identification—and not aggressive behavior emulating a sadistic guard. First, there was a sudden, terrifying capture. The hostage was stunned, shocked, and often certain that he or she would die. Then the hostage became like an infant. He couldn't talk, eat, move, or use a toilet without permission. But then, little by little, small acts of kindness by one of the captors evoked feelings that were deeper than relief. "We knew they were killers, but they gave us blankets, cigarettes," one Dutch ex-hostage told me, and then went on to explain his sense of warmth and compassion towards the Moluccans who chose not to kill him (Ochberg, 1978). I realized this must be akin to the infant's feeling that accompanies the relief of thirst, hunger, wetness, and fear of neglect—a primitive gratitude for the gift of life, an emotion that eventually develops and differentiates into varieties of affection and love.

The captor often develops reciprocal feelings of attachment, and when he does, we on the outside, concerned with rescue, have an advantage. The hostage holder wants to protect the hostage. But both captor and hostage have little trust in us and may actually come to hate us. We are the common enemy.

So I defined the Stockholm syndrome for the FBI and Scotland Yard negotiators in memos at that time as involving three conditions:

1. Positive feelings from hostage to captor
2. Reciprocated positive feelings from captor to hostage
3. Negative feelings by both to authorities managing the crisis

That definition stuck. I never named the Stockholm syndrome; I defined it. A few years later I wrote about it in several articles with FBI agent Tom Strentz and in a book with David Soskis (Ochberg & Soskis, 1978). In 2003, 30 years after the incident in Sweden, some reporters tracked me down to reprise the events and to evaluate the significance of siege room bonding. The significance of Stockholm Syndrome goes beyond rare instances of kidnapping and hostage taking. It explains aspects of attachment to battering husbands and incestuous fathers. It explains confessing to accomplished interrogators. It is not just conscious, willful behavior to avoid punishment. It is regression and recovery of a powerful, primitive feeling toward a giver of life.

LATE 1970s

When I returned from the year in Europe, things were not the same at NIMH. Bert Brown, a Kennedy Democrat who held the fort during the Nixon years, was under siege. The Secretary of Health, Education and Welfare (HEW) was Joe Califano. The Assistant Secretary for Health was Julie Richmond. And Gerald Klerman, a Harvard psychiatrist, was brought in to run the new conglomerate called ADAMHA—the echelon below Dr. Richmond and above Dr. Brown. One too many alpha males.

Betty Hamburg now worked at NIMH and David Hamburg advised both Califano and Richmond. Bert Brown pushed the boundaries with Klerman far past the protocol for loyal subordinates. Richmond backed Klerman, not Brown. David Hamburg was unhappy with the way his wife was treated at NIMH, and in a short while Bert Brown was fired. He tried to muster support from Senator Kennedy and other old allies, but there were new Democrats in town and it was their turn to rule.

I was in trouble, too. Bert's successor, Herb Pardes, didn't want me as his associate director. By then I was the number two psychiatrist at NIMH, responsible for congressional and constituency relations. That was a sensitive political position, one that the director fills with his own handpicked loyalist. So I arranged to be designated Associate Director for Crisis Management and went to work for the Secret Service. I also became the male member of the Committee on Women of the American Psychiatric Association (APA).

WORKING WITH WOMEN

We were a heck of a committee, we gals.[3] We kept Hysterical Personality Disorder out of the Diagnostic and Statistical Manual (DSM). We picketed meetings until the APA trustees agreed to boycott states that refused to ratify the Equal Rights Amendment. We brought Gloria Steinem to rally support. And we paid close attention to the concerns of victimized women.

The grass roots movement to provide shelters for battered women began to pick up steam and could have received grants from the NIMH. Some psychiatrists wanted to link shelter services with community mental health centers. But my women colleagues saw how mental health management would imply mental illness on the part of the battered spouse. "The kiss of death," we all agreed, and we kept the systems separate. I still had a policy position at the NIMH and some leverage, which made a difference.

Judith Herman had not quite finished her landmark book *Father-Daughter Incest* (1982), but we knew and respected her (she eventually replaced me on the committee). Ann Burgess and Linda Holstrom had defined the rape trauma syndrome by then (Burgess & Holstrom, 1974), but there was little support or sympathy in mainstream psychiatry for the victim of sexual assault. We raised the consciousness of colleagues as best we could, using the traditional methods of workshops, seminars, articles, and effective personal advocacy within the various APA committees and councils.

We invited Marty and Allie Symonds to meetings and digested the meaning of "the second wound." Both Marty and Allie were psychiatrists, but it was Marty, a former beat cop who put himself through med school, residency, and analytic training, who coined the term. It referred to the wound inflicted by the callous detective, the crass physician, the angry husband—after the rapist or the mugger did his damage. This second wound, inflicted with insensitive words, often cut deeper than the first.

Sue Salasin played a major constructive role, beginning in the late '70s and well into the '80s. She worked in applied research at NIMH, had survived a near fatal physical assault, and yearned to help victims of violence everywhere. We chaired many meetings together, introducing clinicians, researchers, and policy leaders who shared an interest in victims. We linked the APA Committee on Women to the NIMH and established ties to the National Organization for Victim Assistance. Sue introduced me to Yael Danieli and Bessel van der Kolk before they became prominent leaders in our field.

Our overlapping networks of APA and NIMH participants, while not explicitly feminist, had a feminist agenda. Men occupied most of the positions of influence in government and academia, defining victimized women as flawed, feckless, or contributing to their own victimization. It took scientific evidence and political muscle to turn the tide. These "alpha females," connected to one another by strong bonds of respect, spoke a different language than their male counterparts, who were far more concerned with turf and pecking orders.

SEEDS OF THE INTERNATIONAL SOCIETY FOR TRAUMATIC STRESS STUDIES

This was the period in which the seeds of the International Society for Traumatic Stress Studies (ISTSS) were sown. The Vietnam War was over, but Vietnam vets had little clout within the VA. They were outnumbered, stigmatized, and neglected. Slowly, the attitudes changed and the Vietnam generation found its voice. Prominent psychiatrists like Jack Ewalt[4] spoke about "not blaming the warrior for the war." I had opposed the war in the '60s but saw the veterans as victims in the '70s—and I did not consider *victim* a dishonorable term.

We didn't have the diagnosis of PTSD back then. But we did have the observations of military psychiatrists, veterans themselves, and writers, reporters, and poets who documented shell shock and battle fatigue. I had the experiences of a different type of combat vet—the survivor of hostage ordeals and persons imprisoned by terrorist groups.

My colleagues in the Committee on Women knew about the aftermath of battering, rape, and incest. Common clinical insights eventually became a common language with a unifying diagnosis.

It took Charles Figley to pull it all together.

CHARLES

Charles Figley needs no introduction to anyone reading this chapter. We met in the '70s, when he was organizing the special interest group that preceded the ISTSS.

Charles might have been the first person I met who was younger than I but could have been my father figure. He organized, encouraged, facilitated, and collaborated. He did the dirty work, like taking notes, filing reports, raising money, and traveling out of his way to meet you. He had a vision—a global network of trauma specialists, well trained and well educated. He invented a field.

I was more than willing to help. Charles asked me to serve on his board; I served. Charles asked me to write a position paper; I wrote. Charles asked me to edit a book on treating victims; I took a deep breath, consulted my wife (knowing she would say, "Do it"), and I did. That book, *Post-traumatic Therapy and Victims of Violence* (Ochberg, 1988), was very difficult for me. I tried to make it an APA task force product with Marty and Allie Symonds as partners, but both had writer's block and took years to make progress. We began in the early '80s, and only when they said, "Go on without us" could I take over the project and finish the job. We published in 1988. My chapter authors were the stars of the field, many of whom became renowned trauma experts.[5] I didn't consider myself a trauma treatment expert (back then there were no experts), but I felt I had a job to do, deputized by Charles Figley.[6]

Something happens in your forties if you've been a young leader. You learn to enjoy working for younger leaders or you become an ornery old coot. My experience with the Committee on Women certainly helped me. There was no way I'd ever lead that group, and simply being a member was a high privilege. When we were all walking down a hotel room corridor, gabbing away intently, and suddenly the group entered a ladies' room, I knew there were limits to my membership. But I figured that was an important lesson and I let it sink in.

RECENT INFLUENCES AND OUTCOMES

Later on, in the '80s and '90s, and this decade, I met people who became very significant to me personally and professionally.

Governor William G. Milliken appointed me director of the Michigan Department of Mental Health, a cabinet position with 17, 000 employees and a budget close to $1 billion. He was the last of a generation of moderate Republicans who conducted the business of government with decency, dignity, and warmth. He respected and attracted advocates who sought power to provide resources for the underserved. That job didn't last long. An economic collapse forced me to lay off 5,000 state workers. I lost my budget, my political support, and my freedom to innovate. I left my office shortly before the governor left his.

Mary Janice Belen of the Sisters of Mercy hired me to build and staff a new hospital. That job included the authority and resources to create the first residential treatment facility for victims in America.

We called it the Dimondale Stress Reduction Center (Ochberg & Fojtik 1984).

William A. Dart and Kenneth B. Dart entrusted me with half the assets of the Dart Foundation and later with its semiautonomous division, Dart Innovations. This foundation allowed me to create or cocreate the Michigan Victim Alliance, the Dart Center for Journalism and Trauma, the Critical Incident Analysis Group, the National Center for Critical Incident Analysis, and Gift From Within.

All of these entities have websites with their histories, functions, and goals detailed.[7] All collect remarkable assemblages of overworked volunteers and underpaid staff.

My most significant achievements in the trauma field may be the seeding and nourishing of these networks. For example, if the Dart Center continues to improve the profession of journalism, we may have a day when the general public understands trauma the way trauma experts understand it. And we will have less rewounding of victims and more judgment and reason in our responses to violence.

If the Critical Incident Analysis Group (and its successor, the National Center for Critical Incident Analysis) progresses as a forum for scientists, journalists, humanists, and crisis managers, we may understand and avoid debacles like Waco and 9/11. I doubt we can avoid certain acts of terrorism and mayhem, but we can avoid a rush to judgment and miscalculation based on passion and prejudice.

If Gift From Within grows and evolves to reach millions rather than thousands, the trauma field will be less a society of experts and more of a consumers' movement, helping its own victimized members become survivors, demanding and receiving their due.

I'd like trauma scholars to build upon these opportunities, and to recognize the worlds beyond the walls of one's university or discipline or current stream of funding.

We have a science based on ancient principles—keen perception, rigorous analysis, and modest claims of new truth as new truth slowly becomes evident.

We have a species—our human species—that is capable of advanced intelligence and primitive cruelty.

What could be more exciting or productive than harnessing our intelligence to overcome our cruelty?

Frank Ochberg, 1968

REFERENCES

Burgess, A., & Holstrom, L. (1974). Rape trauma syndrome. *American Journal of Psychiatry, 131,* 981–986.

Daniels, D., Gilula, M., & Ochberg, F. (Eds.) (1970). *Violence and the struggle for existence.* Boston: Little, Brown.

Graham, H., & Gurr, T. (Eds.) (1969). *Violence in America: Historical and comparative perspectives.* Washington, DC: US Government Printing Office.

Herman, J. (1981). *Father-daughter incest.* Cambridge, MA: Harvard University Press.

Lindemann, E. (1944). Symptomatology and management of acute grief. *American Journal of Psychiatry, 101,* 141–148.

Ochberg, F. (1978). The victim of terrorism. *Practitioner, 220,* 293–302.

Ochberg, F. (Ed.) (1988). *Post-traumatic therapy and victims of violence.* New York: Brunner/Mazel.

Ochberg, F. (1991). Post-traumatic therapy. *Psychotherapy, 28*(1), 5–1.

Ochberg, F. (1993). Post-traumatic therapy. In J. P. Wilson & B. Raphael (Eds.), *International handbook of traumatic stress syndromes* (pp. 773–783). New York: Plenum Press.

Ochberg, F., (1996). The counting method for ameliorating traumatic memories. *Journal of Traumatic Stress, 9*(4), 873–880.

Ochberg, F., & Fojtik, K. (1984). A comprehensive mental health clinical service program for victims: Clinical issues and therapeutic strategies. *American Journal of Social Psychiatry, 4*(3), 12–23.

Ochberg, F., & Soskis, D. (Eds.) (1982). *The victim of terrorism.* Boulder, CO: Westview.

Willie, C., Kramer, M., & Brown, B. (Eds.) (1973). *Racism and mental health.* Pittsburgh: University of Pittsburgh Press.

ENDNOTES

1. Erich Lindemann, M.D., is best known for his seminal article on pathologic grief, published after the Coconut Grove fire (Lindemann, 1944). Although he was a wise and compassionate man—a wonderful clinical mentor—he completely missed the fact that his sample of bereaved survivors were exposed to horrifying imagery and must have had symptoms we now recognize as PTSD.

2. Thirteen staff reports to the National Commission on the Causes and Prevention of Violence are available from the U.S. Government Printing Office, beginning with an excellent historic overview (Graham & Gurr, 1969).

3. Our members were Elaine Hilberman Carmen, Elissa Benedek, Brenda Solomon, Nanette Gartrell, Dorothea Simmons, Janet Ordway, Katherine Falk, and Theresa Bernadez. Jean Shinoda Bolen was an active collaborator.

4. Jack Ewalt, M.D., ran the VA Mental Health Division after retiring as distinguished professor and chairman of the Harvard Medical School Department of Psychiatry. He was once one of the most powerful figures in academic psychiatry, loved, feared, and respected, depending upon one's ability to stay in his good graces.

5. Contributors were Ann Burgess, Yael Danieli, Charles Figley, Anne Flitcraft, Carol Hartman, Judith Herman, Mary Merwin, Richard Mollica, Carol Mowbray, Frank Ochberg, Walton Roth, Edward Rynearson, Bonnie Smith-Kurtz, Evan Stark, Bessel van der Kolk, John Wilson, and Marlene Young. Dave Hamburg wrote the foreword.

6. My technique for treating flashbacks and haunting memories, invented in the late '80s and reported in the mid-'90s, never achieved the popularity of EMDR and other methods, although it is simple and effective (Ochberg, 1996). A general philosophy of treatment did have impact (Ochberg, 1991, 1993).

7. www.mivictims.org/mva; www.giftfromwithin.org; www.dartcenter.org; www.healthsystem.virginia.edu/internet/ciag; www.criticalincident.org

11

Life, Trauma, and Loss

BEVERLEY RAPHAEL

It has been a challenging experience for me to review my own career and try to write objectively about it—to review the complex motivations; the issues of chance and opportunity; and most particularly how people in everyday life, both those close to me and those famous, have influenced me. I recognize that what I have written is from this time and place and is just one view of this particular part of my life and work experience.

WHAT WERE THE EVENTS IN MY LIFE THAT LED TO MY INTEREST IN TRAUMA?

One cannot fully separate one's professional development from elements of personal life experience. As a child during the Second World War, I felt the sense of threat about the possibility of a Japanese invasion of Australia; the general environment of anxiety generated by a "world war"; the changes in small-town life, with concern and alarm for the future; the building of an air raid shelter at our home—all these led me, as a very curious child and avid reader, to think of war and its consequences. Mass communication was not as it is now; therefore the uncertainty of threat, the lack of the images that are so much now part of our view of the pain of war, left much to the imagination. Every country town had its memorial to the soldiers who had left their homes and died in the First World War: one in five Australian men had joined that distant fight, from a total population of 4 million. A beloved "uncle," a family friend, had gone to war, survived Changi, the main prisoner-of-war camp in Singapore during

WW II (nearly 15,000 Australians were held there) and come back a changed man; others from our town died. Death, loss, and the impact of war, the news of its ending with the atom bomb and Hiroshima, continued to have an impact for many years after the celebrations of peace. The postwar period of my adolescent years was filled with reading, much of which included the survivalist literature of that time, response to the threat of nuclear war, and the ongoing "cold" war. With the postwar migration, confrontations also occurred for Australians, with learning from those who had survived them, of the horrors that war and refugee experience had brought to Europe.

As a medical student I learned more about life and death, and as an intern I saw its realities at close hand. In my first years as a young doctor, I commenced in a primary care or general practice. At the beginning of that time I personally experienced a life-threatening illness, a blood dyscrasia, but fortunately I recovered. Through this I learned of the difficulties doctors have in discussing such situations with their patients but also of the powerful nature of the will to live, the fighting spirit.

Most important, in those years of general practice I worked in a very big veterans practice, treating many who had survived the Second World War and had psychiatric disabilities. My curiosity about these men's experiences and why they were labeled as "inadequate personality" or "anxiety neurosis" led me to learn something of their ways of dealing with what had happened in the war as well as the strong cultural prescription of the time: that "men" did not talk about these things. My interest in and involvement with veterans has stayed with me throughout my work in mental health. However, my interest in trauma, loss, and grief was also built up from other sources.

I commenced training in psychiatry in Australia in 1964 and had fairly wide-ranging experiences. I was very fortunate to work with Professor David Maddison during those years. He had spent a sabbatical with Gerald Caplan in the United States and brought back a strong commitment to testing crisis intervention and to prevention in mental health (Raphael, 1971). This led to my doctoral research, which involved a randomized controlled trial of a preventive intervention following the crisis of conjugal bereavement with high-risk recently bereaved widows (Raphael, 1977a).

In a theoretical framework of crisis intervention, I then extended this model of "preventive intervention" to other life crises, including hysterectomy, first pregnancy, and later to response to accidental injury. These studies involved extensive community work and liaison with other agencies as well as visiting people in their own homes. This outreach and community involvement skill, which began in general practice, followed on with my work as a community psychiatrist in the first wave of the community mental health movement. It was honed in this research outreach and has proved to be of great value in my work with disaster-affected populations.

On Christmas Eve 1974, Cyclone Tracey hit Australia's far northern city of Darwin, destroying a large part of it. The television images vividly portrayed the devastation of the impact. Because of my work in the crisis intervention model, I was asked to provide training for those who would work with evacuees to Sydney and to be involved for the response to those so displaced. I provided guidance to the doctors and health workers involved and saw and assessed some of the evacuees myself (Raphael, 1975). But more than anything I learned of the chaos of disasters and the aftermath, of the lack of understanding of mental health reactions (no mental health person was allowed to go to Darwin at that time), and of the complex mental health impacts that might follow.

I took up my first major academic appointment in 1975–1978 as associate professor in psychiatry at Australia's largest veterans hospital at the time, continuing clinical work with veteran populations, including Vietnam veterans. During this time I also commenced a research project looking at those affected by accidental injuries of the moderate range (compensable and noncompensable) and the risk of developing morbidity, including "traumatic neuroses," with the aim of developing preventive approaches. This study commenced well, but I learned then and subsequently that stakeholders may not "want" prevention, as lawyers and unions advised those affected against participation, so that lack of follow-up negated this study.

Pursuing also an interest in opportunities for prevention in the early stages of life following major crises, I carried out a study, of children 2 to 8 years of age following the death of a parent, again with the aim of assessing factors that could mitigate the risk of adverse mental health outcomes following these tragic life events (Raphael, Field, & Kvelde, 1980).

In January 1977, a major rail disaster occurred in Sydney when an overhead concrete-slab bridge crashed onto a commuter train, causing 83 deaths. This was the first time an emergency mental health response was implemented in an Australian disaster setting. My team was placed initially at the city morgue, where we worked with police and the coroner's office helping the bereaved to identify the dead and in providing crisis outreach and follow-up counseling over the ensuing months (Raphael, 1977a; 1979–1980). In this program, I learned of the resilience of many people, of how such deaths had traumatic components added to the bereavement, and of the difficulties of an outreach program when the resources provided in an emergency could not be sustained. This was the first outreach program where a systematic and independent evaluation was carried out (Singh & Raphael, 1981).

This resulted in my ongoing involvement in many subsequent Australian disasters, including the Ash Wednesday Bushfires in February 1983; then, in my emergency assessment review of mental health needs, I took with me a young psychiatrist who has subsequently become well known in the field of trauma (McFarlane & Raphael, 1984; McFarlane, 1986). This also led to the development of a consultancy model to assist disaster responders and leaders through the management of this process (Raphael, 1983a).

Over the years from 1974 onward I have had the privilege of working with those responding to many of the major disasters and incidents that occurred in Australia during this time: earthquakes, floods, fires, and bus crashes, to name a few. Most of my work has been in acting as consultant to governments, supporting health and mental health workers, working with emergency services and recovery organizations, working with media and engaging with affected populations, and providing preventive and treatment interventions for some of those affected (Raphael, 1983a, 1986; Wilson & Raphael, 1993).

Another experience in 1993–1994 influenced me profoundly and further shaped my interest in the field of trauma and grief. An Aboriginal woman colleague invited me to join her in a consultancy to develop a national mental health plan for indigenous Australians. My travels with her and my meetings with Aboriginal people across Australia, from urban to remote communities, confronted me with trauma and grief from past colonization, abuse, assimilation policies, and ongoing stressor exposures, with multiple premature deaths as well as much violence, and poor health (Swan & Raphael, 1995; Raphael & Swan, 1997; Delaney, Raphael, & Wooding, 2003). I learned of the impacts of trauma and grief across generations on health and well-being. Indigenous Australians have 20 years less life expectancy than nonindigenous Australians and poorer health on all health indicators as well as ongoing and profound social disadvantages. I also learned further of survival, courage, and resilience. These experiences changed me profoundly and personally.

Two other major events have been very influential in more recent times. Preparation for mental health response should a disaster or terrorist attack occur during the Sydney Olympics (2000) led to engagement with the horror of potential terrorism and its impacts. This process involved the setting in place of systems of mental health response; the training and development of an evidence-based manual (New South Wales Health Department, 2000); the preparation, planning, and holding of exercises as part of an expert professional health and emergency response system; and my role and responsibilities as the mental health controller in this system were important challenges and learning experiences.

No disaster or terrorist attack occurred at that time. Australia's distance from catastrophe continued and the atmosphere of that time was the "best ever."

Yet a year later, September 11, 2001, affected us tremendously, as the reality of mass violence hit home. Prior to this I had been working with U.S. colleagues to contribute to a consensus statement entitled *Early Intervention After Mass Violence* (National Institute of Mental Health, 2001).

This plan of response was completed after September 11. In Sydney, we met people arriving on inbound U.S. planes. We set up a support program for the U.S. embassy, as well as telephone help lines. My daughter and son-in-law were living in San Francisco during this time, and I shared their shock and fears.

Following this and the heightened state of alert, there were "white powder" incidents (i.e., anthrax threats) and ongoing arousal and concern. Yet Australians settled back to their usual activities, with some underlying view that the "lucky country" was safe once more. Then, a little more than a year later, the Bali bombings brought terrorism close to Australian shores. We mobilized health and other emergency responses, with mental health as a key part of these. We set in place responses to deal with the extensive loss and grief, trauma, and traumatic stress in diverse and dispersed populations. We are still providing outreach to those affected (Raphael, Dunsmore, & Wooding, 2004).

All these events and many others, including my ongoing work with veterans of many wars, my clinical work with bereaved and traumatized populations, my own research and the research of my students have consolidated and strengthened my interest in trauma and grief and also my interest in how we can prevent the violence that so often contributes to morbid outcomes (Raphael, 2002). My interests have also extended to the questions of how populations can adapt to ongoing but uncertain threat, build resilience, and remain hopeful, trusting, compassionate, and attached to families and their societies, and ultimately how they can deal with trauma and grief when they occur.

WHAT HAVE BEEN MY GREATEST ACHIEVEMENTS AND CONTRIBUTIONS TO THIS FIELD?

It is difficult to list achievements in any field separately from the drives and motives that have influenced one's actions. Perhaps "achievements" are best viewed as areas of greatest satisfaction and opportunities to contribute. One cannot judge them without bias, nor are they separate from all the others who have been involved with me in the processes. Most particularly there is my family—whose members have nurtured and supported me through the events and difficulties of life with love and understanding.

So, from my own point of view, I see as important the contributions of developing mental health roles in response to disaster and more recently to terrorism. I have built on my research, my understanding of the great contributions of colleagues to this field, my clinical experience, my work in responding to disasters, and my understanding of systems.

First, my research has looked at *bereavement as a stressor* and in the individual psychological, social, and mental health concomitants with the aim of developing appropriate mental health responses

(Raphael, 1974, 1977a). This model provided a framework to understand this life stressor and reactions to it, both normal and pathologic. Risk factors could be delineated and linked to the development of pathology. The "traumatic circumstances" of some deaths were identified as contributing a further stressor component that could interfere with resolution (Raphael & Maddison, 1976). This conceptual model provided the basis for developing preventive intervention for those at higher risk, tested in a randomized controlled trial with individuals in the community. It was subsequently translated into an intervention program, implemented, and evaluated (Raphael, 1977a, 1977b; Singh & Raphael, 1981). The significance of bereavement as a disaster stressor, one that can profoundly influence mental health and social outcomes, has continued as a major theme of my work. A number of doctoral and other research students have carried this work with bereavement forward. It provides a model that also shows the interconnectedness of knowledge, skills, and response to both the personal disasters of everyday life and mass disasters.

Both at the time of my early research in bereavement and progressively through my clinical work with affected populations, and because of work with those psychologically traumatized, I came to understand the different phenomena of bereavement reactions and traumatic stress reactions (Raphael & Martinek, 1997). This strong theme also evolved from the excellent work with children of Pynoos and coworkers (Pynoos et al., 1987a, 1987b), which more clearly highlighted the traumatic stress reactions to life threat, the bereavement reactions to loss, and their relationships to particular pathologic outcomes. This theme of different, multiple, and interacting phenomena of stressor reactions and outcomes is, in my view, significance. This field requires much further research into psychophysiologic aspects, as these reactive processes evolve and are related to mental health outcomes. The effectiveness of counseling and other interventions dealing with these in preventing adverse outcomes also needs further research in the disaster context. The understanding of life threat stressors leading to traumatic stress reactions and loss leading to bereavement reactions is a key element that moves from the narrow view that all postdisaster or mass violence outcomes should be viewed and researched through the lens of psttraumatic stress disorder (PTSD). The most long-term and disabling consequences encompass both these and other stressor impacts, which require specific assessment and intervention (Raphael & Martinek, 1997; Raphael, Martinek, & Wooding, in press).

Systems are impacted by trauma and mass events. *Systems will respond.* Understanding the nature of these systems and how mental health may be integrated with these in its response is important in positively influencing outcomes. In the period after the cyclone that destroyed the Australian northern city of Darwin at the end of 1974, I was asked by the professional body the Royal Australian and New Zealand College of Psychiatrists (RANZCP) to develop a report recommending mental health response to disaster (Raphael, 1976). To do this, I met and talked with people who had been involved in every level of political, social, and community response. Mental health was *not* seen as part of this system of response. Nevertheless, all these groups saw the "human factor" as significant and felt that it was essential to understand and take this into account. When discussed further, this human factor covered personal reactions, personality, behavior in the face of stress, barriers to functioning and not "getting over it," and trying to understand "what had happened." The model developed took into account and mirrored the systems of emergency and recovery organizations as well as state and federal government systems. Mental health's integration into systems of response and action has taken place progressively over the years since. This has led to formal and identified roles for mental health as a component of emergency and recovery systems. This formal, structured role delineation and systems approach is critical in the face of disaster or terrorism. It brings status to mental health well beyond these contexts.

The development of *evidence-based guidelines* for responses to disaster and terrorism has provided a strong framework for clinical responses. These were developed to prepare for the Sydney Olympics should such events occur at that time. The manual and associated training have been invaluable in response to the events that have occurred and have been implemented internationally. They have also provided the basis for response to the Bali terrorist attack. The manual and the training have contributed to building the capacity for mental health response in New South Wales, in Australia, and elsewhere. The manual is currently being updated.

Opportunities to contribute *internationally* have come through a number of sources: links with Scandinavian researchers (Raphael, Lundin, & Weisaeth, 1989; Weisaeth, 1989), the publication of *When Disaster Strikes* (1986) and its translation into Japanese, writings in this field, collaboration with U.S. colleagues (Raphael & Wilson, 2000; Wilson & Raphael, 1993), and consultancies with the World Health Organization. These have all helped me link in collaborative relationships with workers in mental health in the fields of grief, trauma, disaster, and more recently terrorism.

A Prevention Framework

Commitment to prevention in the mental health field has been sporadic and until recent decades poorly supported by evidence. Trauma, loss, and disasters are fields where prevention of adverse mental health outcomes could potentially be achieved through intervention with affected populations who are at heightened risk (Raphael 1979–1980). Such strategies need also to recognize the resilience of many, even in the face of horrific events. However, an adequate set of prevention strategies is yet to be developed, tested, and evaluated in disaster and terrorist settings, although there is much data that could contribute. This could also be linked to population surveillance for mental health and potential impacts and their monitoring.

Recognizing Resilience and Personal Growth

Learning from those involved in response to disaster and those exposed and affected has highlighted the potential for resilience in such populations. Our first study of rescuers and other responders after a rail disaster showed that many experienced a positive re-evaluation of life, and negative impacts were variable (Raphael et al., 1983–1984). Experience clinically and in consultation since that time has shown that trauma, loss, and grief may be horrific, but they may also bring out the best in people: altruism, courage, maturation, and hope.

The major way in which I feel I have contributed to this field could perhaps best be summarized as the *development and implementation of mental health policy for disaster preparation, planning, and response.* These policy initiatives have been built on the evidence available and what is known of good practice and consensus. They have provided the bases for programs that have been implemented in response to disaster. The opportunity to do this has been invaluable, but this whole process needs to have much stronger cycles of program implementation with fidelity, evaluation, research and trials, implementation, and further evaluation. These stages are only beginning both in Australia and elsewhere.

WHO ARE PEOPLE WHO HAVE INFLUENCED ME TO MAKE THESE CONTRIBUTIONS?

My family, and especially my parents, influenced me in my childhood. They held liberal views, encouraged my curiosity and education, and provided an environment of freedom that was unusual for a small country town. They were always interested in and concerned about others and compassionate toward people who suffered or were in trouble in some way. My mother would always lend a listening ear to those troubled, and my father was a practical, sociable man, responding often to community needs. Maybe this set the scene for me to become a psychiatrist, or maybe it contributed to my interest in grief and trauma in people's everyday lives.

Teachers in my high school years were influential in that they opened doors to the rest of the world, as did my interest in reading, particularly works that challenged with tales of grief and trauma, such as *War and Peace*. Teachers in medical school were also interesting, but the people who influenced me most, both then and as a young doctor, were my patients. They influenced me through their trust and sharing of their diverse experiences and their clear messages of how important it was to have someone listen and hear, and how people should *never* be pre-judged. Each and every one of them had something new for me to learn. Their stories, their pain, and their suffering were often profound: for instance, the veterans, including some from World War I who had been gassed; the survivors of POW camps; women who had been raped; girls struggling with unwanted pregnancies and abortions; parents who had suffered the traumatic deaths of children.

In my training to become a psychiatrist I was influenced by clinicians, teachers, and distinguished leaders in this field as well as those who had contributed in theory, writing, and research, including Sigmund Freud, Karl Menninger, and many others. As a researcher, my interest progressively focused on stressful life events and biopsychosocial reactions to life experiences. Thomas Holmes and George Engel visited Australia, and I was privileged to meet them. My interest in prevention research was strongly influenced by David Maddison, then professor of psychiatry at the University of Sydney, who encouraged me to take up studies in the field of bereavement as a life stressor, potentially leading to psychiatric morbidity for some, and the opportunity to test the effective-ness of preventive interventions for those at heightened risk (Raphael & Maddison, 1976). His early encouragement and support strongly influenced me in my academic career and its development.

Another important influence was John Bowlby, who generously con-tributed to my conceptualization and research in the field of bereavement, both with adults and children, and through his classic contributions on attachment, separation, and loss. He also encouraged me to write my first book, *The Anatomy of Bereavement* (1983b), which is still in print.

As I progressively moved from a focus on bereavement to work more broadly with disaster-affected populations and to understand more about trauma, Lars Weisaeth of the University of Oslo showed me the importance of trauma and traumatic stress through his work with a wide range of traumatized populations in peace and in war and through his linking me to Leo Eitinger with his follow-up of Holocaust survivors, demonstrating the longer-term impacts on health and life.

My friend and colleague Carol Nadelson has also influenced me, parti-cularly in terms of her work with women who had been traumatized through rape and other adverse life experiences. Alfred Freedman has been a strong and ongoing influence through our shared experience in a WHO consultancy to China; subsequently he has been a source of wis-dom about the challenges of translating research and understanding across international boundaries.

The work of a great many colleagues in the field of trauma, with their excellent conceptualizations and research, has been significant in diverse ways. John Wilson has been influential, thanks to the energy and enthusiasm he has brought to his work with me and others. Bob Ursano has "shown the way" with his insights, his many studies, collaboration, creativity, and broad-ranging work in the fields of disasters, terrorism, and multiple contexts of trauma.

Robert Lifton, Bob Pynoos, Yael Danieli, Terry Keane, Charles Figley, and more recently Arieh Shalev, Zahava Solomon, Matt Friedman, Carol North, Cam Ritchie, Pat Watson, Richard Mollica, Richard Bryant, Derek Silove, and many others have all stimulated my thinking. It is often difficult to identify specific contributions, as the interactions with others are subtle yet ongoing; often it is only later that you realize the pivotal value of a query raised, a conceptualization touched upon, or an interesting research finding.

As I noted earlier I was profoundly affected by my experiences with my colleague Pat Delaney (Swan) and my relationships with and shared knowledge from Aboriginal Australians (Raphael, Swan, & Martinek, 1996).

I have learned an enormous amount from people in disaster settings, from people responding, from people under threat, from patients and groups who have experienced trauma and loss in such circumstances. I have learned in ongoing ways from veterans, police, and ambulance officers, from soldiers, nurses, and doctors. I saw and assessed about 200 survivors of a peacetime naval disaster 30 years and more after it occurred, and their cumulative stories gave a shared experience, as did the evaluation of trauma impacts after many, many years.

You also learn from those closest to you, in particular your children. My daughter has shared many of my experiences of working in disasters with my absences and commitment to disasters and emergency response since her early childhood. Her good challenges to me have influenced my understanding of how this work impacts the self and one's loved ones—an aspect that should never be ignored but that can enrich one's work in this field.

HOW WOULD I HOPE CURRENT AND FUTURE SCHOLARS MIGHT BUILD ON MY WORK?

It would be my hope that future scholars would look to new methodologies to answer questions generated not only by my work but the work of many others.

First, there is a need to better research and understand *resilience* in populations affected by disasters and terrorism. Understanding these traits, coping strategies, and the role of personal, community, and environmental variables will constitute a much stronger basis for prevention strategies to prevent adverse mental health outcomes. With many years' experience in prevention and population health (Raphael, 2000) as well as clinical care, I remain concerned that it is still so difficult to orient services to prevention strategies.

Perhaps, however, one of the greatest challenges is to focus on the *prevention of violence*, for it is this human and social attribute that contributes so much to incidents that impact profoundly on mental health.

Second, there is the need to research the *impact of and adaption to terrorist threat over time.* Does resilience protect from this type of threat? How does such ongoing threat influence mental health and well-being, and general health over time? Does it lead to greater morbidity in the population broadly, or for vulnerable groups—for instance increased anxiety or depressive symptoms or disorders? Does it lead to paranoid views, to loss of capacity to trust? Or does it strengthen and mature those so threatened? Do people retain compassion, or does compassion fatigue take over and impact on personal responses as well? Of particular concern must be impacts on development, particularly with children and young people. There is an urgent need to research and establish optimal strategies for children and young people so that their emotional, cognitive, and behavioral development is not negatively impacted.

Third, it would be important to further develop *intervention strategies* for those *bereaved and traumatized* through exposure to disaster or terrorism. While some evidence exists for some interventions, such as those focusing on trauma and grief, programs built on such evidence have had only limited testing and evaluation in circumstances of disaster or terrorism. There also needs to be better understanding of the complex and multiple stressors involved, their interactions over time, and the factors that influence positive adaptations as compared to the evolution pathology, and how intervention strategies may influence these.

Further exploration of the *phenomenology over time of reactions to stressors,* such as death encounter and traumatic stress reaction, loss and grief reactions, and the interactions that may occur between these would be helpful in terms of the relationship of such phenomena to the development of pathology and the determining of appropriate interventions. The contribution of prior stressor exposures, especially trauma and loss and their reawakening, need to be better understood and more systematically researched.

Fourth, there is a need to better understand the emergency and longer term reactions and how strategies may support and influence these positively (Raphael & Wooding, in press). Of importance is further research into models such as psychological first aid and whether different debriefing models may lead to positive or negative outcome in terms of mental health for specific populations or applied at different times (Raphael & Wilson 2000). One may also consider how the environments of response can promote positive mental health or at the least do no harm.

A whole field of research is needed to explore the nature of the *stressor exposure of "human malevolence,"* knowing that others have attacked deliberately, have intended to kill and destroy, and may do so again. We know little of these processes and their ultimate effects on mental health.

Prospective population-based surveillance and screening with nested studies could contribute further to understanding the impacts of these exposures over time.

How to *describe and measure systems,* both spontaneous and formal organizations, and to evaluate their contribution to effective response to disasters and terrorism—how to optimize their contribution to response and outcomes—is another important field for future research. This will be relevant before, during, and after incidents as well as over time. There is also a need to research media impacts and seek opportunities to positively influence outcomes. And inevitably the nature of political responses and their impacts, positively and negatively, should be explored.

Vulnerable populations have been variously described: those with pre-existing mental or physical disability, the socially disadvantaged, the young, minority groups, those previously traumatized, and so forth. *Understanding vulnerability and protective factors* and providing interventions that can mitigate risk while at the same time empowering such populations is an area of need.

Occupational mental health and safety programs for emergency workers, responders, and rescue and recovery personnel need to be developed, building on available evidence about tours of duty, training and preparation, support and recognition, and active learning from operational review and debriefing. Significant research and development effort is required in this field.

What skills and knowledge can be provided to the *population as a whole,* as universal prevention to lessen risk of adverse mental health impacts is a further important question. We do not know and we need to research this to deal with threat and impacts of incidents.

Human attachments, the strength of family, affection, trust, and empathy for others, are all central to society, as are human rights. How response to terrorism and threat of terrorism can be dealt with so that the core of social and personal life, the foundations to love, work, and play are not destroyed, is an ongoing challenge. Vaillant (2000) has shown how positive mental health is a nebulous concept yet involves the above and hopefulness for the future. It needs to be constantly considered and understood, valued and developed, as do the community strengths of social cohesion and capacity. Scholars and researchers need to address these themes vis-à-vis trauma and traumatic futures.

Work in the fields of disaster, trauma, loss, and grief *challenges* us all with the recognition of human suffering, with which we may identify and empathize. The challenge needs also to extend our creative drive to find and develop new methods for researching disaster and trauma while still recognizing the "gold standards" of epidemiology and randomized controlled trials. We need to do better in the chaos and the evolving fields of the future, to better deal with the trauma and grief of both the past and the present and of the times to come. But mostly we need to recognize and build on the good, peaceful, accepting, courageous, compassionate, altruistic, and affiliative behaviors that can be mobilized by trauma, grief, and disaster—to research these and enhance them for more positive futures.

Beverley Raphael, 1972

REFERENCES

Delaney, P., Raphael, B., & Wooding, S. (2003). Suicide and self-harm. In S. Couzos & R. B. Murray (Eds.), *Aboriginal primary health care: An evidence-based approach* (2nd ed.). Melbourne: Oxford University Press.

McFarlane, A. C. (1986). Chronic post-traumatic morbidity of the natural disaster: Implications for disaster planners and emergency services. *Medical Journal of Australia, 145,* 561–631.

McFarlane, A.C., Raphael, B. (1984). Ash Wednesday: The effects of a fire. *Australian & New Zealand Journal of Psychiatry, 18*(4), 341–351.

National Institute of Mental Health (2001). *Mental health and mass violence: Evidence-based early psychological intervention for victims/survivors of mass violence. A workshop to reach consensus on best practices* (NIH Publication No. 02-5138). Washington, DC: U.S. Government Printing Office.

New South Wales (NSW) Health Department (2000). *Disaster mental health response handbook.* Sydney, Australia: NSW Health and the Centre for Mental Health.

Pynoos, R. S., Frederick, C., Nader, K. Arroyo, W., Steinberg, A., Eth, S., et al. (1987a). Life threat and posttraumatic stress in school-age children. *Archives of General Psychiatry, 44,* 1057–1063.

Pynoos, R. S., Nader, K., Frederick, C., Gonda, L., & Stuber, M. (1987b). Grief reactions in school age children following a sniper attack at school. *Israeli Journal of Psychiatry and Related Sciences, 24,* 53–63.

Raphael, B. (1971). Crisis intervention: Theoretical and methodological considerations. *Australian & New Zealand Journal of Psychiatry, 5,* 183–190.

Raphael, B. (1974). Bereavement and stress. *Bulletin of the Postgraduate Committee in Medicine*, University of Sydney, *30*(3).

Raphael, B. (1975). Crisis and loss counselling following a disaster. *Mental Health of Australia*, 14, 118–122.

Raphael, B. (1976). Death, dying and patient care: The patient and his family. *Australian Hospital*, 2, 10.

Raphael, B. (1977a). Preventive intervention with the recently bereaved. *Archives of General Psychiatry*, 34, 1450–1454.

Raphael, B. (1977b). The Granville train disaster: Psychological needs and their management. *Medical Journal of Australia*, 1, 303–305.

Raphael, B. (1979–80). A primary prevention action programme: Psychiatric involvement following a major rail disaster. *Omega*, 10, 211–225.

Raphael, B. (1983a). Psychiatric consultancy in a major disaster. *Australian & New Zealand Journal of Psychiatry*, 18, 303–306.

Raphael, B. (1983b). *Anatomy of bereavement*. New York: Basic Books.

Raphael, B. (1986). *When disaster strikes: How individuals and communities cope with catastrophe*. New York: Basic Books.

Raphael, B. (2000). *A population health model for the provision of mental health care*. Canberra: Commonwealth of Australia.

Raphael, B. (2002). *Violence and prevention*. Paper presented at The Second World Conference for the Promotion of Mental Health and the Prevention of Mental and Behavioural Disorders. London, September 11.

Raphael, B., Dunsmore, J., & Wooding, S. (2005). Terror and trauma in Bali: Australia's Mental Health Disaster Response. In Y. Danieli Browm, D., & Sills, J. (Eds.) Trauma and Terrorist, Binghamton, NY: Haworth Press.

Raphael, B., Field, J. & Kvelde, H. (1980). Childhood bereavement: A prospective study as a possible prelude to future preventive intervention. In E. J. Anthony & C. Chiland (Eds.), *Preventive psychiatry in an age of transition*. New York: John Wiley & Sons.

Raphael, B., Lundin, T., & Weisaeth, L. (1989). A research method for the study of the psychological and psychiatric aspects of disaster. *Acta Psychiatrica Scandinavica Supplementum*, 353, 80.

Raphael, B., & Maddison, D. C. (1976). The care of bereaved adults. In O. W. Hill (Ed.), *Modern trends in psychosomatic medicine* (pp. 491–506). London: Butterworth.

Raphael B., & Martinek, N. (1997). Assessing traumatic bereavement and post-traumatic stress disorder. In J. Wilson & T. M. Keane (Eds.), *Assessing psychological trauma and post-traumatic stress disorder* (pp. 373–395). New York: Guilford Press.

Raphael, B, Martinek, N, & Wooding, S. (2004). Assessing traumatic bereavement. In J. Wilson & T. M. Keane (Eds.), *Assessing psychological trauma and post-traumatic stress disorder* (2nd ed.). New York: Guilford Press.

Raphael, B., Singh, B., Bradbury, L., & Lambert, F. (1983–84). Who helps the helpers? The effects of a disaster on the rescue workers. *Omega*, *14*(1), 9–20.

Raphael, B., & Swan, P. (1997). The mental health of Aboriginal and Torres Strait Islander people. *International Journal of Mental Health*, *26*(3), 9–22.

Raphael, B., Swan, P., & Martinek, N. (1996). Inter-generational aspects of trauma for Australian Aboriginal people. In Y. Danieli (Ed.). *An international handbook of multi-generational legacies of trauma*.

Raphael, B., & Wilson, J. P. (Eds.) (2000). *Psychological debriefing: Theory, practice and evidence*. Cambridge, UK: Cambridge University Press.

Raphael, B., & Wooding, S. (In press). Longer term mental health interventions following disasters and mass violence (greater than 1 month). In E. Ritchie, M. Friedman, & P. Watson (Eds.), *Interventions following Mass Violence and Disasters: Strategies for Mental Health Practice*. New York: Guilford.

Singh, B., & Raphael, B. (1981). Post disaster morbidity of the bereaved: A possible role for preventive psychiatry. *Journal Nervous and Mental Disease*, *169*(4), 203–212.

Swan, P., & Raphael, B. (1995). *"Ways forward." National Consultancy Report on Aboriginal and Torres Strait Islander mental health.* Parts 1 and 2. Canberra: Australian Government Publishing Service.

Vaillant, G. E. (2000). Adaptive mental mechanisms: Their role in a positive psychology. *American Psychologist, 55,* 89–98.

Weisaeth, L. (1989). The stressors and the post-traumatic stress syndrome after an industrial disaster. *Acta Psychiatrica Scandinavica Supplementum, 355,* 25–37.

Weisaeth, L. (2000). Briefing and debriefing: Group psychological interventions in acute stressor situations. In B. Raphael & J. Wilson (Eds.), *Psychological debriefing: Theory, practice and evidence* (pp. 43–57). Cambridge, UK: Cambridge University Press.

Wilson, J. P., & Raphael, B. (Eds.) (1993). *International handbook of traumatic stress syndromes.* New York: Plenum Press.

12

Choices Made, Promises Kept

ZAHAVA SOLOMON

WHAT LED TO MY INTEREST IN TRAUMA?

One's professional life is inevitably intertwined with one's personal life. As an Israeli, my professional choices were strongly influenced by Israel's sociopolitical situation and by the events in my family which stemmed from it.

The state of Israel was established after some 2,000 years in which the Jewish people were stateless wanderers, living in various countries of Europe, the Middle East, and North Africa. The establishment of Israel as a sovereign Jewish state, after most of European Jewry was exterminated in the Nazi Holocaust, thus seemed to usher in a new era in which we would live safely and securely in our own land. That was the hope. It has not materialized.

Instead, Israel has become something of a laboratory for war stress. In the past half-century or so, our small country has known six organized wars, an undeclared war of attrition, and countless terrorist campaigns. As a citizen who has lived through much of the strife, as a wife whose husband, like most Israeli men, was a reserve soldier; and as a mother whose son and daughter, like most Israeli youngsters, both did mandatory army service, I could not but be aware of the vital role that our army plays in our collective and individual existence, as well as of the high toll that the ongoing strife can take—on fighters, their families, and other civilians. For me, trauma study is not merely an academic but also a deeply personal matter.

During the Sinai campaign of 1956, I was 6 years old. I remember my mother trying to hide her fear as she explained that she was taping up the windows so that they wouldn't break in the event of shelling and covering the shutters with black paper so that the light wouldn't seep out of the cracks. I remember her listening nervously to the hourly radio news broadcasts and waiting anxiously for my father's return.

When the next war, the Six-Day War, erupted in June 1967, I was in the 11th grade. The war itself lasted only 6 days, but the 3 weeks that preceded it were filled with excruciating anxiety. Egypt, Syria, and Jordan had moved their armies right up to our borders. Only 3 kilometers separated my parents' home from the Arab forces. The Voice of Cairo, broadcasting in Hebrew, was conducting a scare campaign aimed at demoralizing us. Though we went on with our lives, the danger was palpable and terrifying.

I vividly remember my mother, who had spent her adolescence in Auschwitz and who had already been through the War of Independence and the Sinai campaign, whispering quietly, as if to herself, "Till when? How many more wars do I have to go through in my lifetime?"

The Israeli victory was a tremendous relief but produced an unrealistic euphoria. People made victory albums glorifying the heroism and achievements of our soldiers. Then, with the Yom Kippur War in October 1973, this short-lived sense of power and strength evaporated.

By this time I was married. For 8 months, I was the wife of a combat soldier on the Syrian front. I spent my days waiting for news of him. At night, I'd return to the college dorms exhausted and crawl into bed to a recurrent nightmare: heavy boots sounding on the pavement, slowly approaching my house, and soldiers coming to tell me that my husband had been killed. I'd wake up three or four times a night, covered in a cold sweat. My husband sent short postcards: "Everything's fine. Don't worry. Take care of yourself." They were splattered with mud and less than reassuring.

When he finally came home on leave, instead of my usually energetic husband, I had a man who was physically and emotionally exhausted, introverted, and decidedly disinclined to tell me about his experiences or to share his feelings. It was only later that I learned something about what he had gone through. Practically the only inkling I had at the time came from his talk in his sleep: jumbled words about planes circling overhead.

At the end of the first semester—my husband was still on the front—we had to write a paper for a course in psychopathology on the emotional reactions of soldiers in combat. I read the pioneering works of Kardiner (1947) and Grinker and Spiegel (1945) on the psychological reactions to combat of American soldiers in World War II. Oddly, their findings seemed remote. At that point, I still made no connection between what they wrote and what my close friends were going through.

The turning point in my career came with the Lebanon War, fought in 1982. When it began, I had been working in the newly formed research branch of the IDF (Israeli Defense Forces) mental health department. This was my first job in Israel shortly after I returned from the United States, where I had completed my doctorate in psychiatric epidemiology. I took the job not out of any special interest in combat stress but simply because it was the best offer.

With the outbreak of the war, my reading and the strong personal feelings I had in connection with war seemed to come together under serendipitous circumstances. The men in the department, mostly therapists, were organized to treat combat stress reaction (CSR) casualties in special treatment stations at the front and along the northern border. The women were left idle.

Wanting to contribute, I saw an opportunity to fill what was to me an obvious need in the IDF medical corps for clear and comprehensive information about the psychiatric casualties. I thus suggested to the female mental health officers in the department that we collect and organize all the data that were accumulated. We began to set up a casualty file. We recorded the number of casualties, examined the clinical features for common patterns, and looked at data on predisposition and types of treatment interventions.

With this work, I found my direction. After about 2 months, a cease fire was signed and I began to organize my first research project. I knew that the subject would be combat reactions. From that point on, almost all the studies I conducted were on one or another aspect of manmade trauma.

By the next two wars, the first Gulf War of 1991 and the armed Intifada that broke out in the fall of 2000, I was a mature scholar, well recognized in my field. But these wars too made their mark on my research.

In contrast to previous wars, in the first Gulf War it was the civilian population that was targeted, while our army was not engaged in active fighting. In the event of a possible chemical or gas attack, most of us collected our gas masks from the pickup stations organized by the army. But, to the last minute, we also told ourselves: "Nothing will happen."

Our anxiety level rose considerably when the air-raid sirens sounded and the only protection we had was sitting in our gas masks in rooms that were "sealed" by taping plastic sheeting over the windows and taping doors plugged with wet rags at the bottom. Our household expanded from 4 to 11 when relatives and friends moved in with us for company and safety.

At work in the mental health department, it was my research that kept me on an even keel. The war offered me yet another opportunity to study the psychological reactions of people to real-life stress under real-time conditions. But it seemed cynical to take advantage of the situation to further my career. Most research on the psychological effects of national disasters is carried out post hoc. Mental health professionals in an area hit by disaster are supposed to spend their time minimizing the pathogenic effects of the stressor, not researching it.

Fortunately, a friend persuaded me otherwise. There was nothing I could do about the war, he insisted, so I might as well make something useful out of it—for myself, certainly, but also to shed light on how war affects a civilian population. The research I carried out during the rest of the war helped me to cope with the uncertainties of those days and to get through them with relative equanimity.

The first Gulf War was frightening but caused little damage. The El-Aqsa intifada, which is not yet over, has been another matter entirely. Hundreds of Israelis have been killed and thousands injured, most of them in suicide attacks carried out in the middle of crowds, but also in drive-by shootings or intrusions into their homes. People of every age and station have been hurt, and attacks have occurred throughout the country: both in the settlements and within the internationally accepted borders.

By now I was no longer with the army. I was a full professor and director of the Adler Research Center at Tel Aviv University. Afraid for myself, my family, and my friends, I was no longer deterred by any notion of illegitimate "benefit" and felt that I had to learn more about how such violence affects people. Along with colleagues, I thus set out to assess the effects of the terror on both Jewish and Palestinian people, focusing mainly but not exclusively on children.

All the wars I described, including the Holocaust, which my mother, uncles, and aunts survived and memories of which my mother vividly shared with me since my childhood, have had a profound effect on my life and work. My secondhand experience of the Holocaust, I believe, sensitized me to the effects of the seemingly endless wars in Israel. In retrospect, I have come to realize that my research is tremendously important to me not only for my career but also personally. My investigation of the traumatic effects of war and terror are my way of fighting my fears and also, I believe, of asserting mastery and meaning in place of the sense of powerlessness that trauma produces.

WHAT WERE MY GREATEST ACHIEVEMENTS AND CONTRIBUTIONS TO THIS FIELD?

Although I write this section in the first person singular, I must begin by emphasizing that I did much of my research in collaboration with colleagues and students and also that I owe a considerable debt to researchers in other countries and times.

Over the last 24 years I have conducted several large-scale studies, prospective as well as cross-sectional, of groups at risk for trauma:

mainly soldiers, including ex-POWs and their wives, but also Holocaust survivors, along with civilians, both children and adults, exposed to the war and terror in Israel. The findings have been published in 6 books and 50 book chapters, more than a dozen monographs, and more than 200 articles in scientific journals in several languages. The studies deal with the acute reactions to traumatic stress; the development, course, and sub-types of posttraumatic stress disorder (PTSD) (e.g., reactivated, delayed) over a 30-year span; vulnerability and resilience factors, including per-sonality attributes and social and cultural factors; societal attitudes toward traumatized individuals; and issues of countertransference. There are also several studies evaluating various treatment modes and the role of compensation in PTSD. In addition to satisfying scientific curiosity, the various studies were aimed at increasing our understanding of human responses to man-made disasters and ways of coping with them. In gen-eral, these studies have raised public awareness and influenced public policy toward the traumatized individuals, especially with regards to the treatment and compensation of traumatized soldiers in Israel.

Some of the studies that I believe have made a contribution are briefly described below.

Acute Combat Stress Reaction

During and after the 1982 Lebanon War, my colleagues in the IDF and I documented the diagnosis, treatment, and course of CSR. These data enabled us to draw an initial empirically driven clinical taxonomy of CSR—to the best of my knowledge, the first of its kind—which subse-quent analysis revealed to be polymorphic and labile (Solomon, Mikulincer, & Benbenisty, 1989). All in all, we were able to show that the symptoms of CSR are normal defenses aimed at preserving ego integrity, and that what distinguishes these behaviors in CSR is the extreme form they take and their interference with functioning.

Longitudinal Study

Along with data routinely collected for every Israeli soldier before induc-tion (age 17), the data collected on the battlefield served as the basis for a 20-year follow-up study that compared CSR soldiers with matched con-trols and also combat soldiers who did not have a recorded CSR. The assessments, carried out four times over the two decades (1, 2, 3, and 20 years after the Lebanon War) covered the long-term psychiatric, social, and somatic consequences of participation in war. The findings of the first three follow-ups revealed very high rates of PTSD among CSR casu-alties and much higher levels of general psychiatric symptomatology, impaired social functioning (at work, in the community, and in the family), and somatic problems than the non-CSR controls. These and other findings, which are collected in my first book (Solomon, 1993), clearly show that the breakdown on the battlefield constitutes a major rupture in the CSR casualties' psychological structure. The 20-year follow-up revealed that the clinical picture in the clinical and nonclinical samples took a different course with time. The study is still going on.

Repeated Exposure

The frequent wars in Israel have resulted in the repeated exposure of both soldiers and civilians to war-related stress. The question of the psychological impact of such repeated exposure is thus a vital public health issue in Israel. There are few direct studies of this issue. Along with my colleagues, I studied the impact of prior exposure to war on the ability to cope with subsequent adversity in several studies: "Soldiers in the Lebanon War" (Solomon, 1993); "POWs of the 1973 Yom Kippur War" (Solomon, Neria, Ohry, Waysman, & Ginzburg, 1994); "Holocaust Survivors During the Gulf War" (Solomon & Prager, 1992); and "When Confronted With Life-Threatening Illness" (Hantman & Solomon, submitted). The findings of these studies show that the power to withstand stress declines with every recurrent exposure and with the magnitude of the exposure.

Subtypes of PTSD

Two subtypes of PTSD, reactivated and delayed-onset, were the focus of several of my studies. Based on clinical observations, my colleagues and I formulated a four-category taxonomy of reactivated stress responses (Solomon, 1993).

Delayed-Onset PTSD

Following the Lebanon War, there seemed to be a snowballing of war-induced injuries with delayed onset. Clinicians and policy makers had doubts about the validity of this diagnosis. There were few empiric studies of delayed-onset PTSD at the time. The Lebanon War provided a unique opportunity to carry out such a study.

First, we reviewed medical records in order to determine which cases were truly "delayed" and to calculate their rate and latency period (Solomon, Kotler, Shalev, & Lin, 1989). We then assessed the psychosocial status of delayed-onset versus chronic PTSD casualties and analyzed the implication of pre-, peri-, and posttraumatic personal, personality, and situational variables to delayed onset. The findings showed that delayed-onset PTSD was less severe than chronic PTSD. They also showed that delayed-onset casualties reported more personal resources than chronic PTSD sufferers but that they also reported having experienced more intense battle stress, less social support in battle, and less social support at homecoming than controls. These findings help to answer two important questions: what explains the difference in time of onset of chronic and delayed PTSD? And what explains why delayed-onset casualties broke down at homecoming even though they coped with the battle itself as well as the non-PTSD controls? (Solomon, Mikulincer, Waysman, & Marlowe, 1991; Solomon, Mikulincer, & Waysman, 1991a, 1991b). Delayed-onset PTSD is still understudied and requires more scientific attention.

Civilian Responses to the Stress of War

During the first Gulf War in 1991, Israeli civilians suffered 39 missile strikes in densely populated areas and were exposed to the threat, albeit unrealized, of chemical and biological attack. The government's policy of restraint left citizens with no more recourse than to huddle with gas masks in "sealed" rooms. My book *Coping with Induced Stress: The Gulf War and the Israeli Response* (Solomon, 1995) documents the real-time peritraumatic coping and cognitive, emotional, and behavioral responses of the Israeli population both during the war itself and 1 year later.

The book is a compilation of studies carried out by myself and numerous other Israeli mental health professionals. The studies show elevated levels of distress (e.g., sleep disturbances, social disintegration, depression, anxiety, and PTSD), along with rapid habituation and the continuation of normal life. Coping in various sectors of society was assessed, including families, children, Holocaust survivors, evacuees, mentally ill patients, and Israeli soldiers. We also assessed gender differences in coping and the role played by mental health professionals during this largely psychological war.

Alongside the impressive yet anecdotal study of Londoners during the Blitz, this work carried profound implications for societies under threat.

Treatment Effectiveness

Of all my many studies, the one that perhaps generated the greatest interest was on front-line treatment. First developed by Salmon in 1919, this was the official IDF treatment for CSR casualties in the Lebanon War. It has the advantage of being applied on the battlefield, when the CSR first occurs and before it develops into chronic PTSD. Its efficacy had been documented in clinical observations, but no systematic empiric investigation had been carried out, largely because of the great difficulty of doing systematic research on the battlefield. The approach also raises moral concerns, because the successfully treated soldier is sent back to the battlefield; this is one of the core principles of the treatment.

The evaluation compared the outcomes of the CSR casualties who were treated by the front-line approach with those who were treated behind the lines. The findings showed that those who received front-line treatment were more likely to rejoin the battle than the others and less likely to suffer from PTSD (Solomon & Benbenisty, 1986). The findings were enthusiastically received by the IDF and were almost immediately translated into operational strategies.

Recently we assessed the long-term effects of front-line treatment. The findings, obtained 20 years after the war, show that the CSR soldiers who received front-line treatment had lower rates of posttraumatic and psychiatric symptoms than those who did not receive front-line treatment; they experienced less loneliness and reported better social functioning.

Secondary Traumatization

The effects of trauma often extend from the traumatized persons themselves to people who are close to them, especially their families. My colleagues and I conducted a series of studies examining secondary traumatization in wives of traumatized soldiers (Solomon, Waysman, Levy, Fried, Mikulincer, Benbenishty, Florian, & Bleich, 1992) and in combat soldiers whose parents were Holocaust survivors (Solomon, Kotler, & Mikulincer, 1988). The studies on the afflicted veterans' wives, which documented the detrimental effects of their husbands' condition on their own physical and mental health, led to the recognition of their plight by the Ministry of Defense and to the provision of psychological assistance.

POWs

During the Yom Kippur War, hundreds of Israeli soldiers were captured and imprisoned by the Egyptians and Syrians. In 1991 we conducted the first comprehensive study of these POWs. The findings, which showed substantial rates of psychological distress and disability, revealed the former captives' enduring but invisible wounds. This study turned out to be the impetus for a film and together with this led to the initiation, by the Rehabilitation Division in the Ministry of Defense, of an outreach program to all POWs from all of Israel's wars. Such outreach was the first of its kind in Israel or, to my knowledge, elsewhere. In 2003, a second assessment of these POWs was undertaken to determine the effects of time and aging. The data are being analyzed as I write these lines.

Attitudes and Countertransference

One of the central themes of Zionism was the spiritual and psychological rebirth of Jews in their historic homeland, transforming them from passive, dependent victim to a strong, resilient, self-reliant people. The many traumatized individuals who made up Israel's population were included in this aspiration, and their sufferings went unrecognized or were denied legitimacy.

In a series of studies, we examined the attitudes of the public, including Knesset members (Solomon & Israeli, 1996), military physicians (Inbar, Solomon, Aviram, & Spiro, 1989), and military and civilian mental health professionals to various groups of trauma survivors such as traumatized soldiers and Holocaust survivors (JTS special Issue; Solomon, 1995). The findings of these studies revealed the shift from denial to recognition and acceptance of the survivors' plight. This was particularly noted with regard to Holocaust survivors, who are now treated with utmost respect. A similar yet less pronounced trend was observed with regard to traumatized soldiers. This is a long way from the disgrace that was associated with psychological breakdown on the battlefield in the 1948 War of Independence.

Terror

Finally, the outbreak of the second intifada, marked by deadly suicide attacks and other forms of terror against Israeli civilians, led me to carry out, along with colleagues and students, several large-scale studies on the effects of the ongoing terror. We examined the immediate responses and coping of the general population (Bleich, Gelkopf, & Solomon, 2003), as well as more specific effects on the aged, rescue workers and social workers, and Palestinian and Jewish students (Society & Welfare, Special issue; Solomon & Dekel, 2004).

Two very large scale studies assessed the effects of ongoing terror on adolescents. They covered the adolescents' resilience, psychological growth, PTSD, general distress, and attitudes toward peace and explored the roles of ideology, religion, social support, and personality attributes in mediating both the salutogenic and pathogenic effects of the terror. The study findings highlight the need for both mental health intervention and peace education.

In summary, these studies we conducted have raised public and professional awareness of the psychological toll of trauma and led to a fair number of policy changes in Israel, which have enabled the provision of treatment and rehabilitation of the traumatized and their significant others.

WHO HELPED AND INFLUENCED ME IN MY RESEARCH?

My parents, Bracha and Moshe HaElion, bestowed on me their love of knowledge and their sensitivity to the sufferings of others. Both of them actively encouraged me to pursue my education in the helping professions. I was also influenced by their strenuous efforts to rebuild their lives after the Holocaust and by the many emotional difficulties they had in its wake. This, in fact, was a strong driving force in my professional life, though it took me many years to recognize it.

My mentor was Professor Evelyeen Bronet, my dissertation adviser in the Psychiatric Epidemiology Program at the University of Pittsburgh. Her remarkable analytic abilities and high standards of meticulous research were coupled with a warm personality and outstanding generosity. She was also a lifelong model both as a teacher and scholar. The very close ties that I developed with most of the graduate students I advised were modeled, to a great extent, on the relationship Evelyeen Bronet had developed with me.

My other teacher and lifelong colleague was the late Professor Victor Florian. He was a dear friend whose superb coping with a severe physical handicap aroused my endless admiration, and awe as well. Our friendship lasted 30 years, until his untimely death in 2003. Victor's writing, much of which dealt with the fear of death, influenced my conceptions of the fear of death as the chief cause of combat stress reaction.

Professor Joseph Eaten, a pioneer in psychiatric epidemiology, was my teacher at Haifa University. I benefited from his consistent encouragement to explore uncharted territories and to open new fields of research.

I have always preferred working with others to working on my own. Colleagues and students have thus been great sources of inspiration. In particular, a large number of persons were instrumental in the long-term CSR study that I began in 1982. Professor Yossi (Joseph) Schwarwald and the late Professor Mati (Matisyohu) Weisenberg worked with me on designing the study. These professors, one a social psychologist and the other a clinical psychologist, greatly enriched the project with their knowledge and experience. Professor Mario Mikulincer joined this team, and I have been blessed by working with him also on the 20-year follow-up.

None of us had any experience either in combat or in treating traumatized soldiers. To our aid came Dr. Danny Enoch, former chief psychiatrist of the IDF and a decorated hero. His insights about the clinical picture of CSR and the effects of recurrent exposure to combat and his concept of time perception in PTSD casualties have had formative effects on my work.

Over the years, many colleagues in the IDF's Department of Mental Health have shared their knowledge and experience with me. Among them are Dr. Shabtai Noy, who introduced me to the American military psychiatry literature, Dr. Ron Levi, Dr. Rami Sklar, Prof Avi Bleich, and Professor Steve Hobful.

The study of the Yom Kippur POWs also entailed considerable teamwork. A number of individuals were especially involved. Dr. Yuval Neria, a former student and today a friend and colleague, enhanced and enriched the study by his sensitivity and clinical insight.

For years I was blinded by the view that the salutogenic effects of manmade trauma should not be assessed. Dr. Mark Waysman's study on resilience and positive change opened a new avenue of research for me. The findings of the study I carried out under his impetus led me to assess salutogenic effects along with pathogenic ones in subsequent studies.

My former students and colleagues, Dr. Karni Ginzburg, Dr. Racel Dekel, and Dr. Giora Zakin have enriched my understanding of the role of personality attributes as coping mechanisms, including attachment, hardiness, and repression.

I owe a great debt of gratitude both to scholars who wrote before me and to some of my contemporaries in the profession. The writing of clinicians and researchers who treated "shell shock" patients in World Wars I and II influenced my studies of combat stress reaction. The writings of Grinker and Spiegel, Kardiner, and Bartemeier were of particular interest, as was the collection of papers edited by Mullin and Glass on neuropsychiatry in World War II. Salmon's observations of the British and French armies' experiences in World War I and the formulation of front-line treatment were a major source of inspiration. The work of many others, including Linderman, Caplan, Menninger, Glass, and Artiss in conceptualizing crisis intervention as it pertains to traumatized soldiers inspired my series of studies on front-line treatment. Archibald's pioneer longitudinal studies paved the way to my own longitudinal studies.

Researchers of the Vietnam era generally focused on PTSD, not CSR. Charles Figley was an important exception. His 1978 compilation, which includes an outstanding chapter by Kormos on CSR, and his own insightful review of the literature, as well as, later, his two edited volumes (*Trauma and Its Wake*), became important and often consulted references for me. His writings also influenced my thinking and research on secondary tramatization.

In these early years several remarkable pioneering studies on Vietnam by Laufer, Kadushin, Hendin, and Pollinger-Haas on veterans, and later by Rosenheck on secondary traumatization in offspring of the traumatized veterans, had great effect on my work. More recently, the seminal work in the ECA studies and particularly the influential study of Kessler, Bromet, and Hughes (1995) and the Vietnam readjustment study (Kulka, Schlenger, Fairbank, et al., 1990) greatly expanded our knowledge of the epidemiology of PTSD.

In terms of conceptualization of issues of stress and coping, the writings of both Bruce Dohrenwend and Richard Lazarus and also meetings with them were most meaningful.

Horowitz had been most influential and I am still trying to validate, in our follow-up, his conceptualization of the interplay of intrusion and avoidance.

Over the years there have been many others whose work has profoundly affected my thinking and work. As they are too numerous to mention I shall name only a few: Terr, Pynoos, Yule and Saigh in regard to children, McFarlaine and Green with regard to longitudinal studies.

HOW WOULD I LIKE TO SEE OTHER SCHOLARS BUILD ON MY WORK?

Understanding Vulnerability and Resilience

Findings consistently reveal considerable variability in responses to traumatic stress. Being able to identify markers of resilience could have enormous public health benefits. For example, in situations where traumatic events cannot be prevented, the ability to identify persons who are likely to be resilient to stress can improve the selection of personnel for high-risk occupations (e.g., military service, rescue work). Along similar lines, better understanding of what makes for effective coping may serve as a basis for coping enhancement training aimed at enabling persons to better withstand traumatic stress.

Assessing Acute Stress as a Risk Factor for PTSD

Acute stress reactions in the course of a traumatic event are potentially transient, so that the symptoms pass within a short time. However, persons who sustain such an acute reaction are at greater risk than others for PTSD. Therefore it is crucial to further identify markers of acute stress reactions as potential predictors of long-term pathology.

Studying Methods of Intervention

Another major challenge in our field is to devise effective evidence-based interventions for the treatment of PTSD in its various subtypes. In particular, modes of crisis intervention should be developed and their effectiveness rigorously evaluated as they are applied. In addition, intervention techniques should specifically focus on blocking or arresting the crystallization of acute stress reactions into chronic PTSD. It is thus important to begin intervention as early as possible, with an emphasis on prevention.

By prevention I mean both inhibiting the development of disorder before it occurs and interrupting or slowing its progression.

Understanding Prolonged and Repeated Trauma

A major concern for traumatologists is the long-lasting implications of growing up and living in conditions of prolonged or repeated trauma. This issue is of special interest to those of us living and working in stress-ridden areas like Israel.

Studying Traumatic Experiences of Children

Childhood is a formative time, both physically and mentally, and the experiences we have during that time may have long-lasting effects. Some symptoms and problematic behaviors serve children well in coping with harsh realities. Psychic numbing, for example, may help them keep their fear and sorrow at bay. If such behaviors continue after the threat is over, however, they are dysfunctional and become symptoms of psychological distress. It has also been suggested that repeated exposure to war from a young age may lead to long-lasting personality changes. These contentions need to be systematically assessed.

Children's moral development may also be affected by trauma. Under circumstances of war, for example, killing is not murder and appropriating another person's property is not stealing. This hypothesis should be put to the test in rigorous longitudinal studies. Finally, our basic assumptions about the world are formed in childhood. Studies by several research groups including mine have suggested that children traumatized by war come to see the world as dangerous, unpredictable, and unsafe and people as malevolent and untrustworthy.

There is a pressing need for multifaceted large-scale longitudinal studies starting in infancy and following individuals until old age to assess psychological vulnerability, resiliency, moral development, attitudes toward the "other group," and future orientation.

Studying Secondary Traumatization

Those surrounding the traumatized individual are often vicariously exposed to the adverse effects of trauma. In future research, it is important to assess risk factors for secondary traumatization. There is also a need to assess the nature of the process of "contagion" between the traumatized individual and those interacting with him. This is particularly important in light of findings indicating that while the environment plays a role in the recovery process, it may also contribute to the chronicity of the posttraumatic disorder.

Conducting Interdisciplinary Research

My last suggestion for future research concerns methodology. It is important to try and bridge the gap that currently exists between psychologists and sociologists on the one hand and those studying biological aspects of trauma on the other. Complex models of etiology and treatment are necessary and must be assessed empirically. In addition, at least some of the research should be designed to include the active participation of trauma survivors in formulating the research questions, defining the methodology, and in interpreting and disseminating the results. Survivors may bring to the research the insights they gained from their first-hand experience, while their participation in the research may help to restore some of the self-confidence and self-esteem that they lost with their traumatization.

Zahava Solomon, 1986

REFERENCES

Belenky, G. L., Noy, S., Solomon, Z., & Jones, F. D. (1985). Contemporary Israeli studies in combat psychiatry. *Annales Medicinae Militaris Fenniae, 60,* 105–110.

Bleich, A., Gelkopf, M., & Solomon, Z. (2003). Exposure to terrorism, stress-related mental health symptoms, and coping behaviors among a nationally representative sample in Israel. *JAMA, 290(5),* 612–690.

Grinker, R. P., & Spiegel, J. P. (1945). *Men under stress.* Philadelphia: Blakiston.

Hantman, S., & Solomon, Z. (2004). *Reactivated trauma: Elderly Holocaust survivors cope with aging and trauma.* Manuscript submitted for publication.

Inbar, D., Solomon, Z., Aviram, U., & Spiro, S. (1989). Commanders' attitudes towards the nature, causality and severity of combat stress reaction. *Military Psychology, 1,* 215–233.

Kardiner, A. (1947). *War stress and neurotic illness.* New York: Hoeber.

Kessler, R. C., Broment, E., & Hughes, M. (1995). Posttraumatic stress disorder in the National Comorbidity Survey. *Archives of General Psychiatry, 52,* 1048–1060.

Kulka, R. A., Schlenger, W. E., Fairbank, J. A., et al. (1990). *Trauma and the Vietnam War generation: Report of findings from the National Vietnam Veterans Readjustment Study.* New York: Brunner/Mazel.

Levy, A., Witztum, Z., & Solomon, Z. (1996). Lessons relearned: When denial becomes impossible: Therapeutic response to combat stress reaction during the Yom Kippur War (1973) and the Lebanon War (1982). *Israel Journal of Psychiatry and Related Sciences, 32,* 89–102.

Manor, I., Shklar, R., & Solomon, Z. (1995). Diagnosis and treatment of combat stress reaction: Current attitudes of military physicians. *Journal of Traumatic Stress, 8,* 247–258.

Ofri, I., Solomon, Z., & Dasberg, H. (1995). Attitudes of therapists toward Holocaust survivors. *Journal of Traumatic Stress, 8,* 229–242.

Salmon, T. W. (1919). The war neuroses and their lesson. *New York State Journal of Medicine, 51,* 993–994.

Shalom, D., Benbenishty, R., & Solomon, Z. (1995). Mental health officers' causal explanations of combat stress reaction. *Journal of Traumatic Stress, 8,* 259–269.

Solomon, Z. (1985). Stress, social support and affective disorders in mothers of pre-school children—A test of the stress-buffering effect of social support. *Social Psychiatry, 20,* 100–105.

Solomon, Z. (1993). *Combat stress reaction: The enduring toll of war.* New York: Plenum Press.

Solomon, Z. (1995). *Coping with war-induced stress: The Gulf War and the Israeli response.* New York: Plenum Press.

Solomon, Z. (1995). From denial to recognition: Attitudes toward Holocaust survivors from World War II to the present. *Journal of Traumatic Stress, 8,* 215–228.

Solomon, Z. (1995). The effect of prior stressful experience on coping with war trauma and captivity. *Psychological Medicine, 25,* 1289–1294.

Solomon, Z. (1995). Therapeutic response to combat stress reaction during Israel's wars: Introduction. *Journal of Traumatic Stress, 8*(2), 243–246.

Solomon, Z. (1995). Trauma and society. *Special Section: Journal of Traumatic Stress, 8(2),* 213–214.

Solomon, Z., & Benbenishty, R. (1986). The role of proximity, immediacy, and expectancy in front-line treatment of combat stress reaction among Israelis in the Lebanon War. *American Journal of Psychiatry, 143,* 613–617.

Solomon, Z., & Dekel, R. (2004). The effects of terror on the Israeli society. *Editorial: Society & Welfare, Special issue, 24(2),* 121–123.

Solomon, Z., Garb, R., Bleich, A., & Grupper, D. (1987). Reactivation of combat-related post traumatic stress disorder. *American Journal of Psychiatry, 144,* 51–55.

Solomon, Z., & Israeli, U. (1996). Knesset members' attitudes towards combat stress reaction casualties. *Israel Journal of Psychiatry and Related Sciences, 32,* 103–113.

Solomon, Z., Kotler, M., & Mikulincer, M. (1988). Combat related post-traumatic stress disorder among second generation Holocaust survivors: Preliminary findings. *American Journal of Psychiatry, 145,* 865–868.

Solomon, Z., Mikulincer, M., & Benbenishty, R. (1989). Combat stress reaction: Clinical manifestations and correlates. *Military Psychology, 1,* 35–47.

Solomon, Z., Mikulincer, M., & Jakob, B.R. (1987). Exposure to recurrent combat stress: Combat stress reaction among Israeli soldiers in the 1982 Lebanon War. *Psychological Medicine, 17,* 433–440.

Solomon, Z., Mikulincer, M., & Waysman, M. (1991a). Delayed and immediate onset post-traumatic stress disorder: The role of life events and social resources. *Journal of Community Psychology, 19,* 231–236.

Solomon, Z., Mikulincer, M., & Waysman, M. (1991b). Delayed and immediate onset post-traumatic stress disorder: II. The role of battle experience and personal resources. *Social Psychiatry and Psychiatric Epidemiology, 26,* 8–13.

Solomon, Z., Mikulincer, M., Waysman, M., & Marlowe, D. (1991). Delayed and immediate onset posttraumatic stress disorder: I. Differential clinical characteristics. *Social Psychiatry and Psychiatric Epidemiology, 26*, 1–7.

Solomon, Z., Neria, Y., Ohry, A., Waysman, M., & Ginzburg, K. (1994). PTSD among Israeli former prisoners of war and soldiers with combat stress reaction: A longitudinal study. *American Journal of Psychiatry, 151*, 554–559.

Solomon, Z., Oppenheimer, B., & Noy, S. (1986). Subsequent military adjustment of CSR casualties—A nine year follow-up study. *Military Medicine, 151*, 8–11.

Solomon, Z., & Prager, E. (1992). Elderly Israeli Holocaust survivors during the Persian Gulf War: A study of psychological distress. *American Journal of Psychiatry. 149*, 1707–1710.

Solomon, Z., Waysman, M., Levy, G., Fried, B., Mikulincer, M., Benbenishty, R., Florian, V., & Bleich, A. (1992). From frontline to home front: A study of secondary traumatization. *Family Process, 31*, 289–302.

Witztum, E., Levy, A., & Solomon, Z. (1996). Lessons denied: A history of theraputic responses to combat stress reaction during Israel's War of Independence (1948), the Sinai Campaign (1956) and the Six Day War (1967). *Israel Journal of Psychiatry and Related Sciences, 32*, 79–88.

13

Memoirs of a Childhood Trauma Hunter

LENORE TERR

GETTING STARTED IN AN ALMOST NONEXISTENT FIELD

I met the very first psychiatric patient of my career, "Miss Anne Jones," in September 1962. It was late to start a residency because I had taken a couple of months off to have a baby. Anne Jones, a single mother from a Detroit suburb, voluntarily signed herself into the University of Michigan hospital, stating "If you don't stop me I'm going to kill my child!" I believed her. Not only did she threaten her 5-year-old girl, Wendy, but as a new mother, she also threatened me.

Anne Jones was a high school graduate with no past mental illnesses, no family history of psychiatric hospitalizations or suicide, and no problems with street drugs or alcohol. The man who got her pregnant was long gone. After Anne gave birth to Wendy, she didn't leave home. She stayed with her widowed mother. Then, when Wendy was 3½ years old, Anne tried to drown her in the bathtub. Thinking better of it, Anne rushed the coughing, choking girl to a local emergency room, where the ER team said, "Don't worry. Accidents happen." Several months later, shortly before she signed herself into the our hospital, Anne had once again indulged in a murderous attack, this time taking a hot teakettle to her daughter. Trying another emergency room, Anne confessed, "I did it!" But this ER team, like the others, failed to believe

185

her. "Kitchens are dangerous places," Anne was told. "Try and be more careful."

This was physical child abuse of the most dangerous kind. But what came first, the chicken or the egg? In the early '60s, when I met Miss Jones, the dynamics of child abuse were not worked out. I decided to meet the young "egg," Wendy. Perhaps knowing Wendy might help me to understand Anne. I found the kindergartener to be an angry bundle of energy. According to her mother's reports, Wendy said "no" to virtually everything Anne asked of her. When she was particularly enraged, Wendy smeared her feces on the back screen door. Except for the fecal smearing, Wendy was much the same with me. But in my view, there was no question: Anne was the angrier of the two. After a series of interviews, the original source of Anne's rage became clear—Grandma had "up and died" on her just before the first homicidal attack. Suddenly, unexpectedly, a young mother's touchstone had been removed. Without Grandma in place, neither Anne nor Wendy could cope. Anne didn't know how to be a mother. Wendy didn't know how to be a child.

I read most of the literature available at the time and realized that the best medical paper on the subject had just been printed that July—in the *Journal of the American Medical Association*. It had been written by a team of Colorado physicians, including a child psychiatrist (Kempe, Silverman, Steele, Droegmuller, & Silver, 1962). My patient was opening up new territory that was almost unexplored. I wrote a letter to each department at our hospital. I would assess every case of child abuse they sent me—as part of a clinical research study. Eventually, during 4 years of residency and fellowship, I evaluated 10 cases. In those days, 10 was apparently all that a 700-bed hospital could muster up. Ten cases or no, I was hooked.

In those days, psychological trauma was fragmented into "battered child syndrome," "battle fatigue," "rape," "incest," "accident," "torture," "civilian casualties of war." There were professional meetings for a number of separate organizations dealing with one or the other of these. So I chose "battered child syndrome" as my first field for research, and I asked the gifted University of Michigan social worker and psychoanalyst Selma Fraiberg to take me into her research group. Selma was studying blind babies at the time; by watching her techniques, I learned how to carefully observe the smallest, least verbal youngsters and to write about them. Rather than Selma's subject, blindness, rubbing off on me, however, my subject, trauma, eventually rubbed off on her. When I finished my training at Michigan and left for a Cleveland faculty position at what is now known as "Case" (it was Western Reserve when I began teaching there), Selma Fraiberg's group at Michigan started to study child abuse. Her classic paper "Ghosts in the Nursery" followed (Fraiberg, Adelson, & Shapiro, 1975).

Another very different source of inspiration for me at Michigan was a huge figure in American forensic psychiatry, Andrew Watson, M.D. Dr. Watson, who looked like Michelangelo's "Moses" (without the horns), taught me how to take part in the legal system, consult with agencies, and form educated opinions about child-related politics. All of these skills helped. He insisted that I teach in law schools, and he got me my first law school job—at Case. Andy was coauthor with me of "The Battered Child Rebrutalized: Ten Cases of Medical-Legal Confusion," the first of two papers I wrote on the 10 University of Michigan cases (Terr & Watson, 1968). From the beginning, Andy forced me into the kind of bravery that has subsequently served me well. Toward the end of my child fellowship at Michigan, Andy insisted that I come with him to Washington to meet a small group of juvenile court judges who, at that meeting, outlined the first child abuse statutes and set up the first child protective services agencies. Through this system we have eventually come to uncover many, many more than 10 cases in America.

My period of full-time teaching in academia—at Case Western Reserve University—lasted 5 years. I published "A Family Study of Child Abuse," exploring the dynamics of what makes people hurt their kids and how kids alter their personalities to adjust to these abuses (Terr, 1970). I began collecting new cases in Cleveland with A. Scott Dowling, M.D., another young faculty member. We made movies of neglected and abused infants and their mothers. By watching the babies closely on our clinical research unit, we discovered that a number of these damaged children were clutching their hands at midline. Bringing the hands together at 5 or 6 months of age is normal and expected. But the young babies we followed were unable to release their joined hands in order to explore. For years, pediatricians had been calling this phenomenon the "praying mantis position" and associating it with infantile malnutrition. Scott and I realized that what we were seeing was an important failure of mental development in the second half of the first year of life. The failure was costly. At least temporarily, it would stop the child from exploring and thus limit the child's intellectual growth. Child abuse carried more than an emotional price. It was costing intelligence.

Case Western Reserve nominated me to be an NIMH "Career Teacher," and I eventually became one of those chosen nationally to receive a government salary, travel expenses to visit various programs of interest, and a yearly meeting to be attended by the other career teachers. I visited René Spitz and his Denver "infant" group, including the young Bob Emde and Bob Harmon, the UCLA child program, San Francisco (which I didn't dream would someday become my home), Stanford, Michigan, Emory. I was particularly taken with the research work of one of the other young career teachers whom I met—George Vaillant, M.D. [see Vaillant's *Adaptation to Life* (1977) for his long-term studies of normal Harvard men]. In George, I recognized that the psychology of a phenomenon—and the years-long trail that a behavior or a defense might weave through a person's life—was well worth the tracking effort. Long-term study became one of my interests. I began thinking about watching whole lives, such as those of artists and historical figures, to trace childhood trauma. I also became curious about finding trauma among the "normals."

I decided to interview a series of children who had killed other youngsters, and to compare them with children who had almost been killed by other children. I saw five of each. I could barely tell them apart. This led to no publication, but it stimulated considerable thought. Why were the two groups so much alike? I stopped writing and took time off to think. What we really needed to do was to study one group of children—hopefully including both genders, all social classes, and various racial and cultural backgrounds—who had experienced a single unquestionably traumatic event. Then we would know what "childhood trauma" was. Then we'd be able to observe, organize, and perhaps unify our ideas. I went to one of my bosses at Case Western Reserve University, a distinguished professor and clinician. "What we need is a single long-term study of the effects of one horrible event on a group of normal kids," I said. In response, he told me, "Everything that needs to be known about childhood trauma is now known."

I hit the medical library. It took me a year. Nothing very much was known, I concluded. What was out there were truisms such as "Nervous mothers make for nervous kids" (Carey-Trefzer, 1949; Bloch, Silber, & Perry, 1956) (not necessarily true), or "Childhood separations from parents are bad for children" (Freud, A. & Burlingham, 1942; Bowlby, 1951) (true, but not necessarily related to trauma). The physical elements of child neglect were beginning to emerge (Patton & Gardner, 1963), but the psychological elements of terror and fright in young people were still uncharted. There was no central core to the far-flung information about hurt and harmed youngsters. A research study might create the beginnings of a core. I needed to get out in the field. I needed to explore the effects of one event on many kids' lives. But first, something had to happen. I waited for 8 years.

HUNTING FOR THE CORE AT CHOWCHILLA

On July 15, 1976, twenty-six schoolchildren from the town of Chowchilla in California's Central Valley disappeared, along with their school bus and driver. The evening afterward, with a whole world searching for them, they turned up at an abandoned Alameda County rock quarry, bedraggled, dirty, hungry, and dehydrated. It turned out that they had been kidnapped. Their school bus, in fact, had been commandeered at gunpoint by three young men in stocking masks, and it had then been driven into a dry slough. The kids had then spent 11 hours being bounced and jostled along back country roads in two totally blackened vans. In the middle of the night the vehicles stopped. The youngsters were ordered to "get down into that hole," actually a buried moving van in an abandoned quarry. They heard dirt and rock being shoveled onto them and then remained entombed for 16 hours. A boy leaned against a skimpy wooden pillar and the roof began to collapse. This impelled two bigger boys, a 14-year-old and an 11-year-old, to climb onto the ceiling and work feverishly to dig them out. Once an opening was established, the bus driver helped each child to escape into the Alameda night. He found a pay phone and called the police. A couple of medical doctors examined them all on their arrival at Santa Rita Prison, the closest county facility. "Everyone's all right," the physicians said. But was this true? *Here* was my study.

In 1976, I lived and practiced psychiatry in San Francisco. Five years earlier, both my husband, Ab, and I had decided to leave full-time academic medicine because it didn't offer us enough independence, choice, and research time. We loved the Bay Area and looked forward to raising our two children there. We were supporting each other's research and teaching interests, and we had discovered that—other than the 2 or 3 years we spent setting up our practices—we were enjoying our newfound freedoms. Everyone had settled down. I was waiting to get out "into the field" for a research study on trauma. Chowchilla happened, but I continued to wait. I needed an invitation. A Central Valley psychiatrist, Romulo Gonzales, M.D., gave it to me. I had met him at a child custody meeting in November 1976, and he responded to my stated curiosity about the Chowchilla kids by sending me a recent article from the *Fresno Bee*. It said that no child at Chowchilla was being treated and that the parents were complaining. Names were named, and I called the first mother listed, telling her I could offer them a research study and possible suggestions for treatment but no therapy per se. "You are an angel of mercy. You are an answer to our prayers," she said. "Come!"

I did a study of the 23 kids who still lived in Chowchilla—and their families—over the year beginning in December 1976 (Terr, 1979). Four to five years later, I interviewed the kids and families again; I added two kidnapped Chowchilla children I had found in other towns and a child released from the bus just before it was abducted. I set out to discover lasting traumatic problems in this untreated group of youngsters (Terr, 1983a). I then looked for these same problems in an age- and sex-matched "normal" comparison group in Porterville and McFarland, California, two Central Valley towns about a hundred miles to the south of Chowchilla (Terr, 1983b). I found the symptoms of severe externally caused stress in 10 of these comparison kids.

Trauma could, thus, be identified by using the core symptoms and signs I found at Chowchilla. Mental mechanisms—such as omen formation, future foreshortening, perceptual distortion, fears of the mundane, specific trauma-related fears, posttraumatic play, reenactment, characteristics of traumatic memory, how traumatic childhood dreams are expressed and changed over time, and posttraumatic thinking patterns—were worked out from the Chowchilla studies. I found that I could now look at sexually attacked children, incest victims, accident survivors, witnesses of domestic violence, victims of neglect and abuse, or child heroes who had stopped the attacks of others— and if they had been traumatized, I could find the same core signs and symptoms I had observed in the Chowchilla group. The findings from Chowchilla became incorporated by committee into the criteria for posttraumatic stress disorder (PTSD) in the third and fourth editions of the *Diagnostic and Statistical Manual* (DSM-III and DSM-IV). After Chowchilla, it was possible to speak a central language with other childhood trauma researchers and be understood. Chowchilla began the long, long process of unifying the clinical field of childhood trauma. There was still a way to go—cross-cultural studies; studies of more chronic, grinding, repeated childhood events; studies of infants—but Chowchilla had begun to show the way.

At first, the Chowchilla project was not treated with the respect it later received. "Why weren't there infants in your study group?" a colleague asked at grand rounds. "How dare you write about victims while the alleged perpetrators are still working on their appeals?" one of the kidnappers' lawyers challenged me. "We have already known for years about 'omens' after trauma," a small conference of colleagues jumped all over me. ("We just didn't write about them ourselves," they implied). "Why didn't you initially plan a control study?" a research group sponsored by the National Institute of Mental Health (NIMH) criticized. (It was clear, however, that you can't do a control study until you already know what you're looking for.) "In our new unpublished study, we have discovered 'cognitive reappraisals,'" a fellow researcher announced. (That's what I had meant by "omens" when I defined them in the Chowchilla studies).

In the long run, the Chowchilla study turned out to be a unifying force in childhood trauma. It also inspired other researchers to take up field studies. It focused adult specialists on learning more about their grown-up patients' lives by considering their life stories as children. Pediatricians discovered Chowchilla. Through my book *Too Scared to Cry* (Terr, 1992), "pop culture" discovered Chowchilla as well. Chowchilla had been the "international news story of 1976." In 1990, it became a new story to the public once again, but this time the story was about the psychology of children.

The most memorable praise I received for the Chowchilla project came 20 years after the kidnapping. A young psychiatrist doing research on field rodents, called voles, approached me at a meeting and said, "I saw you give grand rounds on Chowchilla when I was a med student at

UCSF. Your presentation made me decide to become a psychiatrist and a researcher." That was Thomas Insel, M.D., who is currently the director of NIMH.

CONSIDERING CHILDHOOD TRAUMA AS NORMAL PSYCHOLOGY

From the beginning of my work on trauma, I have always wondered whether childhood PTSD was the most extreme form of a more general phenomenon affecting every one of us. I wondered, in other words, if PTSD was just the tip of the iceberg. Did developmental psychology allow a place for the smaller traumas of everyday life? I knew that early in his career Sigmund Freud considered trauma, especially sexual trauma, to be a crucial part of his patients' histories. He turned his back on trauma in the mid-to-late 1890s. Perhaps in doing so, Freud had missed something big.

I have always remembered a few quasitraumatic events from my own childhood. They didn't count as heavily as my family, friends, and teachers, but they were always there. A pigeon landed "on my head" when I was about 9 months old. I still see the descending fluttering shape in my mind today. When I asked about it during my childhood, my mother told me the pigeon really came down on the hood of my carriage, not on my head. Did it set up my lifelong fascination with birds? I don't know. But I do understand that it created a fragmentary and partly wrong "traumatic" memory. Then, at 11 months, I remember my paternal grandmother holding me while trying to force something hot into my mouth. Her words ("Have tea"), my awkward position in her arms, and the strange warm liquid are there in my head today. My mother later explained that I had screamed on a train all the way from New York to Cleveland. My dad, a starving artist, had been unable to support the three of us, so my mother and his mother were moving me to Ohio, where Mom's family lived. I guess the tea was supposed to be solace for temporarily losing my father. In fact, we were separated for a year. But I still am unable to drink tea with pleasure.

Thus, I knew from my own early experience that pieces of unpleasant memory can be retained clearly. Might they influence behavior? I knew the answer, at least from my own experience. At 4 or 5, as I played on the shores of Lake Erie, a large wave swept me out to sea. I began to drown—I thought. I saw bubbles and couldn't breathe. I was unable to fight the undertow. My dad found me, picked me up, and carried me back to the beach. After that, I didn't like to swim. I had to—I couldn't graduate from high school without swimming the length of the pool, so I did it. But all my life I have not opted for seaside vacations. When forced into it, I rove the beaches looking for shorebirds and shells. It's odd. My dad tells me that once, in a small boat on Lake Erie, the two of us almost went down in a storm. I was well under age 5, I recall. I was with *him*, however. It is not at all a traumatic memory. In my mind, I was safe. I love boats. I love storms. For me, they represent no peril. It is the swimming that I dislike. One wave created a lifelong aversion. A series of bigger waves set up no problems at all.

After Chowchilla, I set out to explore the widespread trauma-related psychological phenomena of weird experience and the supernatural (Terr, 1984, 1985). I found that problems, like believing in predestination, prediction, coincidence of thought, auras, ghosts, supernatural interventions, were associated clinically with traumatic experience. I found supernatural phenomena in my patients' records. I began to watch and keep careful notes on their memories as well. From the very beginning, their file folders were coded "red."

The lives of artists, writers, and moviemakers fascinated me. Some of them, like Stephen King (Terr, 1989), Alfred Hitchcock (Terr, 1987), and Virginia Woolf (Terr, 1990), had told, and written about, their early psychological traumas. They then went on to lead full lives, expressing themselves through their art. Could you find traces of their traumas in their work? Indeed you could. Many of their expressions were repetitions of specific literal fears, such as King's mechanical monsters (his prekindergartner friend was mutilated and killed by a train). Some traumatic expressions were broader, conveying a sense of total loss of control and dread (Hitchcock's *Psycho* and *The Birds* distantly reflected his helplessness when, at age 5, he was wrongly confined to jail). Virginia Woolf's lifelong problems and literary efforts reflected her sexual traumas. She was an early incest victim (of her much older half-brother), and her fiction avoids all sex, all emotion, all aliveness—yet it lets in the smallest, most minute of details. Reading Woolf's fiction allows one to fully understand the defense of dissociation.

My observations of artists led me to search my "red" charts for child patients' memories of verified early traumas (age 5 or under). By "verified," I meant cases where there were outside confirmations through eyewitnesses, courtroom convictions, confessions, or laboratory proofs. I found 20 such cases out of a total of 32 (Terr, 1988). This study demonstrated that 28 to 36 months of age at the time of the trauma was an approximate cutoff point for retaining whole or partial memories of a traumatic episode. Before this cutoff age, children might either remember bits and pieces (like my spoonful of tea or my fluttering bird) or nothing at all. After the cutoff age, children were less likely to remember the whole story if it was a repeated or long-lasting episode. Grinding, expected traumas were associated with more memory loss than were single, utterly surprising events. This was a counter intuitive finding. It pointed to defenses such as repression, dissociation, displacement, and intellectualization that were blocking memory from consciousness. It also carried biological implications about transmitter, cellular, and anatomic blockages to memory.

My interest in traumatic memory reached its peak with my research for *Unchained Memories* (Terr, 1994). The case of Eileen Franklin, who had "forgotten" a childhood murder for 20 years, was included in the book because of my 1990 testimony at her father's criminal trial, confirming the validity of Eileen's memory return. (Mr. Franklin was convicted of murder by a jury, but his lower court conviction was eventually reversed in federal court because of constitutional violations against his right not to incriminate himself and his right to see all the evidence.)

Unchained Memories quickly found itself enmeshed in an ugly battle, called by the press the "memory wars." These public arguments, media debates, and courtroom battles eventually threatened psychotherapy itself. For a while, the debate also interfered with trauma and memory research. There was no question, however, either before or after these "wars," that memories could change in formation, storage, and/or retrieval. There was no question either that a naive, unthinking, doctrinaire, or even evil mental health professional could implant false memories into a suggestable client's mind. From my case records, I found that traumatic memories could be full, partial, or entirely blocked. They could be totally true, essentially true with false details, entirely false, or essentially false with true details (Terr, 1996).

In 1986 and 1987, after the *Challenger* spacecraft tragedy, I studied normal children of ages 8 and 15 on both coasts of America. In looking at their interviews and at the statistical data they revealed, I found memory to be one important aspect of the rather complex study. The *Challenger* interviews, placed 1 year apart, showed that ordinary schoolchildren, exposed to a televised and/or replayed disaster, remembered it in extreme detail and with—in most instances—considerable accuracy (Terr, Bloch, Michel, Shi, Renhart, & Matayer, 1991).

One could not ignore traumatized or traumatizing patients' memories the way my first patient, Anne Jones, had been written off in her two ER visits. Patients already in psychotherapy, who recaptured a lost memory, had to be stopped in their other therapeutic pursuits for a short time in order to be re-evaluated for the symptoms and signs of psychic trauma. The therapist would have to listen to any shards of memory that the patient might bring. In addition, the patient might be able to obtain external confirmations from family, friends, or neighbors, from written records in old newspapers, police files, or doctors' notes. There was no reason to "throw out the baby" (the usefulness of psychotherapy) "with the bath water" (the few therapists who uncovered wholly false memories).

Today, the memory controversy is dying down. A "conspiracy" lawsuit against me by George Franklin was thrown out of a lower federal court and the Ninth Circuit Court of Appeals before it ever got started (except in the press). It was not taken up to the U.S. Supreme Court. Speaking for myself, I studied memory clinically and enjoyed the challenge. I think I offered clarity to a murky field. Others took up the memory baton with new-found enthusiasm. For me, however, it was time to move on.

UNIFYING THE TRAUMAS ONCE AGAIN: 1991

I was coming to realize that childhood traumas created four relatively permanent problems: perceptual returns: repetitions in action, personality, art, and play; specific literal fears; and a limited sense of the future. I also recognized that the childhood traumas could be divided into two types, the first comprising the results of an unanticipated, sudden event and the second involving the results of a long-standing or repeated series of events. In the first type, the traumatized person behaves similarly to the kidnapped children of Chowchilla. In the second type, the traumatized person resembles the battered babies and neglected toddlers I had studied in Ann Arbor and Cleveland. With chronic unremitting trauma (the second type), a child's personality is massively changed. Numbing, extreme sadness, anger, "hail fellow well met" behaviors, antisocial activities, substance abuse—in various combinations—would most likely ensue. Extreme defenses are utilized. I wrote "Childhood Trauma: An Outline and Overview" in order to offer this newly structured framework to the field (Terr, 1991). No matter what an adult patient's current diagnosis, some medical reflection would have to go into the patient's childhood traumatic history and related findings. In many instances, the trauma—as well as the patient's current illness—would need psychotherapeutic attention.

IDENTIFYING A TRAUMA SPECTRUM

In 1986 and 1987 I administered structured interviews to 153 "normal" children in Concord, New Hampshire, and in Porterville, California, following the January 28, 1986, *Challenger* spacecraft explosion. The kids were compared as to age (third graders versus tenth graders), time (1986 and 1987), and location (East Coast, West Coast). I considered three issues: memory, thinking, and symptoms. A professional paper covered each (Terr, Bloch, Michel, Shi, Reinhart, & Matayer, 1996, 1997, 1999). If I were asked to summarize *Challenger*, here's how it would go: No one who watched or heard about the disaster became a PTSD patient, yet the "distant trauma" had a definite effect. It was strongly remembered (being a one-time, Type I event). *Challenger* was thoroughly thought through, especially by adolescents. Over 14 months, teens harbored increasingly negative and pessimistic attitudes about space, NASA, manufacturers, the media, government, and in a general sense, life. I could begin to perceive that generational attitudes might follow from traumatic events, especially those experienced by large groups of adolescents. Younger children suffered more symptoms. Event-related fears were the most common. Younger children also commonly feared being alone. But all fears dramatically and spontaneously decreased by the second year after the disaster.

The *Challenger* studies sent me back into the field and yielded new, meaningful information. They led to the idea of a "trauma spectrum." Not only could distant traumas, like *Challenger* (or more recently, the Asian tsunami, American anthrax epidemic, and 9/11) temporarily upset normal people, but at times they set up changes that necessitate brief treatment.

PROBING THE TRAUMA SPECTRUM FURTHER

Challenger identified the signs, symptoms, and thinking processes that characterize "distant trauma." Among my own patient files—and among the newspaper accounts and professional case reports and studies that I had collected—I was able to hunt for other problems that were likely additions to the trauma spectrum. These less-than-traumas included such conditions as "close-call trauma" (the effects of missing a disastrous event); "indirect trauma" (the effects of exposure to a fictional or impossible-to-view disaster); "vicarious trauma" (the effects of knowing about an enormous dehumanizing event, such as Hiroshima or the Holocaust); "mass threat" (the effects of anticipating a possible future disaster, such as the Cold War); "mass hysteria" (the conveyance of trauma-related symptoms through exposure to others' symptoms); "copycatting" (taking life-threatening chances due to media or peer exposures); "unqualified event trauma" (conditions set up by events not included in the DSM-IV definitions of traumatic events); and "helper/rescuer trauma" (the effects of working professionally or voluntarily around traumatic events, and dead, injured, or traumatized people) (Terr, Bloch, Michel, Shi, Reinhart, & Matayer, 1999).

Many trauma spectrum symptoms disappear spontaneously because of natural, behavioral conditioning. But some do not. Eventually, it may be wise to prepare mental health workers to use psychodynamic psychotherapy and/or cognitive-behavioral therapy for relatively short periods of time with individuals who do not reach the full PTSD diagnosis. Trauma spectrum represents a widening of the trauma field. But widening does not mean splintering. The field will remain well-organized as long as we keep the core symptoms in mind.

SEARCHING NATURE FOR A CURE TO TRAUMA

The turn of the millennium brought me and the Stanford biostatistician Dan Bloch to the question of how trauma (and the trauma spectrum) spontaneously heals. What do children naturally do to make themselves feel better after a strikingly horrifying event? Just at the time I was wondering about it, a schoolteacher from Columbine High School in Colorado sent me 118 essays, written by juniors 2 weeks after the murderous assault of April 20, 1999, on their school by Dylan Klebold and Eric Harris. These two seniors killed 12 students, one teacher, and themselves. They seriously wounded at least 23 others.

Two weeks after the Columbine attack, junior students from Columbine were given a mandatory but ungraded assignment: "Write an essay of any length about *your own* story from April 20." This became excellent material for a study of the early phases of natural adolescent healing. Before the students graduated in June 2000, their teacher collected permissions (all but seven students could be found and/or gave their permissions). We thus had 111 usable compositions to work with. We decided to rate each essay for "abreaction" (emotional expression); "context" (thinking the trauma through), and "correction" (strategizing corrective actions for the self or for the community). Dan Bloch and I found that abreaction, context, and correction were extremely important and widely used posttraumatic healing mechanisms. Each was used spontaneously by the majority of Columbine kids, whether or not they were particularly close to danger or one of their friends was killed or wounded. Girls exhibited these mechanisms significantly more than boys. Interestingly, in a separate study of the 12-year, once-monthly psychotherapy of a "wild child" who had been horribly traumatized before 13 months of age, I found that the same three healing mechanisms worked very well in the child's individual psychotherapy (Terr, 2003).

EXPLORING NEW AND FUTURE TRAUMAS

After the terrorist attacks of 9/11, I became involved in two projects, still looking for natural healing among kids. One was a drawing project among third-graders in a San Francisco elementary school. At three different times during the 2001–2002 school year, children were asked, "Draw anything and write a sentence about what you've been going through since 9/11." Here, it would be possible to tell if abreaction, context, and correction could be identified in latency-age art work (preliminary report: they can). The second 9/11 project was done, along with Spencer Eth, Reese Abright, and Dan Bloch in Manhattan and Cape Cod. Juniors wrote ungraded essays three times over that same year ("Write an essay and answer a one-page questionnaire on what you've been going through since 9/11.") The analysis, requiring hundreds of man-hours, is not yet complete.

What do I envision for future trauma researchers? An exploration of childhood brain responses will be enlightening. Magnetic resonance imaging (MRI) studies hold some promise in this regard. Animal research (while animal models are not fully applicable to human children) will educate us to a certain extent. Autopsy studies of children killed in horrible ways—especially if substances released in the brain at the time of death are extracted—may help. The pharmacologic development of retroactive memory-erasing drugs for use in emergency rooms may someday prove useful.

What else do we need to learn? It would be good to know more about the effects of trauma in early infancy and toddlerhood. Dual diagnoses in childhood must also be better understood. We're just beginning to find out how trauma looks in children from nonwestern cultures and within various closed subgroups inside America itself. Also, I don't think we yet have enough information about living through horrible childhood illnesses and painful medical procedures. The absence of pain sensation—as so often seen in incest or physical abuse victims—is another interesting field of study for future researchers.

Finally, there is no way to consider the future of childhood trauma without looking toward trauma prevention. When will the general population fully realize that incest is absolutely off limits? When will people truly treat their children like human beings? How can cycles of family violence be broken up? If we do nothing in one generation, we can expect at least a doubling of traumatic incidence in the next. Now, because of current events, we must consider the effects of terror and of terrorism (as a political movement) on kids. We must eventually learn how to use the media to help youngsters. Mental health professionals must taken an active part in public affairs. In the long run, one trauma hunter like me must team up with other trauma hunters around the world. We've got our work cut out for us!

Lenore Terr, 1972

REFERENCES

Bloch, D., Silber, E., & Perry S. (1956). Some factors in the emotional reaction of children to disaster. *American Journal of Psychiatry, 113,* 416–422.

Bowlby, J. (1951). *Maternal care and mental health.* Geneva: World Health Organization.

Carey-Trefzer, C. (1949). The results of who attended the Child Guidance Clinic, The Hospital for Sick Children, Great Ormond Street, London. *Journal Mental Science, 95,* 535–559.

Fraiberg, S., Adelson, E., & Shapiro, V. (1975). Ghosts in the nursery: A psychoanalytic approach to the problems of impaired infant-mother relationships. *Journal of the American Academy of Child Psychiatry, 14,* 387–422.

Freud, A., & Burlingham, D. (1973). Report 12. In *The writings of Anna Freud.* Vol 3. New York: International Universities Press. (Originally published in 1942.)

Kempe, C., Silverman, F., Steele, B., Droegmueller, W., & Silver H. (1982). The battered child syndrome. *Journal of the American Medical Association, 18,* 17–24.

Patton RG, & Gardner L. (1963). *Growth failure in maternal deprivation.* Springfield, IL: Charles C Thomas.

Terr, L. (1970). A family study of child abuse. *American Journal of Psychiatry, 127,* 665–671.

Terr, L. (1979). Children of Chowchilla: A study of psychic trauma. *Psychoanalytic Study of the Child 34,* 547–623.

Terr, L. (1983a). Chowchilla revisited: The effects of psychic trauma four years after a schoolbus kidnapping. *American Journal of Psychiatry 140,* 1543–1550.

Terr, L. (1983b). Life attitudes, dreams, and psychic trauma in a group of "normal" children. *Journal of the American Academy of Child Psychiatry 22,* 221–230.

Terr, L. (1984). Time and trauma. *Psychoanalytic of the Study Child, 39,* 633–666.

Terr, L (1985). Remembered images in psychic trauma: One explanation for the supernatural. *Psychoanalytic Study of the Child, 40,* 493–533.

Terr, L. (1987). Childhood trauma and the creative product: A look at the early lives and later works of Poe, Wharton, Magritte, Hitchcock, and Bergman. *Psychoanalytic Study of the Child 42,* 545–572.

Terr, L. (1988). What happens to early memories of trauma? *Journal of the American Academy of Child and Adolescent Psychiatry, 27,* 96–104.

Terr, L. (1989). Terror writing by the formerly terrified: A look at Stephen King. *Psychoanalytic Study of the Child, 44,* 369–390.

Terr, L. (1990). Who's afraid in Virginia Woolf? Clues to early sex abuse in literature. *Psychoanalytic Study of the Child, 45,* 533–546.

Terr, L. (1991). Childhood traumas: An outline and overview. *American Journal of Psychiatry, 148,* 10–20.

Terr, L. (1992). *Too scared to cry.* New York: Harper & Row. (Paperback, New York: Basic Books, 1992.)

Terr, L. (1994). *Unchained memories: True stories of traumatic memories, lost and found.* New York: Basic Books. (Paperback, 1995.)

Terr, L. (1996). True memories of childhood trauma: Flaws, absences, and returns. In K. Pezdek & W. P. Banks (Eds.), *The recovered memory/false memory debate* (pp. 69–80). San Diego, CA: Academic Press.

Terr, L. (2003). "Wild child": How three principles of healing organized 12 years of psychotherapy. *Journal of the American Academy of Child & Adolescent Psychiatry, 42,* 1401–1409.

Terr, L., Bloch, D., Michel, B., Shi, H., Reinhart, J., & Matayer, S. A. (1996). Children's memories in the wake of *Challenger. American Journal of Psychiatry, 153,* 618–625.

Terr, L., Bloch, D., Michel, B., Shi, H., Reinhart, J., & Matayer, S. A. (1997). Children's thinking in the wake of *Challenger. American Journal of Psychiatry, 154,* 744–751.

Terr, L., Bloch, D., Michel, B., Shi, H., Reinhart, J., & Matayer, S. A. (1999). Children's symptoms in the wake of *Challenger*. *American Journal of Psychiatry, 156*, 1536–1544.

Terr, L., & Watson, A. (1968). The battered child rebrutalized: Ten cases of medical/legal confusion. *American Journal of Psychiatry, 124*, 126–133.

Vaillant, G. (1977). *Adaptation to life*. Boston: Little, Brown.

14

Autobiographical Essay

ROBERT J. URSANO

WHAT WERE THE EVENTS IN YOUR LIFE THAT LED TO YOUR INTEREST IN TRAUMA?

Growing up in a military family, we were always aware of the possibility of loss and the risks in the world, to my father in particular. Military children are always alert to every military training event and to the news on television, radio, and in the newspapers. One is aware that the events in the news may touch your own family and that it has touched the families that your parents know. Born in Heidelberg, Germany, shortly after World War II while my father was assigned there, I heard of the effects of war as seen by my parents and my older sister as a part of the family stories—the unexpected good events and the losses and destruction. My parents taught us that people were always good; events could be bad, evil, or even deadly. But the challenge was to find how to understand the person from across the ocean or across the street from his or her vantage point. Both of my parents suffered losses in childhood, and I marveled at how they had made their lives and dedicated them to values close to their hearts and histories.

Since I had chosen to accept a scholarship from the U.S. Air Force to support myself and my family through medical school, the Department of Defense remained my home and my community. Throughout college and medical school I was most interested in how people changed—first that they did, a fact not all agreed to. In medical school, the stories of people and their life adventures, filled with challenges, traumas, and successes, brought me to psychiatry. As part of my training, I worked at the Yale Psychiatric Institute and listened to the stories of patients with schizophrenia of decade's duration. They had experienced lives that no one else had. They had viewed life through special lenses, sometimes from early childhood traumas. I learned again to listen to people ("They will teach you"), and they always lead you to places that you cannot expect. The skill to listen and to set the context in which people felt safe to tell their stories were and are invaluable skills for working with those who have experienced traumatic events.

After residency, my first position as a psychiatrist was on the staff of the U.S. Air Force School of Aerospace Medicine. SAM, as it is called, is the NIH of the USAF. SAM is the USAF center for research and medical consultation for flyers with serious and complicated medical problems. This was where those who experienced the extreme environments of flying and space were cared for and their health studied. As part of the neuropsychiatry branch, I was given great latitude to explore my interests and develop research ideas. I learned that extreme environments included everything from lower gravity to increased "g" forces and being a prisoner of war in Vietnam. I was fortunate to be at SAM (1977–1979) at the time of the 5-year follow-up of the USAF Vietnam repatriated prisoners of war from Vietnam (RPWs). I wanted to know whether they changed, and if so, how and in what way. These were the first studies I did in trauma, directed at understanding whether people changed (not whether they became ill). We completed a series of studies of the entire group of USAF RPWs and of a special group who had been seen for various medical reasons prior to being sent to Vietnam.

These studies brought me to wondering more about the effects of trauma and to meeting others interested in the area, including Margaret Singer, Jolly West, Richard Rahe, and others. The studies, which found changes and increased illness in those who were RPWs, were important news at the time and contributed to the acceptance that trauma, including military trauma, can lead to psychiatric illness. The studies also contributed to decisions in the federal government to support compensation for psychiatric illness after RPW experiences and to the understanding that even those who were selected and trained for stress resistance could be the victim of psychiatric illness after severe trauma. It was not "poor protoplasm" or "poor upbringing" but rather a toxic exposure similar to other toxic exposures, where the dosage matters and all are at risk with sufficient dosage. This model of toxic exposure provided a language that was compatible with the USAF and a way to talk to leaders and health care providers.

When I came to the Uniformed Services University School of Medicine, our nation's federal medical school, my group working on RPWs quickly met others who had spent their lives researching, helping, and listening to individuals who had experienced war and other natural and human-made traumatic events. The importance of the many extreme environments humans are exposed to took on broader meaning. In December 1985 our group worked with the Gander Newfoundland air disaster, the largest peacetime loss the Army has ever suffered. The second of three planes returning from the Sinai UN peacekeeping mission crashed in Gander, killing all on board. Working with colleagues, now long-time friends, from the Walter Reed Army Institute of Research, we began a series of studies on the effects of various disasters on individuals and communities, in particular focusing on the effects of exposure to death and the dead, a ubiquitous stressor of disasters. Over a series of years, our group has developed an international reputation for our understanding and experience on this particular stressor.

Since that time, we have had contact with nearly every major disaster our nation has faced in the past 20 years, through consultation, education, or research. These have included plane crashes in New York City and around the nation; earthquakes in California and Armenia (former USSR); hurricanes in Florida and typhoons in Hawaii; the Khobar Tower bombing; the USS Cole attack; embassy bombings in Kenya; wars in Iraq; peacekeeping in Somalia; and extensive involvement following the 9/11 terrorist attack, the anthrax attacks, and the sniper attacks in Washington, D.C.

In 1987 we established the Center for the Study of Traumatic Stress (CSTS), of which I am the director. The center is now recognized internationally for its overall excellence and its knowledge and application of knowledge in preparing for and responding to the psychological and behavioral effects of disaster, war, and terrorism on individuals, communities, and organizations. Understanding these effects and planning for them to foster resiliency, recovery, and preparedness is a critical aspect of national need in order to protect the social capital of the nation. The center, a public/private partnership, is part of the Uniformed Services University School of Medicine (Department of Defense) and the Henry M. Jackson Foundation. It is a university-based center of excellence; it operates on public and private funds to support its research education and consultation activities.

The expertise of the center derives from its early history as one of the first groups to address the issues of modern weapons of mass destruction and their psychological and behavioral implications for planning, preparedness, and responses. The center worked in direct simulation exercises of chemical and biological terrorism with the U.S. Air Force. This initiated pioneering work in the traumatic effects of terrorism and weapons of mass destruction—work that has bridged scholarship and practical application. The center held consensus meetings of international experts on chemical and biological weapons and participated in planning for organizational and psychological and behavioral effects beginning in the late 1980s. Prior to September 11, the center held a consensus meeting of first responders, community leaders, scientists, and workplace experts. The recommendations from this meeting served as the basis for congressional and national education and action for responding to the threats of terrorism.

The CSTS has provided extraordinary leadership in advancing an understanding of the traumatic implications of terrorism to national media outlets, all levels of government, the medical profession, our public health system, academic institutions, and the workplace.

The CSTS has provided its expertise to local, state, national, and international groups to assist organizations, communities, individuals, and the nation. As a result of 9/11, the center's unique expertise in disaster mental health and trauma research in terrorism were recognized as essential to national security. The center has provided consultation to numerous organizations that have sought its expertise for real-world applications and solutions for strategic planning, preparedness, and response to terrorism and bioterrorism. This list includes the New York State governor's office, New York City mayor's office, Department of Health and Human Services, National Capital response teams, the Department of Defense, Pentagon 9/11 attack response groups, Homeland Security's Transportation Safety Division, the Carter Center, the World Bank, the National Institutes of Health, the Department of Justice, Department of Veteran's Affairs, the Red Cross, the Washington D.C. Mental Health Department, NATO, WHO, FBI, the U.S. Senate, the House of Representatives, the Library of Congress Employee Assistance and Human Resources Departments, and private industry.

The center's work on bioterrorism in particular resulted in recommendations widely circulated in Congress and used to develop the national strategy to respond to the psychological and behavioral responses to bioterrorism. The CSTS has provided educational outreach to prepare the Congress of the United States, the Supreme Court, and every state in the nation through widely praised materials developed under a grant from the Department of Health and Human Services. Of significance, the Center maintains one of the world's largest databases (more than 17,000 articles, selected for importance and relevance) on traumatic stress following disasters, terrorist events and wars, and preparedness, prevention, and treatment interventions.

WHAT HAVE BEEN YOUR ACHIEVEMENTS AND CONTRIBUTIONS TO THE FIELD?

As noted above, our studies of the Vietnam era RPWs were instrumental in a number of areas, including the new code of conduct for the military.

The Code of Conduct changed to recognize the concept that everyone has a breaking point. This helped ensure disability payments for RPWs. Our multiple studies on the stressor of exposure to death and the dead have, along with those of others, identified this area as important to nearly all disasters. Further understanding the cognitive processes (particularly identification) involved in this stressor response will aid our understanding of stress and also of cognition in high-stress environments. Our work on the importance of first responders/disaster workers has also raised awareness of this often forgotten group to our community and national response to critical incidents.

I was privileged to be the first chair of the American Psychiatric Association's Committee on Psychiatric Aspects of Disaster. During my tenure, we established the Bruno Lima Award for Outstanding Contributions to Disaster Psychiatry by members of the American Psychiatric Association (APA) and the Erich Lindemann Award by the president of the APA to district branches to assist in responding to disasters. We initiated what has now been more than 10 years of annual training of APA members in half-day and day-long courses in disaster psychiatry. I also had the honor and privilege of being the chair of the first task force of the APA to develop the treatment guidelines for posttraumatic stress disorder (PTSD) and acute stress disorder (ASD). In 1999 I was asked to become the fourth editor in chief of the distinguished journal *Psychiatry*. The founder of the journal, Harry Stack Sullivan, was dedicated to operational thinking about behavior and in particular the contribution of social context to behavior, thoughts, and feelings. It has been an honor to continue this tradition by selecting excellent authors and special commentaries.

In the area of public health and preparing for terrorism, I was asked to serve as a member of the National Academy of Science's Institute of Medicine (IOM) Committee on Responding to the Psychological Consequences of Terrorism. The work of this group has led the efforts to integrate psychiatric and behavioral care, postterrorism and disaster, into public health programs. In addition, the IOM document is one of the first to formally recognize the workplace as an important setting for preparedness. I was among the first to advocate for corporate preparedness as a founding member of the Scientific Advisory Board of the American Psychiatric Association's National Partnership for Workplace Mental Health. In this area, the Center for the Study of Traumatic Stress received a grant from the National Institute for Occupational Safety and Health (NIOSH) to conduct the first review for developing a strategic plan for the management of mass violence in the workplace. This study examined preparedness for terrorism in occupational settings. In 2003 we established the first Disaster Psychiatry/Preventive Psychiatry Fellowship program in the nation. The opportunity to obtain an MPH degree and spend a year with the Center brings individuals interested in research as well as health services to the area of disaster psychiatry.

WHO WERE THE PEOPLE WHO MOST INFLUENCED YOU TO MAKE THESE CONTRIBUTIONS?

I have always believed that you can become only what your colleagues (and family) urge, support, and nurture you to become. My colleagues have been superb; they are truly the makers of any accomplishments I have achieved. To name only a few, in college, John Dunne taught philosophy that both encouraged the exploration of inner life and understanding one's motivations for the future. In medical school and residency, Marshall Edelson taught me how to be a scholar and the importance of evidence; Ted Lidz and Steve Fleck taught heart and knowledge of interpersonal relations and meanings. Harry Holloway, David Marlowe, and Carol Fullerton have taught me, shared their knowledge, and pushed me to learn, teach, speak, and think while choosing problems that affect the nation and the world. These are only a few of those who have led me and fought with me to make each idea a possibility and an adventure.

HOW WOULD YOU HOPE THAT CURRENT AND FUTURE TRAUMA SCHOLARS WOULD BUILD ON YOUR WORK?

The need to understand the cognitive responses to traumatic events still looms large. We have treatments directed to cognitive changes but really know little about fundamental cognitive processes in extreme environments like traumatic events. Identification, seeking the familiar, perceptions of safety, belief in exposure, and altered sense of time are a few of the areas of study that have caught our attention. The further integration of our understanding of the psychological and behavioral effects of disasters and terrorism into our public health planning is a necessary area of growth, as is the need to integrate disaster preparedness into our workplaces, corporations, and employee life. PTSD may well be the first psychiatric illness that we are able to prevent. The establishment of a PTSD and extreme stress brain bank will further facilitate this goal and our neurobiological understanding of this and other "event related" disorders, and the question I began with—how, when, and why do we change?

Robert J. Ursano, 1969

REFERENCES

Butler, A. S., Panzer, A. M., & Goldfrank, L. R. (Eds.) (2003). *Preparing the psychological conse-quences of terrorism: A public health strategy.* (Committee on responding to the Psychologi-cal Consequences of Terrorism Board on Neuroscience and Behavioral Health: Lewis R. Goldfrank, M.D., Gerard A. Jacobs, Ph.D., Carol S. North, M.D., M.P.E., Patricia Quin-lisk, M.D., M. P.H., Robert J. Ursano, M.D., Nancy Wallace, C.S.W., Marlene Wong, L.C.S.W., Andrew Pope, Ph.D., Adrienne Stith Butler, Ph.D.). Institute of Medicine, The National Academies Press.

Epstein, R. S., Fullerton, C. S., & Ursano, R. J. (1998). Posttraumatic stress disorder following an air disaster: A prospective study. *American Journal of Psychiatry, 155*(7), 934–938.

Fullerton, C., & Ursano, R. J. (1990). Behavioral and psychological responses to chemical and biological warfare. *Military Medicine, 155,* 54–59.

Fullerton, C. S., & Ursano, R. J. (Eds.) (1997). *Post-traumatic stress disorder: Acute and long-term responses to trauma and disaster.* Washington, DC: American Psychiatric Press.

Fullerton, C. S., Ursano, R. J., Epstein, R. S., Crowley, B., Vance, K., Baum, A. (2000). PTSD in community samples: A measurement problem. *Nordic Journal of Psychiatry, 54,* 5–12.

Fullerton, C. S., Ursano, R J., Epstein, R. S., Crowley, B., Vance, K. L., Kao, T-C., & Baum, A. (2000). Peritraumatic dissociation following motor vehicle accidents: Relationship to prior trauma and prior major depression. *The Journal of Nervous and Mental Disease, 188*(5), 267–272.

Fullerton, C. S., Ursano, R. J., Epstein, R. S., Crowley, B., Vance, K., Kao, T., & Baum, A. (2001). Gender differences in posttraumatic stress disorder after motor vehicle accidents. *American Journal of Psychiatry, 158*(9), 1486–1491.

Fullerton, C. S., Ursano, R. J., & Wang, L. (2004). Acute stress disorder, posttraumatic stress disorder, and depression in disaster/rescue workers. *American Journal of Psychiatry, 161*(8), 1370–1376.

Grieger, T., Fullerton, C. S., & Ursano, R. J. (2003). Posttraumatic stress disorder, depression, alcohol use, and perceived safety thirteen months following the terrorist attack on the Pentagon. *Psychiatric Services, 54,* 1380–1383.

Grieger, T. A., Fullerton, C. S., Ursano, R. J., & Reeves, J. J. (2003). Acute stress disorder, alcohol use, and perception of safety among hospital staff after the sniper attacks. *Psychiatric Services, 54,* 1383–1388.

Holloway, H. C., & Ursano, R. J. (1984). The Viet Nam veteran: Memory, social context and metaphor. *Psychiatry, 47,* 103–108.

McCarroll, J. E., Thayer, L. E., Liu, X., Newby, J. H., Norwood, A. E., Fullerton, C. S., & Ursano, R. J. (2000). Spouse abuse recidivism in the U.S. Army by gender and military status. *Journal of Consulting and Clinical Psychology, 68*(3), 521–525.

McCarroll, J. E., Ursano, R. J., & Fullerton, C. S. (1993). Symptoms of posttraumatic stress disorder following recovery of war dead. *American Journal of Psychiatry, 150,* 1875–1877.

McCarroll, J. E., Ursano, R. J., & Fullerton, C. S. (1995). Symptoms of PTSD following recovery of war dead: 13–15 month follow-up. *American Journal of Psychiatry, 152*(6), 939–941.

McCarroll, J. E., Ursano, R. J., Fullerton, C. S., Liu, X., & Lundy, A. (2002). Somatic symptoms after exposure to death and the dead in Gulf War mortuary workers. *Psychosomatic Medicine, 64,* 29–33.

McCarroll, J. E., Ursano, R. J., Newby, J. H., Liu, X., Fullerton, C. S., Norwood, A., & Osuch, E. A. (2003). Domestic violence and deployment in U.S. Army soldiers. *The Journal of Nervous and Mental Disease, 191*(1), 3–9, 2003.

National Institute of Mental Health. (2002). *Mental health and mass violence: Evidence based early psychological intervention for victims/survivors of mass violence. A workshop to reach consensus on best practices.* National Institute of Health Publication No. 02-5138, Washington, D.C.: Government Printing Office.

Shalev, A., Bleich, A., & Ursano, R. J. (1990). Post-traumatic stress disorder: Somatic comorbidity and effort tolerance. *Psychosomatics, 31,* 197–203.

Staab, J. P., Grieger, T. A., Fullerton, C. S., and Ursano, R. J.(1996). Acute stress disorder, subsequent post-traumatic stress disorder and depression after a series of typhoons. *Anxiety, 2,* 219–225.

Stuart, J., Ursano, R. J., Fullerton, C. S., Norwood, A. E., & Murray, K. (2003). Belief in exposure to terrorist agents: Reported exposure to nerve/mustard gas by Gulf War veterans. *Journal of Nervous and Mental Disease, 191*(7), 431–436.

Ursano, R. J, Fullerton, C. S., & Norwood, A. E. (1995). Psychiatric dimensions of disaster: Patient care, community consultation, and preventive medicine. *Harvard Review of Psychiatry, 3*(4), 196–209.

Ursano, R. J. (1980). Stress and adaptation: The interaction of the pilot personality and disease. *Aviation, Space and Environmental Medicine, 51,* 1245–1249.

Ursano, R. J. (1981). The Vietnam era prisoner of war: Precaptivity personality and the development of psychiatric illness. *American Journal of Psychiatry, 138*(3), 315–318.

Ursano, R. J. (1987). Comments on "Post-traumatic stress disorder: The stressor criterion" (invited commentary). *Journal of Nervous and Mental Disease, 75,* 273–275.

Ursano, R. J. (2002). Editorial: post-traumatic stress disorder. *New England Journal of Medicine, 346*(2), 130–131.

Ursano, R.J., & Dressler, D. (1974). Brief versus long-term psychotherapy: A treatment decision. *Journal of Nervous and Mental Disease, 159*(3), 164–171.

Ursano, R. J., & Benedek, D. (2003). Prisoners of war: Long-term health outcomes. *The Lancet, 362,* 22–23.

Ursano, R. J., Boydstun, J., & Wheatley, R. (1981). Psychiatric illness in U.S. Air Force Vietnam War POWs: Five year follow-up. *American Journal of Psychiatry, 138*(3), 310–314.

Ursano, R. J., & Fullerton C. S. (1991). Psychotherapy: Medical intervention and the concept of normality. In D. Offer & M. Sabshin (Eds.), *The diversity of normal behavior* (pp. 39–59). New York: Basic Books.

Ursano, R. J., & Fullerton, C. S. (1990). Cognitive and behavioral responses to trauma. *Journal of Applied Social Psychology, 20*(21), 1766–1775.

Ursano, R. J., & Fullerton, C. S. (2000). Posttraumatic stress disorder: Cerebellar regulation of psychological, interpersonal, and biological responses to trauma? *Psychiatry, 62*(4), 325–328.

Ursano, R. J., Fullerton, C.S., Epstein, R. S., Crowley, B., Kao, T. C., Vance, K., Craig, K. J., Dougall, A. L., & Baum, A. (1999). Acute and chronic posttraumatic stress disorder in motor vehicle accident victims. *American Journal of Psychiatry, 156*(4), 589–595.

Ursano, R. J., Fullerton, C. S., Epstein, R. S., Crowley, M.D., Vance, K., Kao, T-C, & Baum, A. (1999). Peritraumatic dissociation and posttraumatic stress disorder following motor vehicle accidents. *American Journal of Psychiatry, 156*(11), 1808–1810.

Ursano, R. J., Fullerton, C. S., Kao, T., & Bhartiya, V. (1995). Longitudinal assessment of post-traumatic stress disorder and depression after exposure to traumatic death. *Journal of Nervous & Mental Disease, 183*, 36–43.

Ursano, R. J., Fullerton, C. S., & Norwood, A. E. (Eds.) (2003a). *Bioterrorism: psychological and public health interventions.* London: Cambridge University Press.

Ursano, R. J., Fullerton, C. S., & Norwood, A. E. (Eds.) (2003b). Terrorism and disaster: Individual and community responses to extraordinary events. London: Cambridge University Press.

Ursano, R. J., Fullerton, C. S., Vance, K., & Kao, T-C. (1999). Posttraumatic stress disorder and identification in disaster workers. *American Journal of Psychiatry, 156*(3), 353–359.

Ursano, R. J., & Hales, R. (1986). A review of brief individual psychotherapies. *American Journal of Psychiatry, 143*(12), 1507–1517.

Ursano, R. J., Kao, T., & Fullerton, C. S. (1992). PTSD and meaning: Structuring human chaos. *Journal of Nervous and Mental Disease, 180*, 756–759.

Ursano, R. J., & McCarroll, J. E. (1990). The nature of a traumatic stressor: Handling dead bodies. *Journal of Nervous and Mental Disease, 178*, 396–398.

Ursano, R. J., McCaughey, B., & Fullerton, C. S. (Eds.) (1994). *Individual and community responses to trauma and disaster: The structure of human chaos.* London: Cambridge University Press.

Ursano, R. J., & Norwood, A. (Eds.). (1996). *Emotional aftermath of the Persian Gulf War: Veterans, families, communities, and nations.* Washington, D.C.: American Psychiatric Press, 1996.

Ursano, R. J. and Norwood, A. E. (Eds.) (2003). *Trauma and disaster responses and management.* Washington, D.C.: American Psychiatric Publishing, Inc.

Ursano, R. J., Sonnenberg, S., & Lazar, S. (1991). *Psychodynamic psychotherapy.* Washington, D.C.: American Psychiatric Press. (Translated into Russian, 1992; Persian, 1995; Japanese, 1995.)

Ursano, R. J., Sonnenberg, S., & Lazar, S. (1998). *Psychodynamic psychotherapy: Principles and techniques in the era of managed care.* Washington, D.C.:American Psychiatric Press, Inc. (Translated into Chinese Classical, Chinese Simplified, and Korean, reprinted in China.)

Wright, K., Ursano, R. J., Bartone, P., & Ingraham, L. (1990). The shared experience of catastrophe: An expanded classification of the disaster community. *American Journal of Orthopsychiatry, 60*(1), 35–42.

15

The Body Keeps the Score: Brief Autobiography of Bessel van der Kolk

BESSEL VAN DER KOLK

It is a privilege to have been asked to contribute a chapter to this book on pioneers in the field of traumatic stress. Having been surrounded and supported by numerous colleagues and friends whom I consider to be knowledgeable on the subject of traumatic stress and its treatment, I hope to speak not only for myself but also for the numerous people who have supported and inspired me over the last 30 years.

Like most people interested in trauma, I came by my interest "honestly"—there certainly was enough trauma in my family's background to warrant taking a serious look at what this was all about.

I was born in the occupied Netherlands during the Second World War. My maternal grandfather developed von Economo's encephalitis, or Parkinson's disease, in the flu pandemic of 1919/1921, which killed more people than the entire First World War, and which left my mother's family destitute at a time before there was social security. My paternal grandfather was a scholar and world famous chess player who died in his early forties, again leaving a large family behind in dire straits. Though my parents never talked about these issues, it was obvious that these devastating childhood experiences had left marked scars on their sense of security and trust in the world, which was not softened by their deep religious faith.

My first memories all are related to the end of the Second World War: family members returning from Japanese concentration camps in Southeast Asia and stories about deprivation and death in the Netherlands. My neighbors on either side were reconstituted holocaust survivor families; I never knew which kids belonged to which parents, but I do remember going with them to Yom Kippur services in the synagogue in The Hague, in front of the statue of Spinoza, and the howling. I vividly remember walking around the ruins of my destroyed hometown, where my parents were among the first people to rebuild a house in the devastated section along the coast of the North Sea that had been used by the Germans as a bulwark against a possible invasion of the American and British troops—the landing that eventually took place in Normandy.

I went to the Latin school ("Gymnasium") in The Hague, a strange school where 17-year-olds studied 11 hours of Greek and Latin each week as well as 12 hours of science, in addition to learning four foreign languages—not exactly a setting for a careless adolescence, though I did get to write the school play with my classmates Koot and Bie, who went on to become the foremost comedians in the Netherlands. I was delighted with the opportunity for a change of scenery that came from my uncle, who taught at the University of Hawaii, who had been captured by the Japanese on Java in 1942, and who spent the rest of the war years helping to build a bridge over the river Kwai, which separates Thailand from Burma. From Hawaii I went to the University of Chicago, and thence to Boston, where I did my residency at the Harvard program of the now defunct Massachusetts Mental Health Center. For many people, that institution represented the best of what psychiatry stood for—I believe it selected deliberately for creative individuals, of whom there seemed to be an infinite supply, including Eric Kandel, Robert Post, Allen Hobson, and my classmates David Spiegel, Steve Green, Phyllis Cath, and Phil Gold.

My first job out of residency was to be the last inpatient director of a once venerable psychiatric institution, the Boston State Hospital; it once housed thousands of patients and was spread over hundreds of acres with dozens of buildings, including greenhouses and workshops for the chronically mentally ill. But my real career did not start till the first day I walked into the Veterans Administration Outpatient Clinic in Boston on July 1, 1978, four years after the end of the Vietnam War.

I seemed to hear something eerily familiar on listening to my first patient, Jack, a young lawyer who looked disheveled, having spent the night getting drunk in his office, not wanting to go home because he only had nightmares when he was there and simply could not mobilize any feelings of warmth or connection toward his wife and children. He was irritable, angry, short-tempered, and felt guilty that he was preoccupied with the friends he had lost in Vietnam.

At that time I had a strong interest in the nature of dreams and nightmares and had done some studies with Ernest Hartmann on the possible roles of rapid-eye-movement (REM) sleep in psychopathology. Together we had worked on various pharmacologic manipulations to affect dream sleep. Hence I felt that I could reassure Jack and tell him that a simple pill would take care of his problems with nightmares. Two weeks later, my veteran came in and told me: "I realized that if I were to stop having my nightmares, the death of my friends would have been in vain."

He then proceeded to tell the story of how his father had been a soldier in General Patton's army during the Second World War and that he had been a morose, difficult man who showed very little affection for his family. Whenever Jack had a success in school, his father would say 'You'll never be as good as my friends who died in the war." Unable to gain his father's affection, he was eager to prove himself just as good as his father's friends. As soon as he graduated from high school at age 17 at the top of his class, he enlisted in the U.S. Marine Corps; then, shortly after arriving in Vietnam, he had been made a platoon commander. Within a few months he lost his entire platoon in an ambush while walking at dusk through a rice paddy. Ever since then he could not get the images of his dying friends out of his mind and had been unable to truly feel pleasure or involvement in his life. At that moment I realized that I would probably be devoting the rest of my professional life to understanding and treating trauma. He was a boy who organized his life around proving himself to be worthy of his father's affection and then, after being exposed to events so similar to his father's, was permanently altered: his view of the world, his biology, his conceptions of himself and his capacity to engage with the next generation were all changed.

After seeing Jack I went to the library and asked the librarian to give me all the books she had on "traumatic neuroses." After failing to receive any books for a week, I went back and was told that the library had no books on that subject. Eventually I found one: *The Traumatic Neuroses of War*, published in 1941 and written by Abram Kardiner. Looking further through the literature, I found a series of articles by Henry Krystal entitled "Trauma and Affects," in which he talks about the loss of language following traumatization and the somatization of experience. That was the extent of the available literature at that time to help us understand what we were seeing in the clinic.

Fascinated with the life-like reliving of the trauma during Jack's nightmares, obviously so very different from the dreams about ordinary events—which never linger as isolated images, smells and physical sensations—I started to study the nightmares of returning Vietnam vets. We quickly discovered that these nightmares emerged from stages 4 and 3 sleep and were not part of REM sleep. We also found that when men like Jack started to go into REM sleep, they woke themselves up, thus confirming something that had recently been described by my colleagues Ramon Greenberg and Chester Pearlman, called REM-interruption insomnia. I wondered whether the loss of REM sleep was responsible for the inability to consolidate the residues of trauma memory into ordinary episodic memory.

In our nightmare studies, we also gave the veterans a Rorschach test. This opened my mind to the abnormalities in perceptual processing in traumatic stress. Charles Ducey and I discovered that these traumatized veterans tended to either superimpose precise images of their traumatic experience on the Rorschach cards or to see nothing at all: these guys appeared to be trapped between feeling as they were re-experiencing their trauma or feeling numbed out and alienated when they were not. My colleague Mark Greenberg and I also were impressed that, during the groups that we ran, they seemed to be generally disengaged and numbed out, except when discussing their experiences in Vietnam. Despite their distress, these were the times that they really came to life.

Fascinated by the changes that occur in people as a result of trauma, I kept looking for literature on war neuroses and concentration camp survivors and found almost nothing. In 1984, I organized the first symposium on the subject of PTSD at the American Psychiatric Association, in which Lawrence Kolb and Henry Krystal were the main speakers. This allowed us a get a glimpse of the observations of prior generations. Later I came to know several other people who had worked on these issues during the Second World War, such as Herbert Spiegel and Henry Murray.

In 1981, after posttraumatic stress disorder (PTSD) had become a formal diagnosis in the third edition of the Diagnostic and Statistical Manual (DSM-III), I applied to the Veterans Administration to formally study the psychobiology of PTSD. Their rejection letter started with the sentence, "It has never been demonstrated that PTSD is relevant to the mission of the Veterans Administration." Astounded, I never read the rest of this grant review but started to look around hoping to find work in an institution that had a better grasp of the reality of their patients' lives. I accepted a position back at the Massachusetts Mental Health Center to teach psychopharmacology.

However, after having seen the altered lives of Vietnam veterans, my perceptions of the patients in this hospital for the treatment of chronic mental illness had undergone a marked shift from a few years before. Now I started to see how many of the behaviors of people who supposedly had schizophrenia or major affective disorder also seemed to have been informed by a history of very severe trauma. In their case, however, the battlefield had not been overseas but in their own homes. I was particularly fascinated by patients who were diagnosed with borderline personality disorder and those who were engaged in self-destructive behaviors, most of whom seemed to have extremely hostile/dependent relationships with the hospital staff and with my colleagues. This made me wonder if they were re-enacting their own childhood traumas in the same way the Vietnam veterans I had been treating seemed to re-enact their trauma in their family lives.

I started a small study group for people in the hospital whom we interested in understanding borderline personality disorder (BPD), and soon patients with BPD moved from being the most despised diagnostic category to the one that held the most fascination: after their pathology was reframed as a replay of their childhood trauma, suddenly patients whom everybody had shunned became patients who were eagerly sought after by the residents.

In 1983, Nina Fish Murray wandered into our little study group. She was the wife of Henry Murray, the former chairman of the department of psychology at Harvard University, who was looking around to re-engage her talents in some project at the medical school. She had studied under Piaget and was fascinated by the way children's thinking shifts in the course of development and might be arrested as the result of adverse child experiences. She and I immediately connected and started to explore how trauma affects the way children think about themselves and their surroundings.

Henry Murray, by then in his late 90s, really formed the bridge between the earliest trauma researchers and our generation; he had been analyzed by both Jung and by Freud, and in 1936, during the tricentennial of Harvard University, he had picked Pierre Janet for the honor of being the outstanding psychologist of his age to get the honorary degree in psychology. Henry and Nina Murray had a long history of collecting young and old scholars in their home. The main venue for this was Friday afternoon tea on professor's row at Harvard, and an occasional dinner. During these teas, I got to meet John Bowlby, Paul McLean, Jerry Kagan, Dante Cicchetti, Howard Gardner, and many others. Whenever I told Nina about a colleague who was doing interesting work in the area of traumatic stress, she would immediately invite them to Friday afternoon tea.

Soon there were too many people interested in the topic, and the teas were transformed into the Tuesday evening Harvard Trauma Study group, which met every third Tuesday of the month from 1982 to 1995. This became a hotbed of thinking and studying issues related to traumatic stress. I cockily have said that, at least for a while, Boston became to trauma what Vienna once was to music: the place was teeming with students and investigators of traumatic stress, including Judy Herman, Terry Keane, Roger Pitman, Ann Burgess, Eli Newburger, Mary Harvey, Dante Cicchetti, Rich Mollica, and many others. We regularly had visitors from abroad, like Are Holen and Arieh Shalev, who came to present their work.

By the late 1980s, Judy Herman, Chris Perry, and I had documented that the majority (87%) of patients with borderline personality disorder had histories of severe childhood trauma and neglect, starting prior to age 7. We were also able to document that the vast majority of self-destructive psychiatric patients had horrific histories of childhood trauma and neglect, usually starting at a very early age. This further raised the question for me about neurobiological shifts in traumatized children that might have a major effect on the capacity of self-regulation. Our other work shed light on how various self-destructive activities function to help traumatized people regulate their distress.

While the Massachusetts Mental Health Center had as little interest in the issue of trauma as the VA and called the young Trauma Center "the boutique," eventually closing it down during one of the regular fiscal crises in the Massachusetts Department of Mental Health, there was an intense atmosphere of inquiry and scholarship. This brought me in 1983 to the American College of Neuropsychopharmacology meeting in San Juan, Puerto Rico, where Steve Mayer first introduced me to animal models of inescapable shock. This opened up a new world of being able to conceptualize how the organism is affected by inescapable traumatic events, and that it is possible to measure hormonal and neurotransmitter changes in traumatized people. After returning home, I read every scrap of literature I could find on the biology of inescapable shock and in 1985 published my paper entitled 'Inescapable shock, Neurotransmitters, and Addiction to Trauma," which to my knowledge was the first theoretical paper on the neurobiology of PTSD. It must have been the paper that inspired Charles Figley to invite me to the opening meeting of the Society for Traumatic Stress Studies, which he organized in Atlanta in 1986.

One of the findings that intrigued me about the issue of inescapable shock in animals was that they secrete endogenous opioids in response to the exposure to a traumatic stressor. I had been puzzled by the compulsive re-exposure to traumatic experiences during my time at the Veterans Administration: many Vietnam veterans, despite their expressed horror about Vietnam, walked around with copies of *Soldier of Fortune* magazine, which they scoured for ads to become freelancing soldiers in various emerging republics in Africa. In addition, during our group sessions, and even in individual psychotherapy, it was obvious how excited and even turned on many of them became as they described their traumatic experiences.

I wondered whether there might be a biological basis for the compulsion to repeat that I initially saw in Vietnam veterans, but later also in women who have been sexually abused and other traumatized populations, and which, or course also had fascinated Freud. I thought that the release of the endogenous opioids might be one possible explanatory mode. Roger Pitman, who then was at the Manchester Veterans

Administration in New Hampshire, encouraged me to further explore this hypothesis, and we combined forces to test it. Our study indeed found that traumatized Vietnam veterans, upon re-exposure to traumatic scenes from their time in Vietnam, experienced considerable analgesia, and complex calculations showed that their decrease in pain perception was equivalent to an injection of 10 milligrams of morphine, about the amount of morphine that people get in emergency rooms to treat heart attacks. However, there was no indication that this release of opioids in any way made these veterans feel better; in fact, it might possibly explain something about numbing. This, in turn led to a variety of studies on self-mutilation and analgesia.

This work led to an invitation to put together what probably was the first symposium on the biology of traumatic stress, at the World Congress on Biological Psychiatry in Jerusalem in 1987. I invited Roger Pitman, Arieh Shalev, and Frank Putnam to join me in this enterprise, and we presented an exciting symposium on the neurobiology of trauma. That evening we went for dinner in Bethlehem, where Onno van der Hart joined us. We talked about how surprising it was, with trauma being so ubiquitous, that it took people so long to discover some of the basic neurobiology, as we seemed to be doing in our generation.

Onno, at that point, shook his head and told us that in fact there was a very ancient and venerable literature on trauma and encouraged us to become familiar with at least some of it. He told us about the history of Pierre Janet, who was active in Paris at the Salpètrière and later on at the College de France starting in the 1880s and continuing for many decades. He told us how Janet had been a contemporary of Freud and that Freud in fact had come to the Salpètrière in the late 1880s to study with Charcot and had derived many of his early ideas from his exposure to Janet's work. Later on a rivalry had arisen between Freud and Janet and, after 1910, they refused to speak to each other. He told us that evening in great detail how Janet had a theory of the psychology of action, which addressed dissociative phenomena in traumatized individuals. It turned out that both Frank Putnam and Roger Pitman were familiar with some of Janet's work, and we decided to write a series of articles for the centenary of the publication of Janet's great work on trauma *L'Automatisme Psychologique,* which was published in 1889. So in 1989, Onno and I published a review of Janet's work as a lead article in the *American Journal of Psychiatry*, which was very well received and may have contributed to dissociation temporarily having been taken seriously as a central phenomenon in trauma.

Reading Janet also taught me a great deal about traumatic memory. He described something that any clinician gets to observe but may otherwise ignore: the phenomenon of how trauma returns to people's minds as isolated images, smells, physical sensations, and sounds. Janet's descriptions of traumatized individuals were extremely useful to help me with my traumatized patients and this led to three empiric studies of the nature of memory in traumatized adults, children, and people who had the experience of "awareness" during anesthesia.

COMPLEX PTSD (OR "DESNOS")

By early 1990, PTSD was beginning to be accepted as an official diagnosis. However, the patients whom we saw in our various institutions in Boston seemed not really to be best categorized under the rubric of PTSD; their difficulties seemed to be so pervasive and their current lives were so disorganized that the triad of intrusion, numbing, and hyperarousal seemed not really to capture the essence of what troubled them. Judy Herman and I used to have frequent discussions about these issues, and as DSM-IV started to come up for consideration, we linked up with David Pelcovitz and Sandra Kaplan in New York to further define this issue. Robert Spitzer, the father of the DSM-III, invited us to form a subgroup of the PTSD committee of the DSM-IV to look at the complexity of adaptation to trauma throughout the life cycle. We worked on formulating a more complex adaptation to trauma that we called disorders of extreme stress (DESNOS), not otherwise specified.

Working within the DSM-IV PTSD committee and the field trial group that I co-directed with Dean Kilpatrick, we found that the vast majority of treatment-seeking people had long-term histories of trauma, particularly of early childhood interfamilial abuse and neglect. We also found that in addition to their PTSD symptoms, they had multiple difficulties in the areas of self-regulation, attention, self-esteem, intimacy, and somatization. The results of our study showed that the category of PTSD captures just a narrow segment of the problems that chronically traumatized people suffer from, and this opened the door to the possibility of a dimensional rather than a categorical definition of trauma-related disorder in the DSM.

This issue was heavily debated in the DSM-IV committee; in the end, we voted 19 to 2 to broaden the definition of PTSD to include the DESNOS syndrome. However, this idea died as it went up the hierarchical ladder of the DSM process, and the issue was relegated to a footnote in the DSM definition under the rubric of "associated features of PTSD." To my mind, this was a major missed opportunity to accurately capture the effects of abuse and trauma—the reality of what abuse and trauma does to children and the effect of abuse and trauma on the totality of children's development, resulting in the contemporary reality that our patients with chronic intrafamilial trauma now carry multiple diagnoses. What particular diagnosis a patient receives seems to be, cynically, more determined by insurance reimbursements than by diagnostic accuracy.

MEMORY

In the early 1990s the issue of trauma had become very well established in our culture. Major newspapers like the *New York Times* and popular journals like the *New Yorker* regularly had articles about the impact of trauma and child abuse, and for a while it appeared that society had come to recognize the impact of trauma on people's functioning. At that point, suddenly, a remarkable thing happened. On the one hand, some clinicians started to cling to trauma as the principal, or maybe only, explanatory mode of much of their patients' problems, and many started to trace back all their problems to past histories of sexual abuse, even when patients denied having such a history. On the other hand, quite a powerful movement emerged, the False Memory Foundation, which claimed that most stories about childhood trauma were made up, and/or the result of "the implantation" of false memories in patients' minds by therapists.

I was very intrigued by this controversy and also by the fact that nobody seemed to pay attention to the difference between the quality of memories of trauma and memories of everyday life. In response, we initiated a series of studies, first of people with childhood trauma, later of people who had been raped or victims of car accidents, and ultimately, of patients who experienced "awareness" during surgical procedures.

Our studies clearly showed that memories of trauma exist both as stories/narratives, as "episodic" memories, as well as in the form of physical sensations, images, physical hyperarousal, and physical reliving. We were intrigued by the possible biological underpinning to explain what could be going on in the central nervous system (CNS) that would cause the lack of integration of these fragmented sensory imprints, which we also call memories, even though these implicit memories are qualitatively quite different from the stories that people tell about their past. We therefore began a process of trying to understand what happens in the CNS during traumatic experiences that could cause these elements of the traumatic experience to become fragmented, split off, and have a life of their own.

Later, when we were able to demonstrate that eye-movement desensitization and reprocessing (EMDR) was very effective in integrating these fragments of traumatic sensory imprints, we started to cast around for possible biological mechanisms for the fragmentation and integration of traumatic memories, which eventually led to our current collaboration with the neuroscientist Rodolfo Llinas in exploring the role of faulty thalamic timing mechanisms as being at the root of the fragmentation of traumatic memories.

NEUROIMAGING

The first opportunity to study how the brain processed traumatic memories came while the Trauma Center was located at the Massachusetts

General Hospital, where Scott Rauch headed the neuroimaging center. Scott was interested in some of the notions that Roger Pitman and I had about PTSD and invited us to do a study on how traumatized individuals' CNS is affected by the recollection of their trauma in the first neuroimaging study of PTSD. Our findings were for me a turning point in understanding traumatic stress. The first and most predictable finding was an activation of the area around the amygdala, the part of the limbic system that is involved in threat perception. While people were having their flashback, Broca's area was deactivated. We also found that the activation of the amygdala occurred on the right and not on the left side of the brain. Taken together, our findings suggested that as people relive their trauma, there is a relative deactivation of the left anterior prefrontal cortex, particularly in the speech area, and a relative increase in activation in the right posterior part of the brain.

What this seemed to suggest was that, when people go into their traumatic reliving, their capacity to talk or articulate their feelings is sharply decreased; at the same time, there is increased right posterior activation, which must be responsible for people feeling that they are being traumatized all over again without being able to really analyze that what they were experiencing belonged to the past and not to the present. These findings were in line with the Rorschach study that Charles Ducey and I had done with Vietnam veterans a decade earlier.

WORDS, ACTION AND BODILY EXPERIENCE

This made me wonder about the limits of verbal psychotherapy. After all, if trauma mainly affects the right hemisphere and decreases people's capacity to "know" and articulate what they are experiencing, treatment should primarily address right hemisphere functioning and entail the "processing" of traumatic memories, possibly with means other than language and the creation of a narrative, since both of these are left hemisphere functions par excellence.

With those questions in mind, I was asked to give the keynote speech for the first U.S. Body Psychotherapy conference, which was held in the summer of 1996 in Beverly, Massachusetts. I presented my data under the title "the Body Keeps the Score." Several body-oriented psychotherapists who heard me talk about these issues realized that I did not know anything about working with people's bodily states or even tracking people's arousal states; hence they offered to take me under their wing. Three people in particular stand out who offered to teach me about issues having to do with bodily states: Albert Pesso, Pat Ogden, and Peter Levine, all of whom became teachers of mine at this point.

During the summer of 1996, I reluctantly attended an EMDR training session. Suspicious of the tradition of new fads in psychiatry and psychology, I dismissed this seemingly hokey new method until several of my patients, who were themselves professionals with PTSD, had EMDR adjunctively to our psychotherapy and came back markedly improved in ways that my therapy clearly had been unable to accomplish. During this EMDR training, I was assigned to another student to practice my EMDR skills. My fellow student refused to tell me what he was upset about but did go through the EMDR procedure without communicating the substance of his problems to me.

After 1/2 hour of EMDR, he told me, with much obvious relief: "I think I resolved this issue with my father." At that point it dawned on me that processing trauma is really fundamentally not an interpersonal process but a process of people internally coming to terms with the memories of their past by whatever method they find. I was intrigued by the contradiction between what I had seen and two basic tenets of therapy. After all, for therapy to be effective, one is supposed to have (1) a safe and close interpersonal relationship and (2) an opportunity to articulate and come to terms with traumatic experiences. Clearly neither a warm interpersonal relationship nor a verbal articulation of the traumatic material had taken place, yet by all appearances this patient seemed to have come to terms with something that had bothered him about his relationship with his father.

When I started to integrate EMDR into my clinical practice, I found it to be remarkably useful. At the same time I was very fortunate to have two experienced EMDR trainers working at the Trauma Center, Libby Cole and Patti Levin, and we decided to explore the efficacy of EMDR and do some pre-post neuroimaging. As a result of these studies our group at the Trauma Center became more and more intrigued with the biological basis of PTSD and the developmental impact of childhood trauma, which allowed us to attract some of the keenest young minds a Center can hope for, including Joseph Spinazzola, Jim Hopper, and Debbie Korn. This eventually led to support from the National Institute of Mental Health to compare the best biological treatment, an selective serotonin reuptake inhibitor (SSRI), such as Prozac, with the best possible psychological intervention (for me, EMDR), to see how a biological treatment affected both psychological and biological functioning and how a purely psychological treatment would affect these same parameters.

We found that Prozac and EMDR were quite helpful in the treatment of PTSD, that EMDR alone was better than placebo, but most of all that 6 months after the end of treatment, people who had responded to EMDR basically remained asymptomatic, while the majority of the people who had taken the drug naturally reverted to some of their PTSD issues. In fact, we found that 87% of our adult trauma patients remained entirely asymptomatic 6 months after treatment. In the treated group, both the cortisol levels and the psychophysiologic responses to trauma scripts changed.

Our study showed that acute trauma can be treated quite well with brief periods of trauma processing, with a method that does not rely primarily on words and understanding, and which can do so considerably better than the best available pharmacologic agent. At this time, it is too early to assess the impact of studies like these, but I hope that they will contribute to a continued interest in the psychological processing of traumatic experience, possibly with methods that do not necessarily involve words and understanding.

THE NATIONAL CHILD TRAUMATIC STRESS NETWORK

The Trauma Center in Boston came into being at the Massachusetts Mental Health Center. The initial impetus was the observation that many patients at the hospital had horrendous histories of various forms of childhood abuse. After learning from Vietnam veterans, I came to understand that these patients and the veterans were very much alike—veterans of domestic wars, only at an earlier age than the adults or adolescents who went to war and hence at an earlier developmental level, which would have had a more profound impact on their neurodevelopmental progress.

As a consequence, we developed a great interest on how trauma affected children's development and started to try to attract as many staff members as we could who would be interested in treating young children. Gradually our capacities and interest in treating children increased, but we were increasingly faced with how difficult it was to organize child services and how little institutional and social support there was for the treatment of traumatized children.

In 1998, I received a very surprising and unexpected e-mail from Adam Cummings of the Cummings Foundation, telling me that he wanted to fund a study to discover how trauma affects learning in children. However, recognizing how tenuous the future of our child therapy team was, I countered that even if we were able to do an outstanding study of how trauma affects learning, the likelihood that children would actually benefit from such a study was extremely limited, given the current climate of child services. I proposed, instead, that we work together on setting up a conference of leading child psychiatrists, psychologists, and policy makers to look at the state of the trauma treatment in children to see if we could collaborate on changing that situation.

In November 1999, we held a conference at the Brain Center on Cape Cod with representatives of the Justice Department, the Department of Health and Human Services, and various congressional staffers as well as many leading child psychiatrists and psychologists from around the country. What emerged from the meeting was clear: the need to set up a national center for the study and treatment of childhood trauma similar to what had been done in the Veterans Administration around the issue of posttraumatic stress in Veterans.

We were very fortunate to have several congressional staffers, as well as Bill Harris, a lobbyist for a lobbying action organization KIDPAC, present at the meeting, because the day after this meeting we received a phone call from Ted Kennedy's office to clarify further what was needed to start a National Center for Child Traumatic Stress. From that moment on, the action passed from the offices of clinicians and academics into the offices of policy makers. Six months later, Congress passed a bill authorizing the establishment of a National Center for Child Traumatic Stress.

Ironically, after the Substance Abuse and Mental Health Services Administration put out its request for proposals, the committee convened on September 11, 2001 to decide which applicants would be funded to be part of this new network. Even as the Towers of the World Trade Center were collapsing and the Pentagon was attacked, the reviewers worked across the Potomac, deciding to make UCLA and Duke universities the collaborative organizations to lead this new network for the study and treatment of trauma in children.

CONCLUSIONS AND FUTURE DIRECTIONS

To my mind, the establishment of this National Child Traumatic Stress Network is one of the most important accomplishments that has come out of the work of our field since its inception, which we can roughly place in 1978, with the appearance of Charles Figley's book *Stress Disorders among Vietnam Veterans*; Marty Horowitz's work on Stress Response Syndromes; Lenore Terr's publications about the Chowchilla children; and Henry Krystal's paper on Trauma and Effects.

To my mind, the other great advances are the explosion of knowledge about the biology of trauma: our understanding about the relative roles of the sympathetic and the parasympathetic nervous system; the abnormalities of the hypothalamic pituitary adrenal axis; neuroimaging studies, which have clarified the roles of amygdala activation, hippocampal damage, hypofrontality, and abnormal brainstem and cerebellar activation; the difficulties focusing, concentrating, and taking in new relevant information; the effects of trauma on immunology, the impact of trauma on development as spelled out by investigators such as Frank Putnam, Dante Cicchetti, and Martin Teicher; attachment research, led by Karlen Lyons Ruth, Daniel Stern, Ed Tronick and Alicia Lieberman; and finally the issue that I like to call "leaving Vienna," with all due respect to the enormous and lasting contributions of psychoanalysis for the insights it has offered about human nature, the unconscious nature of psychological processes, and the power of the therapeutic relationship.

To me, "Leaving Vienna" means abandoning the notion that people can understand their way out of trauma. The notion that in order to process and overcome trauma, people need to create a coherent story, does not really seem to hold up. In my opinion, the discovery of EMDR opened up extremely important new ways of looking at what else might be going on in mind and brain that could help people.

When one writes books about trauma, it is inevitable to be invited to present internationally. By looking at how people in other countries and cultures deal with trauma, I learned another lesson about trauma treatment: that there are other treatment options besides drugs and exposure that are rooted in other traditions and that are practiced in different ways in virtually every culture around the globe. These are traditions that focus on helping people settle into their bodies and regain a sense of balance and composure, traditions like yoga, t'ai chi, and other practices that emphasize movement, breathing, and inner awareness.

My first recognition of that possibility came in Beijing in 1992, shortly after the aborted uprising in Tienamin Square. The first morning I woke up, looked down from the 11th floor of my hotel and saw several thousand Chinese in little black shoes and identical Mao uniforms below my window engaged in slow, deliberate movements, moving their hands and feet in slow motion, as if swimming in the air. I was puzzled why so many people would waste their time on such practices until I had spent several days in Beijing. The air was polluted, the Communist Party officials rigid and unfriendly; there was an air of distrust and suspicion. As the days went on, I became more and more uptight. After 3 days I joined the Chinese in the park below my hotel and fell in with their movements. Immediately it became clear what this was about—you can only make it through the day in such inhospitable surroundings if you can find a way of centering yourself, or as the Chinese might say, working with your "ch'i."

The second inspiration came in South Africa in 1997. I had gone there to study the work of the Truth and Reconciliation Commission and their awesome task of integrating that country after years and years of brutal oppression. It was remarkable how the participants in every hearing and ceremony engaged in communal singing and dancing before and after giving testimony. One day, in Springfontein, a mining township outside of Johannesburg where 17 people were killed the day of my visit, I attended a therapy group of women who had been raped. For the first half hour they sat silently with their shawls wrapped around their heads and shoulders, numb and worn down, just like similar groups of women I was familiar with in Boston. Then one woman started to hum and other women softly joined in. They slowly got up and started to sway to the music. Life came back to their faces; they started to dance more vigorously, making eye contact and touching each other gently. By the end of the hour, a real sense of connection and commonality had returned, and the women walked home arm in arm, alive and in tune with each other.

Shortly after I returned home, my former student Dr. Devin Hinton came over to show me his videotapes of healing ceremonies in Cambodia, and I was amazed by some of the similarities between the ritualized movements in a small village in Southeast Asia and those I had seen in South Africa (and on Native American reservations in the southwestern United States). Maybe there was something about communal movement, music, and singing that restored an inner equilibrium once disturbed by trauma.

Since those experiences, we have focused our clinical and research explorations at the Trauma Center on finding right-brain solutions to right-brain problems. We are currently studying the effects of theater programs on PTSD in traumatized kids and we are doing a yoga study (the pilot study showed that yoga was more effective than dialectical behavior therapy in chronically traumatized women). Trauma, which we once defined as being external clearly leaves residues inside the human organism that need to be faced, processed, and reset. It is likely that this is possible only if the human organism is provided with experiences that approximate the original trauma, but that, instead of being overwhelming and leaving people in a state of inescapable shock and learned helplessness, provides them with pathways of concentrated action and sensations of mastery.

Only time and careful research will tell.

ACKNOWLEDGMENTS

I have used the word *we* throughout this chapter because this work always is a collaborative enterprise. I have rarely written an article, and never a research grant or book, all by myself. I pride myself on the warmth, cohesiveness, creativity, support and integrity of my colleagues at the Trauma Center, a truly diverse group of superb clinicians who consistently share their work, debate clinical issues, attract new talent, teach our students, take new workshops, work in places most sane human beings avoid, from homeless shelters to Gaza, and spread the word, with language and action. They are a huge group of more than 50 people, and if I mention some, others may feel left out. But I need to single out my former students who have grown up to become my colleagues and teachers: Joseph Spinazzola, Ruth Lanius, Glenn Saxe, Margaret Blaustein, and Jim Hopper. Aside from the many people mentioned in this chapter, I need to mention several other critical people who have had a major impact on the development of my thinking about the nature and treatment of traumatic stress: my wife, consort, friend, and intellectual companion Betta, a body-oriented psychotherapist, and my friends

Sandy McFarlane, Rachel Yehuda, Ilan Kutz, Marylene Cloitre, and Bob Pynoos who are ever-evolving sources of inspiration; the neuroscientists Antonio Damasio, Jaak Panksepp, Richie Davidson and Steven Porges, who lit up previously unilluminated spaces; and my monthly Boston neuroscience study group.

Bessel van der Kolk, 1973

16

Becoming a Psychotraumatologist

LARS WEISAETH

I was born in April 1941 in Nazi-occupied Norway, the youngest of three brothers. I was the result of a happy reunion between my mother and father, who had been separated from each other soon after the German invasion of April 9, 1940. So my first 4 years of life were spent in an occupied country. In fact, virtually all my memories from those years are war-related, the vast majority of them involving some kind of danger. Despite the fact that I have spent some 1,000 sessions on the psychoanalytic couch, I have no real explanation for why this is the case other than the notion that our brains probably deal with existential excitement and threats in a different way to the other bits of information.

At the same time, the actual contents of my war memories are not entirely of a frightening or sad nature, as the following example illustrates. My earliest memory is that of watching Serbian and Russian concentration camp prisoners building a railway in front of our house. What I remember particularly vividly was the excitement we children felt waiting to see whether the guards would stop us when we tried to give the prisoners some bread. The prisoners would thank us by giving us small toys they had managed to fashion from incredibly basic materials, such as little trays with wooden birds on top that would peck if you pulled a string underneath. At that time, the war was nearing its end, and since Norwegian children were even more "Aryan" or Germanic than even the German and Austrian soldiers were, our "misdemeanors" were overlooked as long as we restricted our resistance to activities that did not involve troublemaking—that is, to symbolic gestures such as wearing red caps or paper clips on our jackets (the paper clips signified that we were "sticking together"). Nonetheless, we were truly afraid of the soldiers.

Trondheim was Germany's main submarine base in Northern Europe, which meant that anyone living in Trondheim was exposed to bombing. At the time I thought we were being bombed by the Germans. I would be 40 years of age before I found out that in fact the bombing had been carried out by the Allies. I remember being perplexed at my father's delight that we were being bombed, that these were "our planes." Then again, how on earth could a 3-year-old have understood the concept of "friendly fire"? And so my childhood interpretation of who the enemy was stayed with me for many years. Fortunately I was spared some of the more gruesome details of casualties, such as the many children who were killed by such bombing.

One of my fondest memories from the war was my grandmother singing Christmas carols in the basement of our house as we waited for the air raid to stop. I suppose that what my grandmother understood well was that distraction—namely, being occupied with something else—was not only a good way of keeping up spirits but also the best form of protection and self-preservation of the psyche, especially when things were beyond one's control. My grandmother also taught me how to count the seconds that passed between a lightning flash and the subsequent clap of thunder, so I could calculate how far away the actual lightning was as well as what actions to take when the lightning was too close.

There have been two occasions in my life when I have I lost best friends. When I was 6, a friend of mine drowned. We were fishing at the time, and I had to go home for dinner before he did. It turned out that I was the last person to have seen him alive. I remember seeing his sobbing mother at the police station. Months would go by before his body was found and I learned from other children that it had been partly devoured by rats. I was not allowed to go to his funeral, nor was such an event even talked about by the children. These were the days when children were to be protected from such horrific events and details. At the age of 20 I again lost a dear friend, this time in a mining accident.

WHY PSYCHOTRAUMATOLOGY?

Looking back at my childhood, I ask myself whether personal experiences have contributed to my interest in psychotraumatology. The answer is that while they did not in actual fact play such an important role in *why* I chose to work in the field, they did play an important role in deciding *which* areas of this field of work I took an interest in and *how* my assumptions that I brought to my work affected my approach. By and large I would consider these minor or moderately stressful experiences to be assets in my own work.

I would later become acutely aware of why I wanted to become a medical doctor and why I would go down the specialized path of psychiatry: I wanted to combine my interest in natural science with my interest in the humanities. But before going to medical school I decided to do my year of military service. The infantry training I received in the army would later serve me well both when I worked as a military psychiatrist, with war veterans of various nationalities, and also when I was on assignments in foreign countries during wars or in the wake of war.

Without a doubt, though, it would be the teaching I did in the department of psychiatry at the medical faculty of the University of Oslo, along with my choice afterwards to work there as a psychiatrist, that would be the deciding factor in why I came to spend my professional life in psychotraumatology—a professional life I began in 1975.

THE FIRST NORWEGIAN STUDIES OF TRAUMATIC STRESS: THE INCIDENCE OF PSYCHOSIS

Norwegian psychiatry between the First and the Second World Wars continued to emphasize the role of stressful life events in the etiology of mental disorders. Ørnulf Ødegård established an international research tradition and became one of the founders of social psychiatry when, in 1932, he published studies on the effects on mental health—in particular psychoses—of being a Norwegian immigrant in the United States (Ødegård, 1932).

Ødegård (1954) demonstrated that the relationship between war and mental health is not always a simple one. Not all aspects of war are negative, nor do they constitute risk factors for mental health problems; some may even have positive effects. During the Nazi occupation of Norway, for example, the prevalence of certain types of psychoses decreased by 15%.

The first Norwegian publications that explicitly addressed the effect of traumatic stress were published as early as the Second World War. These publications reported the frequency rates of war-precipitated psychoses. It was not until later, however, that traumatic stress studies were conducted in a more systematic and comprehensive way.

In his 1958 monograph on war refugees to Norway (Eitinger, 1958, 1959), among whom he found a tenfold increase of psychosis, Leo Eitinger used the label *reactive psychosis* because he considered it impossible to decide how much influence either of the two mentioned etiologic factors could have on the psychoses of the refugees examined; this tradition is reflected in the later work of Retterstøl (1966) and others on reactive psychoses. These conditions are caused or precipitated by psychic traumas that hit a predisposed individual. The traumas are decisive for the onset of the psychosis as well as its course and recovery. In form and content the psychosis more or less directly and completely reflects the triggering psychic trauma in an understandable way. To these criteria is added the notion that these disorders mostly have a favorable outcome and do not end in deterioration. This concept strongly demonstrates the importance Scandinavian psychiatry has given to stress and traumatic related disorders, since these disorders made up 20 to 30% of all admissions to psychiatric departments in Denmark, Norway, and Sweden.

The new classification of psychiatric disorders (ICD-10) hardly accepts the concept of reactive psychoses, which are coded under acute or transitory psychoses even if a Scandinavian study demonstrates an interrater reliability among Scandinavian psychiatrists that is as good for reactive psychoses as for schizophrenia and affective psychoses (Hansen, Dahl, Betelson, Birket-Smith, von Knorring, Ottosson, et al., 1992). The state as to DSM-III is discussed by Retterstøl and Dahl (1983). For the time being, Scandinavia has lost the "battle of reactive psychosis."

TRAUMATIC STRESS STUDIES, SENSU STRICTI

Professor Leo Eitinger may be considered the father of Norwegian psychiatry related to stress, the military, and disaster. Eitinger was himself among the 3% of Norwegian Jews who survived Auschwitz. When he returned to Norway, his observations and clinical experiences as a prisoner in Auschwitz began appearing in Norwegian medical journals. Along with Baastians in the Netherlands, Eitinger was one of few researchers during the first decades after the Second World War to take a greater interest in the victims of aggression rather than in the aggressors.

MY TIME AS A MEDICAL STUDENT

I studied at the medical school at the University of Oslo from 1962 to 1968. By my second year of neurophysiology, we were being taught about the importance of the amygdala for survival responses and of the hippocampus for memory, two favorite brain centers for research at the faculty. I have often wondered why the clinical implications of this research for traumatic stress were not focused on until several years later. During our psychiatric training, we were presented with research findings and clinical cases from concentration camp survivors, war sailors, and several other types of war stress from the exile front, the home front, and the prison front of the Second World War (Strom et al., 1961; Eitinger, 1964; Strom, 1968; Eitinger & Strom, 1973; Askevold, 1976).

Eitinger was also studying torture survivors who had remained healthy, learning much about hardiness, resilience, and the importance of social support and other prerequisites for coping with such trauma. In this way, Eitinger was focusing on protective factors and not just risk factors, which represented an early contribution to the field of coping, topics that were to be of great significance to me later on in my career.

Several of our teachers had themselves been incarcerated in Nazi concentration camps in Germany and Poland. Students at the University of Oslo had either been arrested or deported, while others who had managed to avoid arrest, torture, and deportation remained active in the resistance movement. However, they hardly spoke about their war efforts, probably because modesty was considered a virtue and also because of the need to avoid painful memories. What is striking is that concentration camp syndrome was first delineated by medical doctors who had been CC-prisoners, as was sailor syndrome by doctors who had been torpedoed in the North Atlantic convoy service. What was equally striking was the lack of interest among other mental health researchers.

As a medical student, I remember how impressed I was by how well the somatically severely ill patients coped with their plight. What also struck me was how frequently childhood traumas were reported by individuals who, on the surface at least, appeared to have suffered no psychopathologic effect. Later on in my career, when I became involved in the training of psychiatrists, I would encourage them to interview healthy persons who had a potentially traumatic background. The many issues of resilience fascinated me.

TRAINING IN PSYCHIATRY

In 1970, after a number of residencies in surgery, internal medicine, and district medicine, I set about training to become a psychiatrist. In addition to the regular training program, I opted to train in individual and family psychotherapy. One of my first assignments shortly after starting work at the University Psychiatric Clinic in Oslo in 1972 came when I was invited to take part in a short-term anxiety-provoking psychotherapy research project (Dahl, Dahl, Heiberg, Husby, Olafsen, Sorensen, et al., 1978). Professor Peter Sifneos from Harvard was, at the time, a regular visiting professor, and he became involved in the project, as did David Malan from the Tavistock Clinic, the UK pioneer on short-term dynamic psychotherapy. Measuring changes and outcome after therapy in a reliable way was for me a very satisfactory scientific learning experience.

GETTING INTO TRAUMA RESEARCH

The department at the clinic where I worked had as its head a certain Arne Sund, M.D. Working with Dr. Sund was to prove a deciding factor in the direction of my career. Dr. Sund had served as a medical doctor in the Norwegian field hospital during the Korean War. This military experience was to be a crucial episode in Dr Sund's career and basically spurred him on to concentrate on traumatic stress and other forms of primary and secondary preventive interventions. Dr. Sund had seen the impressive results of forward psychiatry with the applications of the BICEPS (brevity, immediacy, centrality, expectancy, proximity, and simplicity of treatment), and he was eager to try out these principles on civilian cases of traumatic stress. Sund wrote several papers in Norwegian about traumatic stress and in 1976 completed the first comprehensive textbook of stress and disaster psychiatry (Sund, 1976). Another paper by James Titchener in the *Journal of Trauma* (Titchener, 1970) was also very inspiring. At the time, Titchener's article was about the only contemporary work on acute psychic trauma available in the international literature. I was fortunate to visit Cincinnati in 1974 and see Titchener at work with survivors of the Buffalo Creek Dam disaster. That one visit strengthened my desire to start studies in the early aftermath of trauma. Being able to study the *status nascendi* (moment of birth) of a psychiatric condition was a very tempting opportunity indeed.

Norwegian studies of the late psychic sequels of excessive war stress had demonstrated that when a number of years had passed since the stress exposure, the chances of achieving therapeutic success were considerably limited. Sund and I made similar findings in a retrospective study of patients who had been treated in our clinic for civilian trauma-related disorders. We found that when more than 4 years had elapsed from the time of trauma exposure to the time when the patient was referred for psychiatric treatment, the prognosis was very poor. We decided to conduct prospective research in order to identify, at an early stage, risk situations, risk individuals, and risk reactions. In 1975, I began a research fellowship to study victims of accident and violence in surgical trauma departments. However, I had not reached much further than the initial pilot period when an event happened that would make my research project take a dramatic turn (see below). The research project I left was then taken over by my colleague Ulrik Malt, later to become professor and head at the Department of Psychosomatic Medicine at the National Hospital, whose excellent publications rank with the very best in the field (Malt, 1988).

In the summer of 1976, at the Nordic Psychiatric Conference in Finland, I presented a paper in which I introduced the concept of "the traumatic anxiety syndrome," a subacute posttraumatic constellation of symptoms. My hypothesis about this syndrome as a mediating condition was based on literature studies, my own retrospective study, and my examination of acute and subacute cases in the trauma departments. In this syndrome I included (1) triggered imperative recollections about the stressful event; (2) repetitive nightmares (which I suggested could be pathognomonic for this syndrome); (3) traumatophobia, such as avoidance of the site of the event and of related activities; (4) hypersensitivity/increased irritability/anger; and (5) social withdrawal.

THE STUDY OF THE INDUSTRIAL EXPLOSION

On September 15, 1976, an explosion in the Jotun petrochemical plant in Sandefjord, 130 kilometers south of Oslo, set off a gigantic fire that lasted well into the next day. I went to the scene of the accident the next day to start examining employees who had survived the explosion, some of whom had had narrow escapes while others had been severely injured. I recognized various degrees of the traumatic anxiety syndrome in many and was soon ready to adapt my research project to the collective situation at hand. I decided to stay on in Sandefjord for the rest of the year to study and treat the psychic reactions to the disaster. I would come to spend much of the next 4 years providing treatment for survivors while at the same time conducting a series of follow-up studies. The whole study was published as a two-volume monograph, which I defended for my doctoral degree in 1985 (Weisaeth, 1984).

The event in Sandefjord, a potentially traumatic one for the 125 survivors, had a number of key factors; it was unprecedented, it was unanticipated (i.e., it happened without warning), it was violent, and, finally, it was uncontrollable. The tremendous blast killed 6 workers and injured 20, while the fire caused extensive material damage. Neither the explosion nor the fire could be controlled. In terms of effect on people, it was in fact the many narrow escapes that dominated the public eye, especially since the number of dead and injured was much smaller than one would expect for such an explosion.

The task involved 125 industrial workers who had been exposed at work. Since this was a two-shift workplace, I would then need to compare these 125 with another 121 control persons who had been on the parallel shift. All of the employees had undergone regular annual health checks.

Within a year I had moved from the familiar role of a psychotherapist in my safe office environment to working at bedside in surgical trauma units and doing field psychiatric work in a disaster area. I was confronted with people from bereaved families, injured people, uninjured survivors and their families, body recovery workers, witnesses, rescuers, and employees under the obligatory police investigations. These experiences became the start of work that I was to call "operational psychiatry."

All in all, I conducted more than 1,000 personal interviews, of which about half were therapeutic sessions. The 246 employees were studied in a systematic cross-sectional design 1 week after the disaster, then 7 months later and 4 years after the disaster. Therapeutic work was carried out on 52 employees, all of whom were studied in a longitudinal, intensive design. I focused initially on investigating disaster behavior during the impact and the acute posttraumatic stress reactions. The follow-up project was designed as a prospective, controlled, clinical, and interventive study of subacute and long-term posttraumatic stress reactions. The cognitive, emotional, and behavioral responses during the disaster impact were classified and rated as optimal disaster behavior in 37% of the employees who had experienced a high stress exposure, while 34% were rated as adaptive and 29% as maladaptive.

In the field of traumatic stress research, surprisingly few studies had focused on responses during impact, and there was a need to be innovative in constructing reliable variables. Fortunately a detailed miniature model had been built of the destroyed industrial area, so that I could collect very detailed data on the location and movement of each exposed worker. Since they had undergone police questioning and 80% of them had been in the company of others at the time of the explosion, sources of data other than those related to the individual were available. A high level of training and experience predicted optimal or adaptive disaster behavior with a sensitivity of 81% and specificity of 85% (Weisaeth, 1989a). It was found that competence in handling severe danger situations determined the immediate response, which supported survival and rescue efforts. More surprising, however, was the finding that optimal and adaptive disaster behavior predicted a low level of PTSD. This indicated that the posttraumatic stress disorders that developed were illnesses that had started during the exposure, reflecting a failure to cope rather than a failure to recover from a normal posttraumatic stress reaction.

In particular, four dimensions of the disaster stressor turned out to carry risk of psychological traumatization: (1) the severity and location of the traumatic injury, (2) the intensity and duration of the danger to life, (3) the witness experience, and (4) the responsibility trauma as we came to call it—in other words, the choice between incompatible needs to act, such as choosing to save oneself or to help another person.

With regard to the prediction of PTSD, the traumatic anxiety syndrome rated at 1 week predicted PTSD 7 months later with a specificity of 89% and a sensitivity of 96% (Weisaeth, 1989b). As all the symptoms in the proposed diagnosis of PTSD in the draft DSM-III of 1978 had been among the 30 posttraumatic stress reactions I had rated in 1976–1977, I was able to diagnose PTSD according to the DSM-III criteria. The prevalence at 7 months was 37%, 17%, and 4% in the high-, medium-, and low-stress exposure groups, respectively. The only posttraumatic stress

reaction that increased in frequency and intensity during the first half
year after the disaster was irritability. A closer analysis showed the anger
to be secondary to the anxiety response, in particular sleep disturbance. It
was a neurasthenic type of anger and irritability and not a result of viola-
tion of human worth. The secondary development of anger turned out to
be a severe complication to the successful treatment of the PTSD. The
anger created psychological resistance to therapy, contributing to conflicts at work and in the family. There is a strong likelihood that more
intensive treatment with anxiolytic and sleep-inducing drugs in the early
aftermath may well have helped to prevent some of the anger from
developing further. In fact, I was surprised to find that anger/irritability
was not included among the symptom criteria in the DSM-III of 1980; it
was later inserted in the revised 1987 edition. The ability to predict PTSD
was, of course, important for a high-risk prevention strategy. The few
false positives and negatives reduced my worry that unnecessary interventions could be harmful.

As expected and demanded in longitudinal medical research in Norway, I was able to get extremely high response rates—91% in the acute
phase and 100% at 7 months and 4 years among the 246 employees—even though this took much hard work and a number of very good
collaborators in the industrial company as well as the help of their medical officers and nurses.

Counting the number of times I had to call a person on the phone in
order to get them to come for an interview gave me a fairly accurate picture as to the psychological resistance to the examination that each person had. One worrying finding was that 40% of the PTSD cases probably
would not have been identified if it had been up to the person's own initiative to seek help. In other words, an 80% response rate would have
missed 40% of the cases (Wisaeth, 1989c).

The level of effectiveness of outreach in the trauma population may be
more of a problem than the level of efficacy of the interventions offered.
Delayed reactions beyond a few days did not occur. Shock trauma apparently did not leave enough time for the defense mechanisms to be mobilized, which would have contributed to latency and the late debut of
sequels. PTSD 7 months postdisaster was the best predictor of PTSD at
the 4-year follow-up.

However, as time went by, an increasing role was seen for premorbid
vulnerabilities, immature personality being the most important. The
denial of risk that had characterized the immature person before the accident, indicating an ego vulnerable to anxiety, had now given way to an
illusion of centrality where dangers were seen as bound to recur.

The intervention design prevented any firm conclusions as to the efficacy of early intervention. However, it was now clear that the early interview, which combined research and intervention purposes, was not
generally able to prevent the development of PTSD, of which a number of

cases later developed. The overall results of the longitudinal prevention and treatment program were also hard to evaluate, since a random design was not applied. I feel pretty confident, however, that the work prognosis of the traumatized employees has been positively influenced and that the level of work that had been disabled was extremely low. It is perhaps worth mentioning at this point that a striking difference at that time was the absence of any motivation of financial gain.

During the 4-year observation period in the longitudinal study of the industrial workers, I had the chance to study yet another role that anger played in the development of PTSD and in the clinical picture of the disorder.

PEACEKEEPER STRESS

While I was serving as psychiatrist to the 10 national contingents in the United Nations forces in Lebanon for 3 months in 1978, I found a PTSD that differed somewhat from the ones I had studied until then. The soldiers with posttraumatic stress symptoms mainly feared their own loss of their ability to control their anger and, to a lesser degree, external dangers. It was reasonable to interpret this observation in terms of the particular role that peacekeeping soldiers have, particularly their need to be able to control and to refrain from acting out angry impulses, and all this while having to put up with severe stressors such as being fired upon and being exposed to threats, humiliations, provocations, and so on (Weisaeth, 1982). I labeled the condition "The UN soldier's stress syndrome." Fortunately, the labeling did not contribute to an "epidemic" of such states, a risk I was not aware of at that time. In 1993 I directed the large United Nations Interim Force In Lebanon study, which carried out a systematic investigation of the first 26 Norwegian contingents in the peacekeeping force in Lebanon. We found that 5% of the veterans who had completed their 6 months of service suffered from posttraumatic stress, while 15% of those who had cut short their service had such problems (Weisaeth, Aarhaug, & Mehlum, 1993; Mehlum & Weisath, 2002). A worrying finding was the high suicide rate among the veterans compared to a control population—which was later followed up by Siri Thoresen at our institute through her psychological autopsy studies.

A CHAIR IN PSYCHOTRAUMATOLOGY

In 1978 Sund was appointed professor of psychiatry. His duties included special teaching and research within the field of traumatic stress and disaster psychiatry. The fact that his was the third chair in psychiatry at the faculty underlines the importance and kudos this field was being given. In 1978 the term *disaster psychiatry* was chosen for this discipline, mainly because it was a part of disaster medicine and because the traumatic events that it dealt with often shared the collective nature of that field.

A main driving force behind its development was the desire to institutionalize the knowledge base within the field of traumatic stress. It was commonly recognized at the time that many insights that had been gained in this field of science had a tendency to get lost.

As to the question why so much of the research on PTSD up until 1980s had been conducted on war traumatization and not on sexual or violent trauma in children or others was the fact that both military corps and the National Health Service had a duty to care for military personnel.

THE OIL-RIG DISASTER: PTSS-10

In 1980, the oil rig Alexander Kjelland capsized in the North Sea, killing 123 and leaving 89 survivors. Once again we were drawn to the interesting challenge of studying a whole population exposed to the same potentially traumatic event. We applied similar research methods for the survivors in that study as we did with the Jotun explosion. The actual long-term follow up study was conducted by Are Holen (1990). Holen's study confirmed the previous findings, as well as the considerable role of premorbid psychic vulnerabilities in the risk of developing PTSD. We developed an instrument for early screening based on the 1-year follow-up of the survivors after the maritime disaster. This instrument we called the Post-Traumatic Symptom Scale (PTSS-10). Over time, this instrument has shown itself to have a number of excellent psychometric qualities (Eid, Thayer, & Johnsen, 1999; Weisaeth, 2004), and it has been much used internationally. Both irritability/anger and depression are among the 10 items, anticipating the increasing role that the anger response was seen to have according to the DSM-IIIR and the frequent comorbid depression in patients with PTSD.

A LEGACY FOR AND PASSING ON TO THE THIRD GENERATION

After Arne Sund retired in 1984, I was appointed professor of disaster psychiatry. In my military psychiatric research I decided to prioritize on potentially traumatic events that were severely threatening to human lives or caused the loss of human life; this included suicides. In 1997, after several important works in suicidology had been published (Mehlum, 1994), a chair in suicidology was created at the medical faculty, to which my collaborator Lars Mehlum was appointed. This unit of his later became the National Competence Centre in Suicide Prevention and Research.

What were the mechanisms that made training play such an important and protective role in an uncontrollable danger situation such as the industrial explosion? The preventive implications of these findings were met with much greater interest within Norwegian industry and the military than in the psychiatric community. Preventive strategies, such as the selection of personnel, preparation in the form of training, as well as exercises to build resilience seemed to be of much less concern to clinicians than they ought to have been.

The director of the Natural Science and Technological Research Council, a former minister of defense as well as social affairs, saw our potential and provided the funding that would make it possible to launch a series of studies on coping. We studied responses during real-life events, such as coping among rescuers during a disaster (Ersland, Weisaeth, & Sund, 1989); helicopter crashes and the possible link to effects of the crew's earlier underwater escape training and escape training as therapy for PTSD (Hytten & Herlofsen, 1989); firefighter stress during fire disasters and the way positive response expectancies were established by Stress Inoculation Training before moving through smoke labyrinths; evacuating in free-fall lifeboats; and so forth (Hytten, 1989). Our findings were put to use in civilian and military training programs.

We conducted a number of studies on stressful events such as burn injuries, terror incidents, hostage experiences, bank and post office robberies, major accidents, genetic testing for Huntington's disease, and so on.

OPERATIONAL PSYCHIATRY

The research model that we applied after the 1976 industrial explosion, a model combining intervention and psychiatric research, was used more and more regularly. As a consequence, our institute became involved in the organizational development of models for psychosocial interventions after major traumatic events, such as large-scale accidents, disasters, and mass violence. Basically, three models were developed: one for local communities, another for companies, and a final one for communication disasters (Weisaeth, 2004). We managed to achieve a number of promising results as a result of early intervention. One of these was the case of a military unit that was suddenly struck by an avalanche, killing more than half of the soldiers. Of the survivors, none developed PTSD. We also trained in negotiation techniques for hostage situations and were used by the police on several occasions.

OTHER STUDIES AND ACTIVITIES

In one study, Solveig Dahl (Weisaeth, 1989), a collaborator of mine, found that in the case of rape it was not possible to identify high-risk cases on the basis of early posttraumatic reactions. This was because as many as 80% of the victims had considerable stress reactions for the first 3 months. In order to predict later PTSD in the acute phase, Dahl had to combine individual risk factors (previous psychological instability), trauma risk factors (rape with weapon), and social support risk factors (blame from family).

During my service with the UN in Lebanon, I acted for some time as battalion doctor for the Nepalese military contingent, which gave me the opportunity to study the world-famous Ghurkha soldiers, renowned for their lack of fear of death. I was particularly impressed by how deep their religious and cultural beliefs were, beliefs such as reincarnation if ever they should die on the battlefield. This fatalistic outlook on life, in which one's destiny is actually predetermined, influenced the Gurkhas' fear responses, at least when the soldier had time to consider the meaning of possible death (Weisaeth & Sund, 1982).

When Norway took on the responsibility for training psychiatrists in Cambodia in the 1990s, I again had a chance to observe how religion, in this case Buddhism, shaped attitudes toward suffering and death.

Other assignments that gave me great opportunities to learn about how multiple factors operate within the field of traumatic stress included taking part in World Health Organization (WHO) and UN missions to evaluate the effects of war stress in places such as Kuwait, Serbia, Croatia, Bosnia, and Lebanon.

One of my research interests has been to elucidate the similarities and differences in the posttraumatic response to potentially traumatic events caused by natural forces (such as natural disasters and other events considered to be of an accidental nature) and events resulting from human failure or malice. The increased virulence in terms of pathogeneity of these events in the order mentioned, in my opinion, relates to the severity with which human integrity is challenged, attacked, or crushed by the forces unleashed. Thus, the degree of narcissistic injury seems to me to be at the core of psychological traumatization (Weisaeth, 1989d).

With Ellinor Major I had a chance to study the possible transgenerational effects of trauma. Major conducted a study of Norwegian resistance fighters who had survived incarceration in death camps and compared them and their children with comrades from the resistance who had not been arrested, tortured, or deported. Amazingly enough, Major's findings showed that there did not seem to be any increased risk of health problems among the children of fathers suffering from the concentration camp syndrome. Major's findings indicated that a parent exposed to a traumatic event should not share the experience with the children but rather share with them what was to be learned from the experience— that is, the "learning experience" in contrast to the "subjective experience" (Major, 2003). In other words, the effects of World War II in Norway seemed to stop with the war generation.

In the days following the Chernobyl disaster in 1986, I initiated a series of studies along with other Scandinavian colleagues on the population responses to a "silent" trauma: the nuclear fallout (Tønnessen, Mårdberg, & Weisæth, 2002). The results from these studies showed that, while incidents were fairly low, somatization disorders and hypochondria, as opposed to PTSD, were the most common psychiatric outcomes. This underlined the notion that that coping with such events demands great trust in the information given out by the authorities.

Arnfinn Tønnessen and I studied the psychological effects of the use of Prussian blue, a chemical cesium binder that protects animals from being contaminated by ionizing radiation. The effects of using this countermeasure in Norway had proven to be very positive. However, despite the successful application of the same countermeasure among our comparison Russian population in villages around Chernobyl, no similar effect, either real or perceived, was reported. This seemed to suggest very strongly that if people did not believe the information the authorities provided regarding contamination levels before countermeasures were applied (which is likely in the case of Chernobyl), one could expect little if any intervention effect.

Throughout my research I have tried to utilize the comparative advantages that a population like the Norwegian one offers when it comes to longitudinal research. One example of this involves a recent study, as yet unpublished, on the long-term prognosis of combat veterans. During this study, I and a group of fellow researchers examined veterans who had taken part in continual 45-day infantry combat in the Narvik region during the invasion of 1940. Some 60 years after the combat, we were able to trace all the veterans from this one particular battalion who were still alive. They all agreed to undergo a thorough physical and medical health examination. When we checked the records of those who were no longer alive, we found that their life span did not differ in any particular from that of the control group. As many as 70% of the combat veterans we examined had some degree of posttraumatic stress reaction that could be connected to their war experience. We decided to call the conditions for the majority "normal combat veteran complaints," since their stress reaction had not interfered significantly with their lives. This was supported by the fact that when they were questioned, almost none of the veterans said they would rather have done without the war experience. Another finding was that reactions for the majority of them had started during the actual combat or in the immediate aftermath; in other words, delayed reactions were hardly seen at all. We also found a very strong correlation between posttraumatic stress and somatic health problems during the lives of the veterans, which raised the question of the extent of physical risk of long-term suffering from posttraumatic stress. In the control group, a reserve battalion that had seen no combat at all, we did not find a single case of PTSD.

INTERNATIONAL COLLABORATION

Throughout the 30 years during which I have worked in this field, I have come to realize how important international contacts are, not least for the many single researchers from small countries like Norway. I could mention many people in the same field who have inspired me over the years, such as Tom Lundin in Sweden, who as early as 1977 had started prospective studies of disastrous events; Beverly Raphael from Australia was another person who greatly inspire me during her visit to Norway in 1983, as did the great work that was carried out by McFarlane, Bryant, and many others. Another cross-national study that sticks in my mind was the treatise on research methodology in disaster that Raphael, Lundin, and I published (1989). Other important arenas of collaboration have been the NATO work group on military psychiatry, which was established in 1985; the International Society of Traumatic Stress Syndrome (ISTSS), with Robert Ursano and his colleagues at the Uniformed Services University of the Health Sciences from 1986; and the European Society of Traumatic Stress Studies since its founding. In addition, having the opportunity to coedit international books with prominent colleagues has been a great learning experience for me (Danieli, Rodley & Weisaeth, 1989; Giller & Weisaeth, 1996; Van der Kok, McFarlane, & Weisaeth, 1996).

THE WAY AHEAD

On January 1, 2004, my new workplace, the National Centre for Violence and Traumatic Stress Studies, was opened. It is located in a separate building at Ullevål Hospital, Norway's largest somatic hospital. The center is a subsidiary of the University of Oslo; it is a fully government-financed research center with 30 staff members from various health and social science disciplines. The governmental ministries that joined forces to strengthen research, development, teaching, knowledge dissemination, and supervision in the field of traumatic stress are the Departments of Health, Social Affairs, Justice, Defense, and Child and Family.

The center does not have as its objective to do any clinical work but rather to collaborate closely with clinical services. It has four sections that together cover the whole field of traumatic stress. One interesting aspect of the center is that it admits both the perpetrators and the victims of sexual abuse and violence.

To the question of what I personally see as the most urgent research work that needs to be done in psychotraumatology, my reply is this: We should have randomized controlled trials of the efficacy of early preventive intervention. In this era of evidence-based medicine, we cannot expect to be able to go on using up our resources on early intervention without solid evidence on its efficacy, effectiveness, and cost benefit.

I see the traumatic stress field as the most promising for prevention in psychiatry: the population at risk has been clearly defined, we know when potentially traumatic events have occurred (to an increasing extent also in the family context), and we also have the necessary knowledge for the early identification of high-risk cases. What is lacking is an adequate amount of convincing and compelling data on how valuable our interventive efforts are for the individual, the group, and society.

Lars Weisaeth, 1969

REFERENCES

Askevold, F. (1976–1977). The war sailor syndrome. *Psychotherapy and Psychosomatics, 27,* 133–138.

Dahl, A. A., Dahl, C. I., Heiberg, A., Husby, R., Olafsen, O. M., Sorensen T., & Weisæth L. (1978). A presentation of short-term psychotherapy project at the Oslo University Psychiatric Clinic. *Psychotherapy and Psychosomatics, 29,* 299–304.

Dahl, S. (1993). *Rape—A hazard to health.* Oslo: Universitetsforlaget Oslo.

Danieli Y., Rodley N. S., & Weisæth L. (Eds.) (1996). *International responses to traumatic stress: Humanitarian, human rights, justice, peace and development contributions, collaborative actions and future initiatives.* Amityville, NY: Baywood Publishing Company.

Eid, J., Thayer, J., & Johnsen, B. H. (1999). Measuring post-traumatic stress symptoms: A psychometric evaluation of symptom and coping questionnaires based on a Norwegian sample. *Scandinavian Journal of Psychology, 40,* 101–108.

Eitinger, L. (1958). *Psykiatriske undersøkelser blant flyktninger I Norge* [Psychiatric investigations of refugees in Norway – English summary]. Oslo: Universitetsforlaget.

Eitinger, L. (1959). The incidence of mental disease among refugees in Norway. *Journal of Mental Science, 105,* 326–338.

Eitinger, L. (1964). *Concentration camp survivors in Norway and Israel.* Oslo: Universitetsforlaget.

Eitinger, L., & Strøm, A. (1973). *Mortality and morbidity after excessive stress.* New York: Universitetsforlaget, Oslo/Humanities Press.

Ersland, S., Weisæth, L., & Sund, A. (1980). The stress upon rescuers involved in an oil rig disaster, "Alexander L. Kielland." *Acta Psychiatrica Scandinavica Supplementum, 355,* 38–49.

Giller, E, L., & Weisæth, L. (Eds.) (1996). *Post-traumatic stress disorder.* London: Bailliére Tindall.

Hansen, H., Dahl, A. A., Bertelsen, A., Birket-Smith, M., von Knorring, L., Ottosson, J.-O., Pakaslahti, A., Retterstøl, N., Salvesen, C., Torsteinsson, G., & Väisäinen, E. (1992). The Nordic concept of reactive psychosis—a multicenter reliability study. *Acta Psychiatrica Scandinavica, 86,* 55–59.

Holen, A. (1990). *A long-term outcome study of survivors from a disaster—The Alexander L. Kielland disaster in perspective.* Dissertation. University of Oslo.

Hytten, K. (1989). *Studies on stress and coping: Psychosocial and physical dangers. Establishment and manifestiations of negative and positive response outcome expectancies.* Division for disaster psychiatry, University of Oslo/ Department of Psychiatry, The Joint Norwegian Armed Forces Medical Services.

Hytten, K., Herlofsen, P. (1989). Accident simulation as a new therapy training for post-traumatic stress disorder. *Acta Psychiatrica Scandinavica,* Supplementum), 355: 79–83.

Major, E. (2003). Health effects of war stress on Norwegian World War II resistance groups: A comparative study. *Journal of Traumatic Stress, 16*(6), 595–599.

Malt, U. F. The long-term consequences of accidental injury. *British Journal of Psychiatry, 153,* 810–818.

Mehlum, L. (1994). *Clinical studies of suicidal behaviour in the young with special reference to personality disorders.* Oslo: Medical Faculty, University of Oslo.

Mehlum, L., Weisæth, L. (2002). Predictors of posttraumatic stress reactions in Norwegian UN peacekeepers 7 years after service. *Journal of Traumatic Stress, 15,* 17–26.

Ødegård, Ø. (1954). The incidence of mental disease in Norway during World War II. *Acta Psychiatrica Neurologica, 29,* 333–353.

Raphaelm B., Lundin, T., & Weisæth, L. (1989). A research method for the study of psychological and psychiatric aspects of disaster. *Acta Psychiatrica Scandinavica Supplementum, 353,* 1–75.

Retterstøl, N. (1966). *Paranoid and paranoic psychoses.* Springfield, IL: Charles C Thomas.

Retterstøl, N., & Dahl, A. A. (1983). Scandinavian perspectives of DSM-III. In R. L. Spitzer, J. B. W. Williams, & A. E., Skodol (Eds.), *International perspectives of DSM-III* (pp. 217–234). Washington D.C.: American Psychiatric Press.

Strøm, A. (1968). *Norwegian concentration camp survivors.* Oslo: Universitetsforlaget.

Strøm, A., Refsum, S.B., Eitinger, L., Gronvik, O., Lonnum, A., Engeset, A., Osvik, K., Rogan, B., (1962). Examination of Norwegian ex-concentration-camp prisoners. *Journal of Neurological Psychiatry, 4,* 43–62.

Sund, A. (1976). *Psykiatri og stress under kriser, katastrofer og krig.* Oslo: Universitetsforlaget.

Titchener, J. L. (1970). Management and study of psychological response to trauma. *Journal of Trauma 10,* 974–980.

Tønnessen, A., Mårdberg, B., & Weisæth, L. (2002). Silent disaster: A European perspective on threat perception from Chernobyl far field fallout. *Journal of Traumatic Stress, 15,* 453–459.

Van der Kolk, B. A., McFarlane, A. C., & Weisæth, L. (Eds.). (1996). *Traumatic stress: The effects of overwhelming experience on mind, body, and society.* New York: Guilford Press.

Weisæth, L. (1984). *Stress reactions to an industrial disaster: An investigation of disaster behaviour and acute post-traumatic stress reactions, and a prospective, controlled, clinical and interventive study of sub-acute and long-term post-traumatic stress reactions.* Oslo: Universitetet i Oslo.

Weisæth, L. (1989a). A study of behavioural responses to an industrial disaster. *Acta Psychiatrica Scandinavica Supplementum, 355,* 13–24.

Weisæth, L. (1989b). The stressors and the post-traumatic stress syndrome after an industrial disaster. *Acta Psychiatrica Scandinavica Supplementum, 355,* 25–37.

Weisæth, L. (1989c). Importance of high response rates in traumatic stress research. *Acta Psychiatrica Scandinavica Supplementum, 355,* 131–137.

Weisæth, L. (1989d). Torture of a Norwegian ship's crew: The torture, stress reactions and psychiatric after-effects. *Acta Psychiatrica Scandinavica Supplementum, 355,* 63–72.

Weisæth, L. (2004). Preventing after-effects of disaster trauma: The Information and Support Centre. *Prehospital and Disaster Medicine, 19*(1), 86–89.

Weisæth, L., Aarhaug, P., & Mehlum, L. (1993) *The UNIFIL-report,* part I. English revised edition. Oslo: Forsvarets Sanitet/Forsvarets Overkommando.

Weisæth, L., & Sund A. (1982). Psychiatric problems in Unifil and the UN-soldier's stress syndrome. *Air Force Medical Services,1982; 55,* 109–116.

17

From Crisis Intervention to Bosnia: The Trauma Maps of John P. Wilson

JOHN P. WILSON

Looking backward is in the nature of autobiographical work, and one is never sure how well focused the binoculars are in covering a long trail of professional endeavors. When it comes to this autobiography, I've often wished that someone had invented a neurologic probe, a device like an old-fashioned thermometer, that could be inserted painlessly into the brain to extract perfectly preserved memories that could be "down-loaded" and printed out, documenting the exact details of the many journeys that have taught me a great deal about trauma, posttraumatic stress disorder (PTSD), and the meaning of life. The journey started with the crisis intervention work I did in graduate school and continued to my service in doing psychological first aid in Bosnia during the Balkan War (1991–1995).

HISTORICAL FRAMEWORK

To frame a historical perspective, I begin with my graduate training at Michigan State University in 1969–1973, where two diverse pathways laid the foundation for my later work in PTSD. In brief, I came to the study of trauma and PTSD through my interest in altruism. My research interests directed my attention to the larger question of why people fail to act in situations where there are clear-cut needs for intervention without moral conflict about doing the right thing, as seen in historical examples such as My Lai in Vietnam; the Holocaust; and ethnic and genocidal massacres in Rwanda, Cambodia, and the former Yugoslavia. On the other side of the coin was the question of the victim. What happens to victims in different types of everyday-life situations and how strong must their personal need for help have to be before others will act in prosocial ways? These questions were of interest to me during the years of my graduate training and the early part of my academic career. My laboratory studies led me to want to understand what had happened to men who served in Vietnam, as the war raged on unabated during this time period (1969–1973). Were they forgotten warriors and victims of an unpopular war?

On a personal level, several of my closest high school buddies enlisted in the U.S. Marine Corps after high school and served in Vietnam in 1966–1967. They were never the same afterwards. Despite my most sincere attempts to "reconnect" with them after they came home from the war, they were angry, alienated, and short-tempered, refusing to talk about their experiences. I lost my best friend to a war. And when he returned from Vietnam, I asked him: "Willie, what happened over there in Vietnam?" He looked at me expressionlessly and said: "Fuck it and fuck you and everyone else!" He never spoke of the war again. Years later, he called me at midnight after I appeared on the television program *60 Minutes* with Mike Wallace in about 1980 to talk about PTSD in Vietnam veterans. My lifelong buddy said, "Jack, ol' bud, I need to talk to you. Can we meet somewhere?" Like many Vietnam veterans, he was still awake in the early morning hours.

The second historic thread extends back to 4 years of work in a crisis intervention center in East Lansing, Michigan. It was there, on a daily basis, that I cut my teeth working with a wide range of psychological emergencies. Many of those who telephoned for help or walked in had been traumatized: rapes, drugs, divorce, abuse, assaults, suicide attempts, chronic incurable illnesses, or severe mental disorders. I learned a lot from doing crisis intervention and I did not know at that time that this was going to be my clinical "boot camp" for the work with Vietnam veterans, soon to follow.

In 1973 I accepted a position at Cleveland State University, where I reside today. During my first year, 1973–1974, I encountered the first of many Vietnam veterans who were attending the urban university and who sought out my help. This was to be the beginning of a relationship that changed my life forever. Indeed, there are so many stories of importance that happened between 1973–1976 that it is hard to know which ones to write about. I want to share two stories because they represent hundreds of others I came to know very well, about Vietnam veterans struggling to come home from the war.

During my first week of teaching, a youthful, blond, curly-haired Irishman named John Burke walked into my office. He introduced himself as a psychology major and told me rather quickly that he was trying to get his life "together" and had no place to live. He stated without reservation that he was a recovering heroin and alcohol addict who was estranged from his Irish-Catholic family and needed a place to "crash" for a week or so until he could find a job and place to live. I was impressed by John's intelligence, sincerity, intensity, and understated desperation. He never mentioned that he was a Vietnam veteran. Having just purchased a large old colonial home, I invited him to stay with my wife and me until he could get himself situated. He indicated that he was good with his hands and could fix things that needed repair. John said he'd stay no longer than 2 weeks and be on his way.

John moved in and quickly went about his endeavors. Always polite, courteous, and intellectually engaging, he set about fixing cracked windows, leaky toilets, and broken door locks. I was impressed with his handyman skills and willingness to help us fix up our old house. Time went by and John stayed on, continuing to help with repairs, demanding nothing more than a place to sleep. He usually took his evening meal with us before leaving every night for what he called his "cookies and coffee" club meeting. He never mentioned the name Alcoholics Anonymous (AA), but eventually I figured out that is where he went at the nearby St. Ann's Catholic Church.

One night, while working late in my study, John asked me if we could talk. I said sure and sat back to listen. For the next 5 hours he told me for the first time that he was a combat medic with the 101st Airborne Division in Vietnam. He talked about his war experiences and how they led to his use of heroin before the end of his second tour of duty. He explained that he had never discussed his war experiences with anyone and appreciated my willingness to listen. For the next 6 months, we talked about Vietnam every night. John seemed to feel better and looked much more relaxed. His 2-week stay extended to 9 months. He moved out at the end of the school year and did well in his studies and personal life. Four years later, he graduated from the university as a Presidential Scholar and the most distinguished student. He went on to obtain his master's degree and today is an international director of programs involving refugees, war, and torture victims in different parts of the world. He has a wonderful family and remains sober and an active member of AA, despite additional traumatic losses in his life. John remains a cherished friend to this day.

John Burke's life and story about Vietnam moved me deeply. Soon I was meeting other Vietnam veterans in my classes who would introduce me to others outside the university community. including Cleveland's tough inner-city ghetto, Hough, the site of race riots in 1966. The research process snowballed in 1974. I began conducting informal interviews in a pilot study to learn more about the impact of the Vietnam war in veterans' lives. The format was simple: "Tell me about what you were like before Vietnam, what happened in Vietnam, and how have you changed since coming home from the war." Soon, the men requested an opportunity to get together with other "Nam vets" and talk. I started holding "rap" groups at the university on Tuesday and Thursday evenings. These were intense, emotionally powerful experiences. What I encountered in the way of raw emotional intensity surpassed anything I'd ever previously experienced. I had many personal reactions, including the feeling that the real story of what actually happened in Vietnam had never been told to the American people. I identified with the veterans' pain, suffering, alienation, anger, rage, and their feeling of having been forgotten and abandoned by the government and people that sent them to war. The men in the group reminded me of my lost lifelong buddy Willie, whose personal well-being had been snatched in combat with the 3rd Marines in Vietnam. I began to sense the uniformity and common suffering of their postwar lives; the nightmares, flashbacks, isolation, anger, loneliness, loss of identity, binge drinking, and feelings of betrayal and abandonment. In varying degrees, they all shared a "syndrome" of sorts, which was worse for those with hard-core combat, blood-and-guts experiences as well as involvement in the senseless killing of villagers, repeated witnessing of death, dying, destruction, and atrocities. I often had the feeling that I was looking at the tip of an immense iceberg whose depth of dimension scared me. There was something huge lurking beneath the surface, and there was no denying its existence. It was there and about to erupt like a glacier cutting loose and creating a deafening roar in the silence of nature. Working in isolation like other pioneers who have contributed to this volume, I began speaking of the "post-Vietnam syndrome" and using the term *delayed stress reaction* to characterize the pattern of symptoms that develop following attempts at readjusting to American society after Vietnam. For many men and women, now in their early twenties, the full impact of the war stresses had been put "on hold" and later returned with a vengeance. The delayed stress was an emotional time bomb.

By 1975 I felt the need to study more systematically the phenomena of post-Vietnam adjustment among war veterans. I began writing research proposals and, over the next 2 years, had at least a half-dozen rejected. Interestingly, the feedback was always the same, "This is a timely and important subject but not one that is our priority for funding at this time." The message could not have been clearer: America was not ready to take a self-effacing look at the Vietnam War and what it did to the men who fought there. The rejections of the research proposals angered me and caused me to wonder why America did not want to know about what happened to a lot of good men in Vietnam.

America left Vietnam in 1973 and the war ended in April 1975, when North Vietnamese troops and tanks rolled into Saigon. To the men I was working with, the war was not over and in their minds they were still there. By now, I was working along side them in spirit and commitment. It was then that the 'Nam vets started calling me Doc, and soon my colleagues at the university addressed me in the same manner. Today, more than 30 years later, no one calls me John, Professor, Dr. Wilson, or anything else...just Doc. Some of the vets still call me by the Vietnamese name for doctor, "Bac Si."

The rejection of the grant proposals to study the readjustment problems of Vietnam veterans was discouraging. By 1976, I had just about decided to leave this new research interest and return to my laboratory studies of altruism. I was torn as to whether to proceed or return to the safety of academia. But that was not to be. One day a visibly scarred, disabled veteran came in for an interview in my pilot study. His name was Henry Vasil, an engineering student at the university.

Hank was hit at point-blank range by a rocket-propelled grenade (RPG) while manning an M-60 machine gun on the back of an armored personnel carrier (APC) on November 11, 1969, while serving with E-troop, 1st Cavalry, 11th Brigade, Americale Division. The impact of the RPG blasted him off the APC and blew away parts of his hands, arms, legs, head, and chest. When I met him, he was noticeably scarred with shrapnel marks from his head to his knees. After being so severely wounded, Hank spent time in the hospital in Japan for his burns and had multiple surgeries before being transferred to Walter Reed Army Hospital for the next 2 years of additional surgeries and treatments. Hank was a 6-foot 4-inch power weight lifter and state champion athlete in track prior to enlisting in the U.S. Army. When he returned home to his loving, steadfast wife and former high school sweetheart, Sharon, he was a frail, emaciated, tattered and torn shell of his former self; down to half of his top athletic weight and physical condition. Today, Hank remains married to Sharon and has two strong, handsome sons, Scott and Philip. Hank, Sharon, and I remain good friends, and I regard him as one of the most courageous persons I have ever known. Few women have such solidity of character and love for their lifetime mate as does Sharon.

Hank asked me on many occasions how the grant proposals were progressing. I told him that they had been rejected and that I was discouraged and ready to give up. I had strong personal doubts about the prospects of funding or even doing the study on Vietnam veterans. By now it was 1976 and I was about to leave for summer vacation when Hank said, "Doc, have you tried the Disabled American Veterans?" I told him no, and with that he picked up the telephone and dialed Dale Adams, the National Commander, in Washington. Hank spoke with

Mr. Adams, informing him that he was a member of DAV and 100% disabled. He told him about my work and need for research funding and handed me the phone. I remember that Mr. Adams asked smart, insightful questions about my proposed project, to be called The Forgotten Warrior, and asked me how much money I needed to complete the first phase. I told him and he promised to get back to me. I left to attend the 1976 Fourth of July celebration in Boston; when I returned, the university informed me that it had received a check from the DAV to finance the research. The Forgotten Warrior project was now a reality. Just at the point where I thought I would quit and return to the comfort of laboratory research, the tip of the iceberg popped up to greet me and the in-depth study of Vietnam veterans took center stage.

One year later, I testified before the U.S. Senate for the first of six times on my research findings. The day after the testimony, Walter Cronkite's *CBS Evening News* telephoned to make plans to come to Cleveland to do a documentary. Two weeks later, the White House telephoned and asked me if I would be interested in developing an outreach program for the Veterans Administration (VA) and informed me of President and Mrs. Carter's interest in the work and developing dedicated programs for Vietnam veterans. Shortly after that, I met another disabled veteran and quadriplegic named Max Cleland who was the director of the Veterans Administration in Washington and later U.S. Senator from Georgia. At the same time, the Disabled American Veterans decided to launch a 66-city national outreach program to assist Vietnam veterans. As part of a team, I helped design and implement it over the next several years (1977–1980). The idea was simple: create a one-stop service center staffed by Vietnam veterans for Vietnam veterans that could provide assistance and counseling for war-related stress problems (i.e., PTSD, education, jobs, health care, and assistance with obtaining service connected benefits from the VA). Much of what developed through the DAV's national outreach program carried over to the design of the VA's Vietnam Veteran Re-Adjustment Counseling Program (RCS), which began in West Los Angeles in 1979 under the nurturing eye of Senator Alan Cranston, chairman of the Senate Subcommittee on Veterans' Affairs. On August 15, 1979, Congress passed a law (S.7) enabling the Veterans Health Care Act, which appropriated funds to finance the VA's new program dedicated to establishing national outreach counseling centers in satellite locations outside VA medical centers and hospitals. I received a letter of commendation from President Carter, who gave me the pen that he used to sign the bill and an original copy of the bill itself on behalf of my efforts to aid Vietnam veterans. One month later, I received the George Washington Honor Medal from the Freedom Foundation at Valley Forge, Pennsylvania. I did not know it then, but like the veterans I was working with, my life had changed radically in a short time.

The pilot studies begun in 1973, in which I recorded the accounts by Vietnam veterans of how they had been affected by the war, produced a rich amount of material. The methodology included questionnaires and open-ended interviews, during which the men poignantly and painfully described what happened to them in Vietnam. The scheduled 2-hour sessions often lasted much longer. Virtually all of the participants disclosed that they had *never* talked in depth about their combat and war zone experiences. The sessions were emotionally powerful and interrupted by periods of sadness, crying, anger, rage, and quiet, unspoken pride. I found myself becoming more absorbed into their experiences and disturbed by their narratives of guerrilla warfare and the senseless things that happened during the war. There were accounts of search-and-destroy operations, long-range reconnaissance patrols (LRRPs), the burning of villages, atrocities perpetrated by the enemy, confusion about terrain objectives, the horrors of mortar and sniper attacks at night; there were the accounts of being in formidable jungles and rice paddies, and what it was like to be a helicopter door gunner and crew chief, swift-boat sailor in the "brown river" navy, or point man on patrol in an infantry unit. Especially important were the descriptions of how difficult it was for a 19-year-old to sort out what was happening in Vietnam, trying to understand such things as a free-fire and no-fire zones; the omnipresence of Viet Cong soldiers, night and day; the killing, deaths, and the demand for body counts in a war of attrition. So often, the same themes emerged from the interviews: For what did my buddies die? What's this war about anyway? Why are we rejected by American society? Why can't I sleep? Why can't I relax? Why do I need to have a weapon at all times? Why can't I fit in now? How come I'm not the same person I was before going to Vietnam? Why am I so jumpy? Why don't I trust anybody now? How do I know whom to believe anymore? They lied to us in Vietnam about the war and about what was happening in Vietnam. Why do I feel most secure when I am alone and drinking my Bud beer and Jack Daniels?

By the time the Forgotten Warrior project began, the themes that emerged from the open-ended interviews were clear and beginning to make sense. The war experience produced a great deal of ideologic and attitudinal change. Red-blooded 18- and 19-year-old boys fresh out of high school were sent to the other side of the world to fight a war against the possible spread of communism, the dreaded "red horde" domino theory we'd been taught about in high school during the 1960s. At that time, the justification for the war was barely credible in an era of Cold War politics and the halo effect of John F. Kennedy's credo: "Ask not what your country can do for you, but what you can do for your country." My lifelong buddies from Columbus, Ohio, who went off to become U.S. Marines didn't know what they were getting into in Vietnam, but they believed in Kennedy's credo and the domino theory of communism. Those beliefs died in Vietnam.

Within a year, the men who survived Vietnam had their worlds turned upside down by the horrors of war, assaults on the truth, political and military betrayal, and the absence of a genuine homecoming and appreciation of their service by American society. There was no doubt that this wasn't the war our dads fought in World War II, and neither was the country dedicated to the G.I.'s and the lack of clear-cut victory in America's longest war.

The changes I was observing in belief systems, attitudes, and political orientation were surface manifestations of a larger inner struggle with identity. Time and time again I would hear the men say, "Doc, I'm not the same person who went to Vietnam, I've changed. I'm not sure who I am anymore." This theme was so prevalent that it became apparent that the stressors of war had intensified and taxed the young-adult developmental task of establishing a sense of personal identity in preparation for future roles. There was an internal set of changes stirring about in the newly returned veterans of America's most unpopular war. They were trying to sort everything out and at the same time find a place in American society in which they could live and get on with life. Feelings of alienation, estrangement, cynicism, and doubt were predominant as the men looked around at successful, prospering peers and mainstream American society unaffected by the war. The war-traumatized veterans had existed in a strange land, the "heart of darkness," and a surreal world of madness: death, dying, and destruction in the abyss of human suffering. And for what? This was the unanswerable question for many of these men.

There was uniformity of concern expressed by the men about their post-Vietnam life. There was confusion about changes in personality and behavior. Reports of sleep disturbance, startle response, anger, irritability, jumpiness, and flashbacks to scenes of combat were universal. Their reticence about talking about the true nature of events in Vietnam honestly was paramount, with fears of being misunderstood, disbelieved, and rejected. Accounts of hyperaroused, "wired up" behaviors were particularly evident among those who engaged in infantry patrols, search-and-destroy operations, and firefights in the jungles and rice paddies. The wired-up behaviors included sleeping with weapons, booby-trapping property, nighttime perimeter patrols of property and backyards with weapons, suspiciousness, being on guard for possible attack by the V.C. or "enemy" forces, and a strong need to make sure that loved ones and children were protected against possible harm.

There was tentativeness in asking me about upsetting and strange behaviors that included flashbacks, nightmares, traumatic memories, periods of acting without knowing what happened (i.e., dissociative flashbacks), the sudden onset of heart palpitations, sweating and emotional states of anxiety, fear and intense anger. Accounts of self-medication with alcohol or marijuana were common, and most men traced the use of substances to the need to "come down" after combat operations in Vietnam.

There were changes in perception of self-in-the-future. Men would say, "Doc, I was 19 when I went to Vietnam in 1967 and now I feel as though I'm 60 years old. I don't know if I've got much of a future or even want one." The confusion about the amount of viable time left to sort out the impact of the Vietnam experience carried over to problems in intimate relationships. Many reported feeling numb and unable to sustain close, intimate relationships. There were accounts of difficulties with friendships and attempts to express inner feelings to others. The usefulness of combat-hardened numbing was now causing difficulties in social relations.

There was fear that to "let go" of the numbed outer psychic skin that had been developed in Vietnam would have bad consequences. It was safer not to feel and to maintain automatic states of vigilance and hypervigilance. The result was increasing degrees of isolation, estrangement, and alienation. Soon, many men were existing in cocoons of isolated numbing and felt trapped in the psychic trauma of their war experiences. It was a dark place that was difficult to share with anyone except for the "band of brothers" who walked together in harm's way.

By the time I testified before the U.S. Senate Subcommittee on Veterans Affairs in 1977, the post-Vietnam pattern of psychological reaction was very clear to me. There was no doubt that it was a multifaceted process that cut across different dimensions of psychosocial functioning: identity formation, prolonged stress reactions, psychobiological disruptions associated with nervous system functioning, social alienation, and disillusionment. I knew that this was more than just a "post-Vietnam syndrome" and that there were variations in the presentation of war-related changes in behavior. There were the symptoms of delayed and posttraumatic stress characteristics. At the same time, work on constructing the VA's readjustment counseling program (RCS) continued in meetings in Max Cleland's office in Washington, D.C. We exchanged observations and, to no one's surprise, we were all like the blind men trying to describe the proverbial elephant. By then we had a good sense of the phenomena of PTSD, which was soon to become a new diagnostic category in the DSM-III, first published in February 1980.

Once PTSD was included in the official bible of the American Psychiatric Association (APA), the doors of science, law, and social policy were opened in ways that few could have envisioned at the time. I believe that the advent of PTSD as a diagnostic category was a critical turning point for both science and the humanitarian treatment of trauma survivors. On a spiritual level, I believe that the power and energy from centuries of human trauma and suffering finally got an official mouthpiece and spokesperson with the PTSD diagnostic category. The ghosts of the past had arisen to set in motion a process of discovery that would transform the scientific and spiritual understanding of trauma forever.

THE PEOPLE WHO INFLUENCED MY WORK

Many people influenced my work. Space limitations prevent a proper acknowledgment for their kindness, generosity, and wisdom.

Robert Jay Lifton's research on Hiroshima and Vietnam veterans was critically influential. Bob gave generously to me in the early stages of the research and has remained an influential thinker and friend through the years. Charles Figley, likewise, has been a friend and collaborator since 1977. Through the years we envisioned and implemented ideas together, such as the International Society for Traumatic Stress Studies (ISTSS). Dr. Jack Lindy has influenced my thinking about the intrapsychic dynamics of PTSD more than anyone else. Our friendship and collaboration has been a creative chemistry and resulted in co-authored books and several chapters. Erik Erikson's work on the cultural determinants of identity formation in the life cycle has been important to my thinking and theorizing, especially his insights into identity diffusion among World War II veterans and displaced Native Americans. Finally, Joel Aronoff, my mentor in graduate school and dear friend, has given selflessly of himself over the decades with eagle-eyed brilliance in criticizing my work.

CONTRIBUTIONS TO THE FIELD

Evaluating one's contributions to the field is a subjective matter and better left to historians. There is a chronology to my work, which begins with *The Forgotten Warrior*, a three-volume series published by the Disabled American Veterans (1977–1980), and continues to the present time (2005) with the recent completion of *The Posttraumatic Self: Restoring Meaning and Wholeness to Personality* (Routledge, in press). In between these anchor points are the following books: *Human Adaptation to Extreme Stress* (1988), *Trauma, Transformation and Healing* (1989), *Anomalous Traumatic Experience* (1992), *The International Handbook of Traumatic Stress Syndromes* (1993), *Counter-transference in the Treatment of Posttraumatic Stress Disorder* (1994), *Assessing Psychological Trauma and PTSD (1997)*, *Psychological Debriefings* (2000), *Treating Psychological Trauma and PTSD (2001)*, *Broken Spirits* (2004), and *Empathy in the Treatment of Trauma and PTSD* (2004). These books contain much of my research and writings, as do monographs and chapters written for other books on PTSD and trauma. Recent international collaborative research on disasters, war victims, refugees, resilience, shame and guilt, traumatoid states, and the terrorist attacks on September 11, 2001, have been published in various journals. Currently, I am working on several new books, including *Culture and Archetypal Forms of Healing from Trauma*.

BUILDING FOR THE FUTURE AND LOOKING BACKWARD

In the task assigned by Dr. Figley, the question of how current or future scholars might build on the accumulated and collective work accomplished is artfully posed. Twenty-four years after the advent of PTSD as a diagnosis, we still do not have an integrative metatheory of PTSD. As the field progresses, we need a comprehensive theoretical model that specifies the relevant variables and processes as well as their interactive effects on patterns of posttraumatic adaptation. The advances in the neuroscience of PTSD, assessment technologies, and life-span study of the vicissitudes of prolonged stress response patterns will permit the creation of a unifying theory of PTSD and its effects on all psychological systems of behavior.

We have come full circle in a century of studies on traumatic stress. The seminal insights of Janet, Freud, and Jung showed that trauma affects unconscious mental processes in discernible ways, which include repression, dissociation, and injuries to the self. Future work is critically needed to understand precisely how trauma affects the inner world of experience in terms of ego identity, the self structure, and personality processes. The inner and outer worlds of posttraumatic adaptation are interrelated. Neuroscience studies of brain-behavior linkages will enable a deeper understanding of the inner world of trauma in terms of learning, memory, information processing, personality development, affect regulation and behavioral dispositions.

Understanding trauma's impact on the processes and viscissitudes of life-span development is in its infancy. How does trauma affect the epigenesis of identity across the life cycle? How does trauma shape the trajectory of ontogenetic development? What factors determine human resilience to catastrophic trauma?

The questions associated with the treatment of PTSD are paramount in clinical outcome studies. Future therapeutic treatments will move beyond the current trend of using a method or technique (e.g., cognitive behavioral therapy, psychodynamic, EMDR, pharmacologic treatment) of psychotherapy to treat PTSD symptoms as a unidimensional entity. Future treatment techniques will be geared to identifying target objectives in terms of specific symptom clusters and applying a range of clinical procedures to address their psychobiological origins and how they were encoded through learning and memory into complex repertoires of behavior shaped by cultural influences. Since PTSD is a multidimensional phenomenon of prolonged stress response patterns, clinical studies will lead to new treatments that are analogous to current medical procedures for treating cancer and heart disease. Underlying psychobiological disruptions in neurohormonal and physiologic processes will be known, and clinical interventions will use specialized techniques to target the cognitive-behavioral manifestations of these disrupted processes.

Today we recognize that traumatic stress reactions are more than a set of psychobiological mechanisms located in the brain and sensory nervous system. The human element of empathy and compassion in the treatment process is critically important. We need systematic studies of transference and countertransference, the matrix of empathy, and the role of the therapists' personality processes in clinical treatments. We need to study the processes of posttraumatic therapy and the inner world of the therapist with the same degree of rigor as we do to the PTSD patient or research subject. Future research will refine levels of understanding, applying state-of-the-art scientific techniques to the in vivo study of therapists during psychotherapy. For example, what would positron emission tomography (PET) scans, magnetic resonance imaging (MRI), or other types of physiologic monitors tell us about the emotional processes of therapists during treatment? Are there psychobiological profiles of high-empathy therapists? Are the brain processes of highly empathic therapists in different states of functioning than those of low-empathy therapists? I have examined some of these questions in the book *Empathy in the Treatment of Trauma and PTSD* (Wilson & Thomas, 2004).

FLASHBACK AND FLASHFORWARD

As a final note, I think that it is important to reflect back on the days prior to 1980 when PTSD became a worldwide reality because of its classification as a separate disorder in the DSM-III.

At that time, we had no professional journals, reference works, or textbooks in the field of traumatology. We had no national or international professional societies concerned with the study of trauma and PTSD. We had no databases like PILOTS (Published International Literature on Traumatic Stress; www.ncptsd.org) to catalogue research findings. We had no national or international centers to study PTSD. We had no national or international hospitals, organizations, and centers to treat victims of torture or trauma or to assist refugees, asylum seekers, and victims of political oppression and terrorism. We had no political advocacy organizations for victims of war crime, rape, violence, terrorism, or sexual assault. We had no private or governmental hospital programs dedicated to the treatment of PTSD. We had no professional societies dedicated to crisis intervention, psychological debriefing, and training programs to assist in times of disaster or emergency. We had no treatment techniques tailored to PTSD. We had no scientific studies of the brain and trauma responses in PTSD. We had no books on the psychological assessment and treatment of PTSD. We had no programmatic social policy or legislative initiatives in the U.S. Congress, the United Nations, or other governmental agencies. We had no awareness of the prevalence and ubiquity of psychological trauma in the daily lives of people throughout the world. We had no media coverage of worldwide traumatic events such as the September 11, 2001, terrorist attack on the World Trade Center Towers in New York or the 2003 earthquake in Bam, Iran, which killed nearly 50,000 people. We had no daily news coverage on CNN of deaths of civilian and military persons in the war in Iraq due to terrorist attacks and guerrilla warfare. We had no websites in computer search engines for PTSD information, alliances, or organizations. We had few avenues of justice to address the wrongs created by trauma in courts, tribunals, or judicial processes, since PTSD did not exist prior to 1980 as a legal entity. We did not have "PTSD" as part of the household vocabulary of people throughout the world. We did not have the collective consciousness that we live in a world of trauma and human suffering and that peace remains elusive throughout the world. But the horrific reality of the tsunami in 2004, which claimed the lives of 200,000 people, brought the world together in humanitarian ways and PTSD took center stage, like a proud child before his schoolteachers.

If there is an overarching humanitarian mission for future scholars, it is to find a way to prevent the conditions in the world that produce trauma, violence, war, and human suffering. Until that occurs, scientific knowledge about trauma and PTSD is critical for the evolution of the species. As Freud (1917) understood, love and hate (Eros and Thanatos) are rooted in the psychology of humans. The forces of hate lead to trauma. The forces of love lead to peace, altruism, and what Buddhists refer to as compassionate wisdom.

John P. Wilson, 1977

REFERENCES

American Psychiatric Association. (1968). *Diagnostic and statistical manual of mental disorders* (2nd ed.). Washington, D.C.: American Psychiatric Association.

American Psychiatric Association. (1980). *Diagnostic and statistical manual of mental disorders* (3rd ed.). Washington, D.C.: American Psychiatric Association.

Aronoff, J., & Wilson, J. P. (1985). *Personality in the social process.* Hillsdale, NJ: Lawrence Erlbaum.

Erikson, E. (1968). *Identity, youth & crisis.* New York: W. W. Norton.

Figley, C. R. (1985). *Trauma and its wake* (Vol. I). New York: Brunner/Mazel.

Figley, C. R. (1986). *Trauma and its wake* (Vol. II). New York: Brunner/Mazel.

Figley, C. R., & Leventman, K. S. (Eds.). (1980). *Strangers at home: Vietnam veterans since the war* New York: Prager.

Freud, S. (1917). *Introductory lecture on psychoanalysis.* New York: W.W. Norton.

Friedman, L. J. (2000). Identit'ss architect. Cambridge, MA: Harvard University Press.

Harel, Z., Kahana, B., & Wilson, J. (1993). War and remembrance: The legacy of Pearl Harbor. In J.P. Wilson & B. Raphael (Eds.), *International handbook of traumatic stress syndromes* (pp. 263–275). New York: Plenum Press.

Lifton, R. J. (1967). *Death in life: The survivors of Hiroshima.* New York: Simon & Schuster.

Raphael, B., & Wilson, J. P. (2000). *Psychological debriefing: Theory, practice, evidence.* Cambridge, UK: Cambridge University Press.

Wilson, J. P. (1976). Motivation, modeling and altruism: A person by situation analysis. *Journal of Personality and Social Psychology, 34,* 1078–1086.

Wilson, J. P. (1977–1980). *The forgotten warrior* (Vols. I–II). Washington, D.C.: Disabled American Veterans.

Wilson, J. P. (1980). Conflict, stress and growth: The effects of war on psychosocial development among Vietnam veterans. In C. R. Figley & K. S. Leventman (Eds.), *Strangers at home: Vietnam veterans since the war* (pp. 123–165). New York: Praeger.

Wilson, J. P. (1989). *Trauma, transformation and healing.* New York: Brunner/Mazel.

Wilson, J. P. (in press). *The posttraumatic self: Restoring meaning and wholeness to personality.* New York: Routledge.

Wilson, J. P., & Drozdek, B. (2004). *Broken spirits: The treatment of traumatized asylum seekers, refugees and war and torture victims.* New York: Brunner-Routledge.

Wilson, J. P., Friedman, M., & Lindy, J. (2001). *Treating psychological trauma and PTSD.* New York: Guilford Press.

Wilson, J. P., Harel, Z., & Kahana, B. (1988). *Human adaptation to extreme stress: From Holocaust to Vietnam.* New York & London: Plenum Press.

Wilson, J. P., & Keane, T. M. (2004). *Assessing psychological trauma and PTSD* (2nd ed). New York: Guilford Press.

Wilson, J. P. & Krauss, G. E. (1979). Vietnam era stress inventory. In J. P. Wilson (Ed.), *Trauma transformation and healing* (pp. 265–308). New York: Brunner/Mazel.

Wilson, J. P., & Krauss, G. E. (1985). Predicting posttraumatic stress disorders among Vietnam veterans. In W. E. Kelly (Ed.), *Posttraumatic stress disorder and the war veteran patient* (pp. 102–147). New York: Brunner/Mazel.

Wilson, J. P., & Lindy, J. (1994). *Counter-transference in the treatment of PTSD.* New York: Guilford Press.

Wilson, J. P., & Raphael, B. (1993). *The international handbook of traumatic stress syndromes.* New York: Plenum Press.

Wilson, J. P., & Thomas, R. (2004). *Empathy in the treatment of trauma and PTSD.* New York: Brunner-Routledge.

Wilson, J. P., & Zigelbaum, S. D. (1986). PTSD and the disposition to criminal behavior. In C. R. Figley (Ed.), *Trauma and its wake* (Vol. II) (pp. 305-321). New York: Brunner/Mazel.